Wisdom in the Family

A Guide to Creating a Family Plan

Stephen Dubrofsky

Lightworker
Publications

Published by:

Lightworker
Publications

P.O. Box 34838

Las Vegas, NV 89133 USA

www.Lightworker.com

Lightworker Books and Tapes and DVD's can be purchased in finer retail stores, on the internet at www.lightworker.com, or by contacting Lightworker at country code 01 702 871 3317.

Wisdom in the Family

ISBN: 978-1-928806-23-3

By Stephen Dubrofsky

Editing & Layout by Tony Stubbs, www.tjpublish.com

Cover art: Uri Cogan

Copyright © 2007 Stephen Dubrofsky

Printed in the USA

Published: Summer 2007

Table of Contents

There are no limitations – You can now create anything you wish.
Be open, adventurous and courageous.
This happens through your attitude, your awareness, and your work.
Be gentle with yourselves, your kids, and your mission.
Your family is now headed in an amazing direction,
a journey which has infinite rewards.
There is no greater reward than self-realization!

Dedication

Rarely is one as fortunate as I was to be introduced to Dr. Al Molyneaux. Al is a jack of many trades and a master of all. As Director and owner of Executive Corporate Edge, Al has over 25 years experience in executive management. In addition to this, Al has perfected a technique he calls *The Trans Programming Experience*. He uses this technique to unlock blockages deep within our psyche. It was through this experience I had with Al that I discovered my creative abilities. Imagination is the greatest gift of all; it is through our imagination that we may experience the infinite. Thank you for introducing me to mine. Thus I am dedicating *Wisdom in the Family* to you, Al.

Acknowledgements

Two years ago, I met Montre Ji. This modest gentleman would never admit to his scholarly ways, but that is exactly what he is — a Master Teacher, one of the best I have met. Montre Ji, pronounced *Montree G,* now lives in Toronto but was born in India where he practiced law and astrology. He now spends his time sharing his wisdom with those of us who choose a path of knowledge designed for deep empowerment. Thank you, Montre, for your wisdom will be forever embedded within *Wisdom in the Family.*

Evangeline Gopaul B.A., R.M.T., I.A.Y.T. incorporates a unique blend of Western and Eastern (Ayurveda & Traditional Chinese Medicine) principles of healing and understanding the subtle and physical aspect of the human body. She acknowledges each of her clients as unique individuals with different needs. Evangeline is first to acknowledge her teachers — Sri Ravi Shankar, Vaidya Rama Kant Mishra, Deepak Chopra and Dr. Gabriel Cousens — as contributing to her love of healing and understanding humanity. In addition to the many gifts Evangeline possesses, you can include writing, for I wish to acknowledge her for the contribution she made in the chapter "In Cultivating Balance."

Hilary, I want to thank you for all of your support, guidance and unlimited patience as well as your unconditional love. You are a passionate, dedicated, wise woman whose life mission is in helping humanity. You are a true friend.

Last but not least, I want to thank you, Rena, for your vision, support and, most of all, undying love. Day or night, you are there to remind me who I am, and your gentle nudges allow me to stay focused. Thank you. You are the greatest.

About the Author

Stephen's academic and professional experience is extensive and focuses not only on the needs of the special needs child but also on a holistic view of how to create a balance between the child, the parent and the school. He has a Bachelors degree in Psychology with an emphasis on child development. His Masters in Learning Disabilities focused on children with learning disabilities, behavior disorders and developmental disabilities. His Masters in Education Administration focused on leadership skills in the workplace and how to maximize performance and motivational levels within the family and school environment.

For the past 9 years, Stephen, as Founder and Director of Parent College, has been working as a family coach. Parent College is designed to empower the caregiver no matter what the circumstance to create positive changes within their situation. It is specifically designed to teach the caregivers how to be an outstanding teacher, guide and advocate to their children.

Not only has Stephen facilitated growth and positive shifts within a quantum of families but as Director of Parent College, he has trained other professionals to go out and do this family work. His experiences have crossed a vast spectrum of special needs including working with child and family services.

He is a strong believer in the cohesive and empowered team dynamic. He is keenly perceptive and sensitive to the challenges of children, is able to see the global picture and is passionate and committed to the development of the child and family.

He can be contacted at: stephen@familyground.com. His web site is:
www.allaboutyourchildren.com.

Preface

And a woman who held a babe against her bosom said,
"Speak to us of children."
And he said: "Your children are not your children.
They are the sons and daughters of Life's longing for itself.
They come through you but not from you,
And though they are with you yet they belong not to you.

"You may give them your love but not your thoughts,
For they have their own thoughts.
You may house their bodies but not their souls,
For their souls dwell in the house of tomorrow,
which you cannot visit, not even in your dreams.
You may strive to be like them, but seek
Not to make them like you.
For life goes not backward nor tarries with yesterday.
You are the bows from which your children,
as living arrows, are sent forth.
The archer sees the mark upon the path
of the infinite, and He bends you with His
might that His arrows may go swift and far.
Let your bending in the archer's hand be for gladness;
For even as He loves the arrow that flies,
so He loves also the bow that is stable."

— Kahlil Gibran, *The Prophet*

Introduction

Wisdom in the Family incorporates as many aspects of family dynamics that we may possibly experience. The book is a practical experience that offers solutions to your problems. Yet the approach, as you will see, is a subtle one. And you will quickly see that ours is not a 'quick fix' methodology.

Yes, the focus is on the family but the answers lie within accessing the powers and potentials within us as individuals. So I use the word 'subtle' and 'gentle' because, anytime we are asked to look within for answers, a strange thing happens. It comes in the form of emotions and discomfort. Our first inclination is to not want to go there. It is threatening and most of us want to retreat, to deny that the answers to our wishes exist within us.

Over the years, our mind has built up defenses – denial, anger, withdrawal, fear, etc. – that do not allow us to 'see the forest through the trees.'

Wisdom in the Family almost surgically and very methodically will help you create an environment that allows you to map out your own plan. It will show you that, by accessing your strengths and unlimited potential, how you can help your children do the same for themselves.

We begin by showing you the picture or paradigm that parents have been operating with for generations, and how we have been conditioned to think and act in the ways we do. It then offers you a new picture and, if you choose, how you may create a new paradigm ... for generations to come.

The book talks about things like:

- Self-mastery.
- Empowerment.
- Stress.
- A holistic way for living – a balanced approach of how we eat, what we are eating, exercise, relaxation, play and the roles these things have in creating a better way.
- How to create balance between the work place and the family.
- 'Re-birthing" – how we can go back to heal some of these old ways we learnt to parent, so we can make room for a new way.
- Television and its effects on our children and family as a whole.
- The connected family.
- How to become better advocates for your children.
- A Family Plan.

This practical model will guide you with information and exercises you can work with and have a hands-on experience of what it feels like to realize that you do have the power to transform the nature of your family.

Bear with us, be patient and gentle with yourselves, as you are embarking on an adventure that will change your life forever, change your children's lives and, believe it or not, change families for generations to come.

We at *Wisdom in the Family* are here to support you every step of the way and honor your courage, passion, dedication and brilliant efforts.

We recognize you as *Wisdom in the Family Trailblazers!*

Welcome to the Club

Wisdom in the Family is not just a book; it is a way of life, a combination of accumulated knowledge and experiences, not just by us authors but by you. I often say that as parents, our primary role is to be good watchers and listeners, and our children will tell us exactly what is going on in their lives while at the same time conveying to us what their needs are in the moment.

Well, this is exactly what we have done in bringing this book to you. This is what we do every day in our own individual practices. We have watched and listened to you, as individuals, as parents and as family units.

We have witnessed and felt your joy and pain, your frustrations, fears, doubts and anger that all parents go through as part of bringing up a family.

We have studied your families and your unique ways of parenting. The whys and wherefores, the do's and don'ts, the guilt, the shame, the regrets, so many things that tend to inhibit your way of achieving harmony within your family.

We have looked at the reasons why so many of us just end up in an abyss where the standard picture is one of chaos and where those moments of tranquility and peace are few and far between.

Do we have answers, you may ask? Of course we do! The answers are simple and are so close yet oh so far.

Wisdom in the Family talks about "how to do" many things. But, truly it is not so much about the specific things that may fix our problems temporarily.

Wisdom in the Family offers you a way to transform your thinking as individuals so you may transform your way of doing things and create a new lifestyle.

It offers you the choice of a new paradigm, a holistic way of seeing yourself as the principal force of creating your own empowerment.

Wisdom in the Family offers you the opportunity to grow *first* as individuals so you are there to provide for your children the opportunity to live life, exploring their own individual potential.

In this picture, we are together yet we are apart. We are observers as well as experiencers. We are guides and teachers not having to feel that our legacy lies in the fact that we must imprint ourselves on our kids to achieve glorification. But the true blessing comes in our allowance of our children to seek their own freedom. This new paradigm is about surrendering old values, about freedom in a way in which you cannot feel until you begin to experience it.

It is about work … lots and lots of hard work.

Have I scared you? I hope not! Because if we think about all the energy we expend in worry, feelings of guilt and so on, we must recognize that this is very hard work as well. What this new paradigm offers you is a way to redirect this energy in other, more positive directions.

The attributes of a healthy and happy family are: inspiration, motivation, sharing, communication, respect, trust, compassion, honesty and love. These attributes cannot be found here; they cannot be found anywhere, for they are just symbols we have grown accustomed to hearing. Yes, we will talk about them, but really the only place they can be found is within yourself. To experience them is to recognize them for what they are and then to practice working with them.

A Generational Picture

The joys of parenthood may be timeless, but the work of combining parenthood and adulthood is harder than ever. Those of us who begin a family today feel more isolated than ever, both spiritually and geographically, from the extended family, from other parents and from the mainstream. Where ready-made support structures once existed, we now have to construct our own: someone to baby-sit, someone to advise us and someone to share our coffee, our complaints, our successes and failures.

Within the community of parents, we are both inspired and confused by the variety of lifestyles among us, including single-by-choice, blended families, late first-time parents, divorced, teenage, dual career, adoptive, traditional and non-traditional. If we have kids later in life, it's tougher to break old habits, from reading the morning newspaper to having time and money to ourselves.

A multitude of thoughts and questions crop up and then there are those issues that just happen and become a cornucopia of feelings and emotions that result in something that feels like chaos.

As if life was not hard enough to balance as a single person growing up, and then comes relationship and marriage and this word 'balance' takes on a whole different meaning. But once we have a child, it's as if all hell breaks loose. We don't know which way to turn.

Some of the issues that arise are:

• How does a child fit into your life and marriage?

- How will it affect your career and home life?
- How will it affect you financially?
- How will you share the responsibilities of a child? What are the responsibilities of having a child?
- How is it going to affect the relationship and are you strong enough to cope with all of the changes?
- How is it going to affect your identity?
- How do you cope with your child's development?

These are just but a few thoughts that happen … and then … you have your second child.

As we know it, interpersonal adjustment and readjustment, temporary balance and intermittent chaos characterize the parental stage of life. There is no perfect order, no 'right' answer or technique that will make everything perfect. If ever a sense of humor is needed, now is the time, because anyone who has been a parent will volunteer that parenting is the most all-consuming job that exists on this planet.

It is about work, life and balance and more work after that is done.

Parenthood

There is more to parenthood than *parenting*. Parenthood is a state of being, a rite of passage – a life stage. It encompasses the spectrum of emotions and experiences you encounter as you take care of your children and yourself.

The challenge of parenthood, beyond the very real demands and rewards of taking care of the kids, is finding out what you are going to make of your own life. How does parenthood fit into your inner world? How does it shape who you are and who you will become? How do you as a parent fit into the outside world of work, family, friends and strangers? And, finally, how does parenthood redefine your intimate relationship with your partner?

For many of you, these concerns are very private – indeed, you may keep them secret from your partner, or avoid confronting them honestly yourselves. If you land that big job, for instance, what you decide to do about your preschooler's care is entirely up to you. Few outsiders want to hear about the trouble you had finding a babysitter or housekeeper, or your running battles about which parent stays home when Alice's fever spikes. In the workplace, this is your private life. And for parents, there is also the personal life of career aspirations, leisure, dreams and your very growth as human beings, for you do not abrogate the right to love and take care of yourselves when you marry or have children. Rather, you hurt the marriage and the parenthood by being less than what you could be.

Yet have we not backed ourselves into a corner by being so private that we allow the pressures and anxieties to build up to such a degree that we are afraid to seek the support that is required as a parent? Life has become so stressful that we are unable to see the picture of what is going on any longer. Primarily focusing on the day to day responsibilities and forgetting to slow down and look at the effect it is having on our lives and family.

Do you feel inadequate and afraid to admit it? As one mother interviewed said, "Parenthood is so full of 'shouldisms' – you should (or shouldn't) express anger; you should (or shouldn't) want time to yourself; you should (or shouldn't) enjoy, feel, want. No wonder we have lost our identity; we are constantly second guessing ourselves and others with us. No wonder we are shamed into secrecy when we don't act the way we think we should. If you do let people know that despite the unconditional love you have for your child, you also have 'bad' feelings such as anger, boredom doubt and frustration; will that make you a bad parent?"

The idealized parent of traditional child care books doesn't catch the flu, is never grumpy and isn't male. But that is the old breed of super-parent. The new breed is even harder to emulate. We live in an increasing complex world where time is taking on a new meeting. That is there is not enough of it. It is moving so fast now that it seems if we try to jump off, within a week we will be left in absolute chaos. Most of us do not even realize that we require breath to live. If we admit to these private fears of inadequacy about our parental and adult performance, we risk losing self-esteem and support.

You may feel that sex and parenthood can't compete. The first practical problems of fatigue, pain and disorientation are gradually supplanted by more subtle changes in attitude. As new parents develop a working partnership, your sexual and emotional relationship may take a permanent back seat. But are you going to tell anyone else – or even each other – how lonely and abandoned you must feel.

You may feel that the life of a parent isn't normal. Life with a child is not familiar, even if you come from a large family. You have never experienced anything like parenthood before and life will never be the same again. Better? Often worse? Sometimes unpredictable?

Parenthood is not typical. As traditional role models vanish for parents – as they have for virtually everybody – we are set adrift in a world where almost any lifestyle goes. The trick is to make yours work for you. Creating a personal design for living is one of the monumental tasks facing every parent.

Parenthood is not static. It is a process of constant adjusting and readjusting. In the chaotic life of a family, are we seeking reassurance from family, friends, experts – a promise that, if we play our cards right, everything will settle down and become 'normal.' We keep on waiting for the dust to settle. We now know differently; things don't simply fall into place even if we devote ourselves single-mindedly to the care of our child.

The most often used parenting slogan is: "There's no one right way to parent." One can also say, "There's no one right way to live as a parent." Why do some parents in the most trying of circumstances maintain a sense of well-being and commitment, while others never are able to get a grip on their lives? After talking and working with many parents, we've found that the difference begins with *attitude, not technique* and *not knowledge.* Positive thinking in parenthood rests on a set of personal principles. It involves the willingness to see parenthood as a time of personal growth, as a testing ground for values and commitments and as a re-evaluation of our spiritual direction.

Can you sense the fragile position in this paradigm? A friend of mine came up with a brilliant idea. As part of the pre-requisite of parenthood, we first need to do an apprenticeship. That is, practice with other families for a period of, say, six months before we begin making plans for our own new family.

Wisdom in the Family will support you in creating your own personal Family Plan based on your needs and where you are in the moment of your social and emotional development. You will see that at its essence, it is about understanding, compassion, trust, honesty and love.

A True Story by Hilary Watson

I remember once taking my lot to Wal-Mart or some store like that. School was going to start soon, so off I went for the jeans, shirts, etc.

I lost one child. The other two were with me, and they dashed off with, "We'll find him, mummy." Suddenly, the third child showed up, so now I had lost two. The third one dashed off yelling, "I'll find them, mummy." They were there one minute and gone the next. I was totally confused. Why would kids do this to their mother?

I turned around and nothing, nada, no kids. Then, over the PA system, I heard, "Mrs. Watson, your sons tell us you are lost in the store, please come to the Customer Service desk."

I went to the desk and the clerk was having the hardest time trying to keep her face straight as she told me how important it was to walk around the store holding hands and not to go wondering off! This frightens the family as they don't know where you are!

I looked at her, raised my eyebrow and nodded. Then I looked at my kids with that 'mummy look' which every kid knows … and had no problems for the rest of the shopping.

That is when the babysitter came into play and it was worth every penny!

To say the least and I think that you will all agree that parenting is full of lessons, life lessons as you will soon see.
If you have a keen eye, interspersed throughout the book are lessons.
At the end of the book is a place for you to list all of them 1 – 15
This may or may not be
A holistic picture of what you are about to face, are facing,
or have already experienced.
ENJOY!
Keep your eyes open, for throughout the book are examples of little life lessons.

Chapter 1

The Demystification of Parenting

Out with the Old

'The Demystification of Parenting' prepares you to go to a place which will hopefully create a greater sense of awareness and connection to who we really are and a blueprint which will lead to positive growth within the family.

The content is a mixture of experiences, introspection's and practical suggestions on how we may transform our family into a more cohesive, cooperative and loving community.

"Parenting is an *attitude* filled with many thoughts,
of fear, distrust, expectations and confusion.
Believe it or not, you have been conditioned to think this way.
To shift these thoughts – and you can –
means to bring growth
and transformation in you,
in your children,
in your family."

stephen@familyground.com

1

tThanks to all of us messengers who are now jumping on the 'parenting' bandwagon. There are more and more of us who are now getting out there, talking, writing, really speaking out and advocating for families.

So what do we say to all of you parents to be, new parents, grandparents, auntie and uncle parents, even to our babysitting parents?

Embrace this onslaught, allow this dialogue to happen, be good listeners and really – yes, really – want to create a new paradigm where change is positive. It is now time to understand that 'empowerment' and 'parenting' are really one and the same.

For too long we have been living in a paradigm that no longer works; we know it but yet we continue to carry on. We are so conditioned that we continue to move from one generation to the next, reenacting what we have learned from our past role models.

We have to ask ourselves, "Are we really enjoying this ride?"

Do we wish to continue it?

Of course not! We must give ourselves more credit than that, after all, of all the animals on this planet we are the only ones with the ability to reason, to problem solve, to look within ourselves and change our ways for the better.

The Traditional Parenting Model

So what is this 'demystification'? Let's look at the existing picture of what it's like to be a parent. Where have we learnt to be this guardian, teacher, advocate and everything else to our children?

We have the ability to procreate, but have we been taught about what it is like to have kids, what we should know, what to expect, and how to use our inherent skills?

Speaking for myself, I was never taught what relationship was like, what it means to be in relationship. It would have been easier for me to build a house at 18 years old than to understand who I was, who that girl was and what to do with her. What were the implications of relationship of having children, and what did family really mean in terms of our varied roles and expectations.

Traditionally, we learn what it is like to be a father or mother from our own parents.

If we indeed are following this paradigm we must ask ourselves, honestly, "If this is setting us apart from who we really are as individuals, is it really preparing us for the job of creating a unique and empowered family unit?"

Is this the first thing that dis-empowers us?

Right from the onset of what is to be a very unique and individual experience; does it seem that we are giving ourselves up? Does this experience belong to someone else? An experience that may have felt right for them? But do we have to accept it as readily as our way?

I have spoken to parents who have adopted the attitude that, "If and when we make mistakes with our children, then we are going to be messing them up, ruining their lives (and ours, as well)."

This may seem dramatic but in this paradigm, we are defeated before we even begin. In this paradigm, every time we make a mistake, chances are we are going to feel some sort of guilt or shame. For sure we are going to feel as if we have done something wrong and with that automatically comes the feeling of 'not being enough.' Whether we know it or not, our children are on the same ride as we are, learning and feeling these things as well.

The cycle has again been reborn

If we maintain this negativity and were to check in with ourselves, then we would agree that our self-esteem and confidence levels are not very high and that chances are this will become a self-fulfilling prophecy.

As previously mentioned, 'parenting' is an attitude more than anything else and we need to rethink and recondition our thoughts so we may change our ways.

When it comes to this attitude of being a parent, it is clear that we are confused, frustrated and, in some cases, lost and that, even though we may not be totally conscious, we are crying out for help.

I know I have embarked on some very touchy and fragile issues here. To be a parent in many ways is a very personal thing. We are in conflict. On the one hand, we are indeed looking for help and on the other, our inner defenses are saying, 'Stay away!'

Maybe then it is time to see ourselves as gentle beings, and that we do not need to place so much pressure on ourselves. We do not have to feel alone.

At times, because we are so close to the problem and things are so intense, we may not be able to see the answer so readily, whereas another loved one can offer us a different perspective.

A good manager or leader will always seek out other opinions before making a decision. Ask yourself if have you been 'hardwired' to believe you have to do it all by yourself.

The old way of educating our child has changed

In a perfect world, we would feel comfortable knowing that we, and our child, would have access to programs and personnel that would assist in the care and teaching of our child, and help to guide us through our challenging times. But during the past several years, due to declining funding, we can no longer make this assumption.

Part of the answer is that, as parents, we must now take on a greater degree of involvement in the management of our child's educational, social and behavioral needs. It is now time for us to recognize and take responsibility for creating significant academic and social growth for our children, both at home and in the educational system.

We have entered into a new time, a time where 'the old way' of educating our children has changed.

We must reassess and develop a strategy as to how we as parents are going to react to these changes in order to provide the best academic and social environment for our children in the coming years.

The 'New Paradigm' for parents and educators is one where we must focus on our intuitive senses, our ability to reflect, to be flexible to see and adapt to the ongoing changes. Not to see us as victims but to tune into the positive attributes within ourselves and our children as the answer to growth and inner well being of the family.

Our role is to re-teach our children the values of self-discipline, courage, compassion and responsibility within an environment that includes large classrooms, under-trained personnel, impatience within the system, and a mentality that the best way to deal with a child is to use a 'quick fix.'

We must empower ourselves. That is, as the ultimate role model, we must take command of the fact that we are the parent, teacher, advisor and advocate for our child. It is our responsibility to know how to assess the problems that may exist within the home and at school, as well as knowing our child's academic strengths and weaknesses.

We need to look at our parenting style and see if it fits the needs of our child, because simply modeling the way in which we were taught and raised may not be the best method for this particular child. We need to look at our schedule and our child's schedule to determine how we can spend more quality guidance and playtime with them.

Teaching them the importance of communication and relationship is paramount.

Whatever plan we create, we must ensure that success is guaranteed, for this will set the groundwork to develop and support self-esteem, responsibility and decision-making skills for the entire family.

As parents, we are 'partners with our schools.' This implies a number of responsibilities, such as expanding our contact and communication with the educators of our child, asking the appropriate and relative questions, and establishing individualized programs that will meet the unique needs of our child.

So what does this all mean? Well, it means that now YOU are the leader of your individual community. You are the principal role model. You are the motivator and the creator of positive energy. You are the one who by being CONSISTENT, FIRM and CARING teaches consistency, responsibility and strength of will. You are your child's partner and in this time of change, you have the opportunity to make every difference.

Being the 'Now' Parent – a Model

Simply speaking, to be a parent is to take on the most challenging job the universe has to offer.

The word 'parent' in parenting is about an attitude. It is a series of thoughts and perceptions that ultimately guides us to how we behave.

When we talk about 'life,' parenting is all about 'life' and what is 'life' but something that just happens at any moment.

We see this happening in our lives all of the time, so why should it be any different when we have kids.

Of course it shouldn't. Our kids are going to be who they are, and since they are experiencing 'life' just as we are, then things will 'just' happen to them as well.

The *big* difference is that now they are happening to all of us and 'life' is now affecting what we call 'a family.'

Now our role is to just do things; many of these things are done 'trial by error.' We have the opportunity to see what happens from the decisions we make. The greatest thing about this is that we have the opportunity to make adjustments based on our decisions.

In this scenario, this thing we call 'guilt' does not exist.

This becomes a 'learning scenario.' We know we are here to learn specific lessons; 'life' will offer these lessons to us and continue to do so until we decide to do something different to change.

This scenario offers us 'choice' instead of 'guilt.' In this scenario, we are given the choice to surrender a lot of the baggage that comes from the past. The baggage we do not have any control of.

In this scenario, we view life as offering us unlimited potential and to experiment with the Power of Intention.

The Power of Intention

I have come to think that a good example for the 'Power of Intention' is the Kramer character on the *Seinfeld* show. Here is a guy who looks weird, acts weird, talks weird and seems as if he should be living on the streets. Yet everything he sets his mind to, he becomes. For example, he picked up a piece of glass from somewhere and made it into a designer coffee table that he then put together as an entire designer magazine of coffee tables. He swam in the infamous polluted Hudson River in New York City and then duplicated this ocean smell into cologne that was then copied by a famous manufacturer. He went to work for an exclusive financial organization, where he just walked into the boardroom and was immediately received as an authority on a subject he knew nothing about.

This is hilarious but through his intention, confidence, strength of will and knowing, he proves he can be successful at whatever he sets out to do. That it is not about what others think of him, but it is really about that he believes in himself. This is a great lesson for all of us to take with us.

So 'Now Parents' see their role as one who is there to:

1. Be the witness to the unlimited potential that exists within our children and uses our unique vantage point to teach to their strengths, focus on their positive attributes and be open to what they have to teach us.

2. Be a good watcher and listener so that we are in a better position to fulfill their needs.

3. Be a true guide for them as you see yourself as the one opening up the doors for them so they may experience the true nature of who they are as individuals, and for what reason and what work they are here to accomplish.

4. Be an 'experiencer,' that is, you are meeting them on their level, experiencing life with them, their joys, their successes, and their failures. You are the disciplinarian, the cheerleader and the advocate for them.

5. Be a teacher, with the awareness of not imprinting your style and temperament on them, for they are to be allowed to be who they are. In addition to this, as their teacher, we have the information to guide our children's teachers about their learning styles, temperaments and best ways to work with them. We are nurturing a partnership with our schools and our children and, at the same time, we are imparting to our children very powerful social and educational mores which promote them in being very productive members of their future community.

6. Use the extended family as integral family members to help problem-solve. You know the old adage, **"It takes a village to raise a child."**

7. Be open to the opportunity that your kids are your teachers as well. As you are watching, notice how they mirror for you the exact issues you wish to change or imprint on them. Use this to take a look at yourself. Get out of the way of your ego. It is essential that you know how your internal dynamics are affecting the behavior of your child. When you change, so will the dynamics. Then as you begin to release this old baggage and you shift, this is the moment that you begin to be each other's teachers.

How magnificent!

You are now growing and developing together. At the same time, look at the nature of the relationship within your family and see how it is changing.

(Write to me and tell me what differences you are seeing and feeling.)

Thinking of Having Kids?

Lesson 1

1. Go to the grocery store.
2. Arrange to have your salary paid directly to their head office.
3. Go home.
4. Pick up the paper.
5. Read it for the last time.

The Self-Reflective Parent

The New Paradigm is about self-reflection and looking at the entire picture in order to effect necessary change within your family. Through this experience, you will begin to see your role and responsibility to your child in a different way. You will see that it is not about the feelings of fear, anger, denial or frustration. Nor is it about the feeling of being sorry for yourself or in being the victim: "What did I do to deserve this fate?"

But it is also about being open to the possibility that you can make a wonderful contribution to your child, and your child to you. You have the opportunity to teach about compassion, understanding and responsibility to another human being by being that compassionate, understanding and loving human yourself.

So let's see all of these obstructions and problems as challenges that allow us to teach another who we really are. We are ready to teach our children to feel better about themselves, safer and more confident. We are ready to experience a higher degree of success as parents. We are really ready to bridge the gap and create a more harmonious family experience.

Then we can say we have done the job we came here to do — to teach, and be taught by, our children!

The Empowered Parent

Awareness … Awareness … Awareness

It is the ability to be aware. As mentioned previously, it is the ability to observe and reflect about what works or what doesn't and our flexibility to change.

The empowered parent will:

*   Look at their parenting styles also the temperaments of their children. They will find ways they can blend the two.
*   Incorporate, diet, exercise, and self in creating balance for themselves and their family.
*   Be flexible when it comes to change.
*   Know how to set themselves apart from their child.
*   Teach about discernment and judgment.
*   Guide rather than threaten.

- Display, compassion, understanding, and love.
- Set limits and structure for their kids and be firm, consistent and loving while doing it.
- Be there to share their doubts, fears, angers with their kids. When they are having a bad day, or have made a mistake, will be right there to share it with their kids. This is what creates safety, mutual respect and understanding in all.

There is No Magic. These *attitudes* and *thoughts* will be those that transform our paradigm.

In conclusion, as you read this, the tendency may be to compare or judge yourself based upon your 'to date' experience of being a parent: "These are the things I am and those I am not." This may be disempowering because you are coming from a place of 'not being good enough.'

The 'Now Parent' or 'being in the moment' parent means to know the past is the past. You are now presenting yourself with the opportunity to change your thoughts and behaviors. Each moment is a new experience, with new choices and new things to look at and new adjustments to be made. There are no 'wrongs' to be done and nor anyone else to be 'bad' or made to feel 'bad.'

Parenting is an ATTITUDE filled with many thoughts,
of Joy, Respect, Fear, Love, Compassion.
Congratulations, you are now creating and
have altered some old thoughts.
You did it!
You are now experiencing growth
and development in you,
in your children,
in your family.

Slowly, slowly, life is a process. "Be gentle with yourself."

Chapter 2

Self-Mastery –
The Road to Empowerment

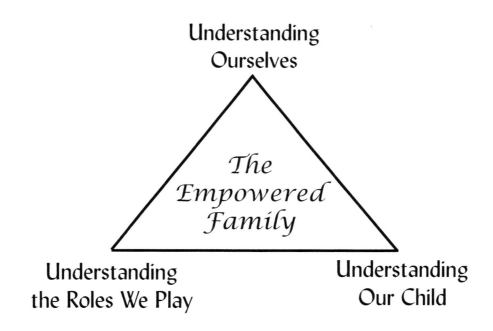

Part I

Three Aspects of the Empowered Family

- The first one is that we must empower ourselves by looking within, and understanding what makes us tick. To be gentle with ourselves and to truly take the time to see the beauty within us, within all of us, knowing we are perceived by our family, friends and associates by the way we behave. Also seeing that our behavior is based directly upon our thoughts and, if we choose to change our behavior, we must be willing to make the commitment to change certain thought patterns.
- The second aspect is to understand who our children are. That they are unique beings, whose sole purpose is to find their way, in their own way. They behave differently from us and each other, they learn differently from us and each other. They all have their own unique interests. They are beautiful beings who are made up of unconditional love. That they are our teachers as we are theirs.
- The third aspect is for us as parents to understand the role we play within the family and that we have free choice in determining if this role *empowers* our family or *disempowers* it.

Empowering Ourselves as Individuals

What follows here is a blueprint to self-mastery. It is a lifelong process so do not get down on yourself by not instantly being able to be in this place of mastery. Instead, use it as a guide to follow. The more of these attributes that you practice, the more empowered you will be as individuals and all the more effective you will be in creating a healthy family.

The benefits are incalculable for yourself and the family you are creating.

Much has and still is being written about some magical process that's going to happen to take us somewhere else, where we will experience a different reality. This sounds great and might indeed happen, but I wouldn't count on it. We all would like to believe in magic but the reality is, it is a combination of *awareness, attitude* and *work* that is really the thing that will bring about transformation.

We are in charge of our own experiences via our consciousness. We will experience other realities only after we change our minds. Only then will it be possible to experience anything other than what we are doing now.

There are no free rides.

An example: Sit in a public park near a beautiful bed of flowers, or choose some other magnificent location. Watch carefully people passing by. Some will stop at the flowers and enjoy them, taking time to smell and touch, soaking in all of the wonder and beauty. Others will walk by, offering no more than a casual glance. Others will not see them at all, and if questioned later will ask, "What flowers?"

A person's state of mind determines his or her experience. Unless you and I have done the work, cleaned up our thoughts, words and actions, we cannot experience other than where we are now. It is also our experience and the way we are viewing it that determines how we perceive the situation. The other variables that apply here are culture, the environment which we grow up in and the values we choose to employ in our life.

The Spirituality of Empowerment

Know what you want first

Be very clear about what it is you feel you need before manifesting it. Once a third-dimensional situation is happening, it requires a lot of undoing if you decide you no longer want it around. Consider your actions carefully. Ensure that what you manifest is good for everyone. If it is a selfish manifestation, you will soon want to be rid of it and it will stay longer than you would like.

The greatest good comes from selfless actions

This transient world can supply to us through our current consciousness any experience we wish to have. After saturating our senses for many lifetimes, we find we are still doing the same things, making the same mistakes, suffering the same emotional pain. All of these experiences have come to us by our conscious or unconscious use of the universal laws of manifestation. They cannot come any other way. This universe does not run by accident. Now you can change your experience by knowingly using the laws for the good of everyone. Your needs will be looked after in ways you never thought possible when you care for your sisters and brothers.

Three little words

- **Honesty**: The honest person radiates a strength that has clarity like the freshness in the air on a clear frosty morning. His or her energy field is clear and open, non-threatening, giving a feeling of trust and dependability.
- **Purity**: The person who displays purity in thought, word and action summons respect from all who come near. The holy energy that manifests around this person is angelic in nature – strong but soft and filled with love.
- **Selflessness**: The person who displays selflessness generates in his or her energy field devotion to the inner self. The ego is transcended through selfless service. Here there is no room for desire, greed and expectation.

Before manifesting anything in your life, read the three little words first and take them into your consciousness so that they become you.

Benefits of living spiritually

The body/mind experience is a direct reflection of our chosen state of consciousness. As we absorb into our beliefs the three little words, our body/mind relationship begins to change. Changing our way of thinking brings change to every cell in our bodies. Negative or fearful thinking cannot exist in the same consciousness as these love-based principles of living. Take these words into you every day of your life, and begin to live them as best you can.

Be ready for the ego's reaction, for it will not give in easily. Be gently persistent with yourself. With everything you do, honor who you are.

Another benefit of inner development is the strength that develops within and around us. There is a purpose about people who live spiritually. They seem to stand still, yet accomplish everything they need to. Amongst the calmness they radiate is a controlled urgency to get things done. When things do not go the way they planned, there is no stress, but an acceptance that all is as it should be, and energy expended has its purpose. They do not hold on to anything they have done, or people they have helped. When they experience anger, they control it and experience it; it is soon gone, and there is no guilt afterwards. By honoring themselves, they let no person abuse them on any level. Within this honoring of themselves, they see themselves in every other soul and extend to others every consideration.

A great inner strength comes from accepting values that change your consciousness. As the transient world lessens its hold over you, a new, more powerful energy releases within you. A primal connectedness that we have covered over comes once again to the fore. By letting go of old stuff, we make room for the new. Really, when you think about it, we could say that by letting go of the new, the old and truthful ways can re-emerge.

Principles of Manifestation

1. Energy follows mind. Therefore, to concentrate energy into any given area is to 'think' about this already being done. There is no room for doubt. Doubt instantly weakens the result or nullifies it completely. When we love someone, there is no doubt in our minds, and love is experienced instantly. Because we have not learned to bring the manifestation into third-dimensional reality does not mean it has not already manifested, for it has. If we did not believe this, then we would not believe that healing energies were of any purpose, because they would never manifest into the third dimension. We all know this is not true. So energy follows thought.

2. Thought: By focusing our thoughts on any place or person, energy related to that thought (corresponding vibrations) will manifest at that point. The result, of course, depends entirely on the type and quality of thought. As this becomes clear to us, our thoughts take on a new meaning and significance. Control of what we think about becomes very important, not only for ourselves but for the whole of humanity. On

our path to self-mastery, controlling our thoughts is the first and most important victory over the mind, which currently we let control us. To ensure success, release the thought completely. To continue to labor over it will hold back the energy and weaken the effect. A clear powerful thought with all of the elements within it needs a split second only, then release. The next time you think about your manifestation, see it and hold the thought of IT IS DONE! Do not allow yourself to get involved in the details again; it is done, completed, finished. Hold that thought and know it to be true. Expect it to come into being. HAVE NO DOUBT.

3. Desire is the fuel that determines the power or energy intensity of the thought you are projecting. If desire is missing, there is no fire or core energy. The will power cannot switch into action when desire is missing. Having no desire stops us from being successful in any part of our lives. This ingredient is often overlooked; it is most important that desire is stimulated. If you do not want to manifest anything at all in your life, then you have no need for desire.

4. Will power is the conduit down which we channel the thought, coupled with the desire – the fuel that makes the will strong and single-pointed. You can liken the will to a pipe; the thought is the water and the desire is the pump that pushes the water to its destination.

5. Balance and Dedication: The final ingredient is balance. A harmonious balance of the three (Thought, Desire, Will) with unshakable faith that it is already in spirit, must manifest the desired result. So bring it into being. Temper each thought with love and dedicate the activity to the inner self.

Exercise 1: Your passion

1. Right now, in this moment, what dreams do you have for yourself?
2. Choose your own way of recording it. Write it if you wish or find a micro-cassette and record it.
3. Listen to your words, your thoughts. What is your heart telling you about this dream?
4. Is this your passion?
5. How do you know?
6. Take this passion, and follow your thoughts as they take you on the journey of making it real.
7. Right now, don't worry about it; you don't have to do anything else … just follow it.

Enjoy the ride!

_____
_____
_____
_____
_____
_____
_____
_____
_____
_____
_____
_____
_____
_____
_____
_____
_____
_____
_____
_____
_____
_____
_____
_____

Part 2

The Practicality of Empowerment

Countless sages have experienced and written about these key elements that have just been outlined.

The next step in the process will offer several ways for you to alter your present day practices – practices designed to shift your existing paradigm within yourself and your family.

We will talk about the following key issues:

1. Impediments to empowerment.
2. Understanding our behavior – a conditioning.
3. Things that *do* empower us.
4. Empowerment and our inner child.
5. What does balance have to do with it?
6. The power of reflection.
7. The power of choice.
8. The power of practicing – where it will lead.

1. Impediments to Empowerment

Our mind is so powerful that if we choose to, we can create anything we wish. It depends on our intent. We also have the power to stay within our existing habits for that is intent as well.

Sometimes consciously and sometimes not we create obstructions that do not allow for us to achieve our goals.

A. Of these the Ego is the most powerful impediment. There are 6 fallacies that make up an ego. It may not be so pleasant to experience these and understand them for what they are.

1. "I am what I have." This means that we allow for our possessions to define who we are. We believe that the more we have the more powerful, the more successful, the better we are as a person. In this case, when we lose our possessions, we lose our sense of self.
2. "I am what I do." In this case, my self-concept is linked to my status in life, my career, my success or failures. The higher the status, the better I feel about myself or so it seems.
3. "I am what other people think of me." In this case, my self-concept is linked to how I believe others think of what I do and say, and where I am in life. In this scenario, I will go out of my way to please others and do what I believe others think is right rather than what is proper for me.

4. "I am separate from other people in life." If this is the case, then I believe I am the center of the universe, and I believe that everything needs to come my way. In this case, my expectations govern my feelings on what I feel I deserve from others. I am setting up myself for total isolation. I feel I can do anything I wish to others. I usually am jealous, not caring of others, greedy and envious.

5. "I am separate from that which is missing in my life." If I do not have, then I am not enough, I am incomplete.

6. "I am separate from the universe." If I do not believe I am part of something, I see myself as an outsider. I feel disconnected and I am paralyzed to do what is necessary to empower myself.

Can you begin to see how our ego interferes; it is built on fear. This describes what happens when we believe our health and well-being depend on outside circumstances. In this scenario, our existence is based on the 'fight or flight" response to protect oneself.

Einstein said, "If our perception is based on fear, then this will act as interference in our ability to achieve our goals." In this case, as a parent creating a family, we are afraid of who we are, we do not really understand our role. We are tentative, reactive and fragile.

If we believe these things, then this is what we become. And because our children are so connected to us, then the question is whether or not they become who we are as well.

B. Resistance is a very powerful impediment. For reasons we may not understand, we become resistant to change. We choose to listen to things that fit in with our beliefs. A sign of being resistant is when we become uncomfortable with what someone asks us to do or say. Is this resistance caused by anger, fear, and trauma?

It usually happens when we are asked to change a habit. For example, do you remember the last time you were on a diet or someone suggested that you quit smoking? You quietly said to yourself, "Why do I have to deprive myself from this dessert?" or, "No way am I going to quit smoking. I love it." Sometimes we don't have to say anything; we just get a feeling in our bodies. A resistant feeling.

This resistant feeling becomes a conditioned response. Does your head feel like it is in a vice, do you get headaches, backaches, etc? Have you ever felt as if wherever you go, you are running into a brick wall? Do you remember the times when someone asked you something and all you wanted to do was change the subject or you wanted to hide in a corner? If you think about it, your mind does actually go into a place of hiding.

It's okay … we all do it. Go ahead next time you feel uncomfortable about something and see where it's affecting your body. In the same way, we have become resistant or conditioned to think and behave as a parent. When something is not working, ask yourself this question, "Am I being asked to look to find a different way?"

It is very natural that the first response we're going to feel would be resistance. The answer is to feel it and continue to move forward. Eventually we will get beyond it and conquer whatever it was we were resistant to.

Exercise 2: Resistance

Go ahead, feel free, and don't hold back. Remember, no one is judging you here. Most importantly, you are not judging yourself.

This exercise is about practicing being truthful and honest with yourself.

There is usually a 'blind spot' here that does not allow you to do this. You can see others very clearly but have difficulty seeing your own truth.

This exercise is about taking full responsibility for your own thoughts and actions. It does not mean they have to be perfect ... just your own.

We know this is not easy so be gentle with yourself and monitor your feelings as you do this.

"Does your truth *empower* you?

Using the above information, talk about any one thing that has caused you to feel resistant. Also, this resistance usually manifests in a certain area in your body. Can you identify where?

After practicing this exercise a few times, do you notice any change?

_____

_____

_____

_____

_____

_____

_____

_____

_____

_____

_____

_____

_____

_____

C. **Stuckness**. Being resistance will often lead us to being stuck. In this case, we leave ourselves with no options; we just stay where we are. We are miserable because we don't understand why the same thing keeps on happening just at different times. When we reach the point of absolute crisis, then we will usually try to find a new way. But look at all of the suffering you have put yourself through.

Exercise 3: Stuckness

Here again you can test out this resistance you have and take it to the next step of being stuck:

- Are you stuck about anything right now? What is it?
- When was the last time you felt stuck?
- What did you do to become "unstuck"?
- Where did this feeling happen in your body?
- Was your solution satisfactory to you?
- If not what would you now do to change your decision?

_____
_____
_____
_____
_____
_____
_____
_____
_____
_____
_____
_____
_____
_____
_____
_____
_____
_____
_____
_____
_____
_____

D. Attachment is a huge impediment. Our lives are based on likes and dislikes. If we like something, we want it more and more. Then we become stuck because we refuse to give up something that indeed may be causing us discomfort. As a parent, we become attached to the way we have learned to do things and not be aware that there are alternatives elsewhere. For example, asking your parents or in-laws how they see things may solve a problem we are having with our child. In this day and age with ADHD (Attention Deficit and Hyperactive Disorder), we become readily attached to having our child on medication to alleviate certain symptoms. As a family therapist, I have seen countless children diagnosed with ADHD who, in fact, are not and do not require medication. In other cases, we have become conditioned to take medication when we are not feeling well. We no longer look for a more natural way to heal our body. We each have our own attachments, which are essentially nooses around our necks. Eventually we feel strangled by it all.

Exercise 4: Attachment
- Make a list of the things you are attached to.
- How long do you think it takes to get attached to something/anything?
- Which ones would you want to detach from?
- What would your plan look like?
- What kind of things/experiences could you get attached to which will enhance your relationship with your family?

_____
_____
_____
_____
_____
_____
_____
_____
_____
_____
_____
_____
_____
_____
_____
_____
_____
_____
_____
_____

Self-Talk

Develop the Habit of Healthy Self -Talk!

"I shouldn't have eaten that chocolate cake! I'm so stupid. I'm just a hopeless case. My family stresses me out and undermines my self-control. I'll never get down to a size 10. I should just give up! "

Do you ever say things like this to yourself? This kind of thinking is called "negative self-talk." It sounds pretty dismal, doesn't it? Let's play the conversation again, this time with positive self-talk.

"I wish I hadn't eaten that chocolate cake! It wasn't a good choice, and I'm smart enough to make good choices. Looking back, I realize I wasn't hungry. I was stressed, and I was only wanting to calm down. So how can I calm down in a healthy, positive way? I'm determined to get to size 10, and mistakes are just part of the learning process."

Which is going to give you more motivation to maintain healthy habits—negative or positive self-talk? Self-talk is internal dialog—the words we use when we talk to ourselves. You can feel calm or worried, depending on what you tell yourself. Your self-talk can influence your self-esteem, outlook, energy level, performance, and relationships with others. It can even affect your health, determining, for example, how you handle stressful events, or how easily you replace unhealthy behaviors with healthy ones.

You can change your negative self-talk with awareness and practice. Learn to recognize negative self-talk, and how to develop the habit of positive self-talk. Below are some types of negative self-talk, paired with positive alternatives.

Replace the Negative with the Positive

Focusing only on problems: This is the essence of complaining. We dwell on the problem, instead of solutions. Instead: Assume most problems have solutions, and ask "How do I want this situation to be different?"

Catastrophizing: Every bad thing that happens is a horrible disaster. Instead: Be realistic in your assessment and stop scaring yourself. Yes, bad things do happen, and many bad things are often inconveniences, mistakes, and foul-ups—not necessarily traumas, tragedies, or disasters.

Expecting the worst: "What if he doesn't like me?" "What if I don't pass the exam?" Expecting the worst does not encourage you to behave effectively. Expecting the worst only promotes anxiety. Instead: Ask questions that presuppose positive outcomes. "How can I make a favorable impression?" "How can I prepare for the exam?"

Stereotyping: By putting others, and ourselves, into preconceived categories, we avoid thinking of people as unique individuals. This leads to strained relationships, and gives us an undeserved sense of superiority or inferiority. It also often deprives us of opportunities to know and understand the giftedness of those whom we stereotype. Instead: Remind yourself that we are all human beings, with unique personalities, each having qualities and shortcomings.

Shoulds: Ought, to, to, must, have to... used carelessly, these words presuppose rules and standards for behavior that do not exist in reality. They imply a consequence for noncompliance, and often evoke guilt. For example, according to the law, we "should" obey posted speed limits, or pay a fine. Is it equally true that "I should be smarter than I am." or "I ought to be married by now."?—Of course not! Instead: Replace the words should, ought, or must with the word "COULD" and realize the gift of choices.

Thinking in Absolutes: We exaggerate reality with words like "always," "never," and "everyone," as in "I always eat too much—I will never be slim." Instead: Replace exaggeration with words that more accurately reflect reality. Example "I often eat more than I need, but I can change that."

All or Nothing Thinking: We distort reality by thinking only in extremes. Our efforts become total failures or complete successes—with nothing in between. Example: "Either I lose two pounds by Sunday, or I quit exercising." Instead: Chunk down your perceptions to see the parts of the whole, which can be positive, negative, and in-between. Give yourself options or choices whenever possible. Example: "I want to lose two pounds by Sunday. Even one pound would indicate that exercise is helping. If my weight stays the same, I'll experiment with variations in nutrition and exercise until I reach my goal."

Negative labels: Negative labels are the tools we use to lower self-esteem in ourselves and others. Example: "I'm stupid," or "I'm fat." When we say phrases like these often, they become a part of our identity and we can begin to dislike who we are. Instead: Remember, people are not their faults or shortcomings. You may engage in stupid behavior occasionally, but that doesn't make you a stupid person. Change your negative "I-am" statement into a statement about behaviors. Example: "I make unhealthy choices when it comes to food." It's easier to change a behavior, than to change your identity.

Blaming: We assign guilt, instead of solving the problem. If we can blame others, then we can feel vindicated in a wrong-doing, and avoid responsibility. Instead: Focus on what YOU can do to promote a solution to the problem.

"Yes but..." Arguments: When someone offers a possible solution to our problems, we "yes but..." and list reasons why the proposed solution won't work.

"Yes but..." says "I'm really not listening to you right now." Instead: Open up to new possibilities and consider alternatives. Really listen to advice and give it a fair hearing, before dismissing it so quickly.

Over generalizing: This is similar to stereotyping and thinking in absolutes. It means that we take a single instance or occurrence, and generalize it to numerous other situations. Example: "Joe is a nice man, and he doesn't want to date me. Therefore: No nice man will ever want to date me." When misused, this kind of generalizing can lead to illogical conclusions. Instead: Ask yourself whether there could be exceptions to your generalization. Does a single occurrence mean it will happen every time?

Now you know what negative self-talk sounds like. Negative self-talk is usually a mixture of half-truths, poor logic, and distortions of reality that perpetuates negative emotions, such as pessimism, guilt, fear, and anxiety. It often occurs when in times of emotional turmoil, or when we are going through stress or a personal transition.

When you catch your negative self-talk, take a deep breath, relax, and remove yourself from the situation. Get up and stretch, or take a walk, or get a drink of water, in order to interrupt your train of thought and get out of the negative rut. Write down some of your negative thoughts and then ask yourself "Are the things I'm saying true? Are there other possibilities and meanings that I could get from these circumstances?" Then replace your negative thoughts with realistic, positive thoughts—and write those down too. Soon you'll stop that self-talk in mid-sentence. If you have difficulty changing your self-talk, you may have clinical depression, and a psychotherapist could help you.

Affirmations

One way to reprogram your self-talk is by repeating positive affirmations until you begin to get a good sense of what positive thinking really sounds like. After all, much self-talk is actually negative affirmations. Our emotions, perceptions, and behaviors are shaped by our most dominant thoughts. Advocates of affirmations theorize that our frequent thoughts represent goals which the subconscious mind strives to actualize. What we most often tell ourselves can become a self-fulfilling prophecy. If you want to explore the power of positive affirmations, follow these guidelines.

Personalize your affirmations with words like "I," "me," and "my." You can't always control circumstances or other people, so make your affirmations about what you can control—yourself. Make your affirmations state your own goals, wants, and values—not someone else's. Some authors say affirmations are best stated in the present tense, because, if affirmations are in future tense ("I will...") your subconscious mind feels no urgency to act NOW. If you feel hypocritical stating affirmations in the present tense (as in "I am slender and healthy") then state your affirmations as a process (as in "Each day I am becoming more slender and healthier.")

Make your affirmations believable and realistic so that you can say them with sincerity. Begin with small, easily achievable goals, and work your way up to bigger accomplishments. "My self control is perfect." is probably more believable as "I have self-control most of the time."

State affirmations in the positive. To say "I don't eat fatty foods," only focuses your attention on the behavior you want to avoid. Instead say "I eat nutritious foods."

Make affirmations short and easy to remember. Catchy slogans stay with us longer than essays.

Repeat your positive affirmations often and positive thinking will become routine.

To maintain positive self-talk, fill your mind with uplifting ideas. Recognize your strengths. Comfort yourself when things go wrong. Let your self-talk be like the soothing, supportive words of a counselor, friend, or mentor. As you improve your self-talk, commit to changing your actions accordingly. Lasting accomplishments come when we change our behaviors as well as our thinking.

Self-talk can work both ways. Experiment with yourself and take one hour to monitor your thoughts as you move through your day. Count the number of positive thoughts and negative ones. This will give you a very good picture of how you are thinking. Remember the adage *what you think is what you do.*

How often do you say, "Oh, I should've done that," or, "If I would've been there, that wouldn't have happened," or, "If I could've done that, then I would've made a million dollars?"

Parenting is about being in the present. Remember, if you live in the past or the future, you can never be making decisions based on what's going on now. You cannot be an effective manager if you are always second-guessing yourself.

More often than not, we're made to feel we're bad. This usually happens when we allow ourselves to listen to other's judgments and expectations. As soon as we do something because we think it's what others believe we should be doing, we are digging our own grave. It is deadly!

This is a huge impediment and very self-destructive.

Exercise 5: Counting
Take one hour each day for one week to monitor your negative and positive thoughts

This will allow you to become aware of exactly what is occupying your thoughts and for how long. It will also show you how much energy you are using for that specific thought.

_____
_____
_____
_____
_____
_____
_____
_____
_____
_____
_____
_____
_____
_____

Exercise 6: Self-Talk
Positive   Negative

Monday
Tuesday
Wednesday
Thursday
Friday
Saturday
Sunday

Counting Journal

Is there a theme to these thoughts? Write them.

_____
_____
_____
_____
_____
_____
_____

Inventory for Shifting
Is the theme: ☐ Positive?   ☐ Negative?

Did this exercise increase your awareness about these thoughts?
☐ Yes   ☐ No

Do you want to change the nature of these thoughts?
☐ Yes   ☐ No

If so, do you feel you have the skills to make the necessary changes?
☐ Yes   ☐ No

What is the specific behavior you are looking to change?
_____

What would you do to help you bring about this change?
_____
_____
_____

A Hint

A valuable technique for defeating negative and self-limiting thoughts that can hamper you from attaining peak performance is the mental interrupt device. When a negative thought enters your consciousness, first you must become aware of it and have a strong desire to remove it for good. To do this, interrupt the negative train of thought by doing something to break and banish the self-limiting pattern. When the bad thought enters, you may pinch yourself and say, "I am strong and weak thoughts are gone," or you may shout out loud or do anything that will divert your attention and remove the negative focus. By *practicing* this technique, you will see a marked decrease in the negative thoughts that most people have, paving the way to the mindset of a true winner.

2. Understanding Our Behavior

What follows is a wealth of knowledge, knowledge that has been spoken by the most deepest, wisest sages of our time. It is through the simplicity of it all that we are not choosing to play out what is necessary to achieve our most desired result.

The Functions of Our Intellect, Mind and Body

It is no coincidence that these days everybody is talking about Mind, Body and Spirit. It is one of those things that, at this point in our evolution, our higher selves know; to achieve fluency, harmony and happiness, we must be in balance. That there is more to life than just stocking up on toys, there is more to life then surrounding ourselves with the material comforts that are being offered to us.

Within the last 2 to 3 years, even our media has adopted a spiritual twist to selling their products. Our awareness and consciousness are being raised as to the direction in which we need to go. All we need do is to jump on to the wagon, use what has been given to us and to change our pictures. One by one.

The answers lie within three things; for us to understand the functions of our *Intellect, Mind* and *Body*. I have always said that life is a puzzle and that we have been given everything that we require solving the conundrums life has to offer.

The ability to *empower* ourselves is here.

All we need do is to understand the processes and act upon this universal wisdom.

- **Intellect** – Simply speaking, our intellect is the place from where we think. It is a place from where our thoughts originate. It is the place from where we develop our discernment and judgment. It is a place where our "will" may be found. It is from this place we can develop our wisdom. Our intellect allows for us to choose and create the paths we journey on.
- **Mind** – Our mind records all the impressions that come from our five senses (sound, touch, sight, taste and smell). It is a place of emotions and feelings. It is where our

ego lies. The function of our ego is to give us the impression that we are the center of the universe and that everything revolves around us based on our perception of the five senses. This, in actuality, is what keeps us stuck. The ego separates us from our physical experience with our ability to connect with our spiritual world. When we master our ego, we *empower* ourselves. We surrender to the drama and know there is something much more important.

- **Body –** The body is the vehicle that houses the five senses, which the mind uses to create a view. It allows for the mind to create a perception or feeling based on the experience that the body is having, which then allows the intellect to make a decision or judgment of what to do and how to act.

As we continue to go through the process of our behavior, you will quickly see that it is not so complicated. We have been behaving like this for eons. Whether we like it or not, we can see that we are wired to react in a certain way. And since we have been doing it so long, there is very little thinking, as it becomes automatic.

To change this, we must stop and use our senses, mind and intellect to alter our attitudes and thoughts so as to create a new way to "be."

The Process –Thunder and Lightning

Please understand that this process happens in a flash; we all do it so you can relax. The *magic* here is to know that we all have our intellect and that is able to change any one of our behaviors affected by this process – at any time and in any place.

1. **Attachment** – "To be associated with something, to have a close relationship to something, devoted to or fond of somebody or something." (Encarta World Dictionary). This is the first step in the process, as we begin to focus on a thought, person, place or thing; we begin to see it as belonging to us.
2. **Desire –** "To want something very strongly, a wish, craving or longing for something." (Encarta World Dictionary) At this point, the cycle or habit has already been born. Once we desire something, we send out an intention to bring it into our lives. It becomes part of our being or behavior and is very hard to let go of.
3. **Anger –** When our desire is not fulfilled, what ensues is anger. The anger grows and festers as a sore. We use our expectations and judgments to fuel our anger and justify the drama we create for ourselves.
4. **Infatuation –** "Thoughtless passion, a great, often temporary and irrational passion for someone or something." (Encarta World Dictionary) At this point, we are so immersed in our attachment, desire and anger that we become 'one–minded' on this particular, event experience or person.
5. **Confusion of Memory –** As you begin taking yourself through this process, you will become aware that you have become so one-pointed that you have forgotten who you really are. Everything else becomes a blank.

6. **Loss of Reason** – At this point in the process, you do not know why or what you are doing. You are just in an automatic cycle, with no rhyme or reason why.

7. **Complete Ruin** – By the time you reach this point, you are totally blind, impotent and have no self. There is nothing left, just total vulnerability. It is like backing an animal into a corner.

Exercise 7: Thunder and Lightning

Using the above 7 steps, track one of your experiences, where you could identify this type of pattern. What would you now do differently to change the outcome of that experience?

_____
_____
_____
_____
_____
_____
_____
_____
_____
_____
_____
_____
_____
_____
_____
_____
_____
_____
_____
_____
_____
_____
_____
_____

Thunder and Lightning: A Case Study

Recently, one of my clients (for the purposes of this exercise we will call him "J") shared with me an experience he had with his wife. This client has been working on his ability to be in touch with his rage and how he uses his anger to block any opportunity for him to grow or achieve any of his goals.

J got into an argument with his wife over her not working and contributing to the financial upkeep of the family. As the argument escalated, both J and his wife became angrier. J knew he was upset with himself because he was unhappy in his job and was totally frustrated that he had not been able to do anything about it. This has been going on for the last few years. He has been afraid to do anything about it because if he leaves, he will not be able to support his family. On the other hand, his wife who has been ill and now fully recovered, has not been able to bring a steady income into the family. J has made her feel so extremely uncomfortable and defensive that she has not worked. Every time J brings up this topic, it sets off an automatic response in both and this adversarial situation is created.

On this particular occasion, J lost total control of himself where his anger escalated to the point where he threatened to kill his wife, and he began throwing glasses against the wall, and vases and plants all over the house. She called the police, who came over to mediate the confrontation. By this time, cooler heads prevailed. J calmed down and his wife chose not to press any charges. Needless to say, the experience left J in a stupor. He had never done anything like this before; he was astounded by his behavior and vowed to seek help to prevent this from ever happening again.

What happened here was an example of 'Thunder and Lightning.' In a flash, both J and his wife went though the seven stages of behavior just described. What is positive is that they are aware that they do have the ability to change this and are beginning to use their intellect differently so as to grow and move on and up in their relationship. They continue to make different choices, thereby creating a new pattern of behavior, one that is more conducive to their relationship.

This is quite empowering for them.

Thinking of Having Kids?

Lesson 2

Before you finally go ahead and have children, find a couple who already are parents and berate them about their...
1. Methods of discipline.
2. Lack of patience.
3. Appallingly low tolerance levels.
4. Allowing their children to run wild.

Suggest ways in which they might improve their child's breastfeeding, sleep habits, toilet training, table manners, and overall behaviour. Enjoy it; because it will be the last time in your life you will have all the answers.

---

3. What Empowers Us?

The idea of empowerment is a very personal thing. What follows here are things that have worked for others. As you read through this information, you will find some things that just feel right for you. There are those you already may be practicing. Keep an open mind and remember that to fully integrate any of these suggestions requires practice.

Keeping a Journal - I love the word 'awareness' and, in my opinion, one of the best ways for us to get in touch with what's going on is to keep a journal. This can easily be done by simply buying a notebook, or you can also keep a daily journal write on your computer. The preference is yours. Once you get into the habit of writing, you will become aware of things you had no idea existed. If done consistently, it will prove invaluable to you.

A good time to journal is early in the morning or before bedtime.

1. Set aside one hour every morning for personal development matters. Meditate, visualize your day, read inspirational texts to set the tone of your day, listen to motivational tapes or read great literature. Take this quiet period to vitalize and energize your spirit for the productive day ahead. Watch the sun rise once a week or be with nature. Starting the day off well is a powerful strategy for self-renewal and personal effectiveness.

2. Use the rubber band method to condition your mind to focus solely on the most positive elements in your life. Place a rubber band around your wrist. Each time a negative, energy sapping thought enters your mind, snap the rubber band. Through the power of conditioning, your mind will associate pain with negative thinking and you will soon possess a strongly positive mindset. *You may want to consider this when you doing your counting exercise.*

3. Laugh for five minutes in the mirror each morning. Steve Martin does. Laughter activates many beneficial chemicals within the body that place us into a very joyous state. Laughter also returns the body to a state of balance. Laughter therapy has been regularly used to heal persons with varied ailments and is a wonderful tonic for life's ills. While the average four-year-old laughs 500 times a day, the average adult is lucky to laugh 15 times a day. Revitalize the habit of laughter; it will put far more living into your life.

4. Enhancing your will-power is likely one of the best training programs you can invest in. Here are some ideas to strengthen your will and become a stronger person:
    *   Do not let your mind float like a piece of paper in the wind. Work hard to keep it focused at all times. When doing a task, think of nothing else. When walking to work, count the steps that it takes to get all the way to the office. This is not easy but your mind will soon understand that you hold its reins and not vice versa. Your mind must eventually become as still as a candle flame in a corner where there is no draft.
    *   You can also build your will-power by restraint in your conduct with others. Speak less (use the 60/40 Rule, i.e., listen 60% of the time and speak a mere

40%). This will not only make you more popular but you will learn much wisdom as everyone we meet every day has something to teach us. Also restrain the urge to gossip or to condemn someone who you feel has made a mistake. Stop complaining and develop a cheerful, vital and strong personality.

5. Make an effort to be humorous throughout the day. Not only is it beneficial from a physical viewpoint but it diffuses tension in difficult circumstances and creates an excellent atmosphere wherever you are. It was recently reported that members of the Tauripan tribe of South America have a ritual where they awake in the middle of the night to tell each other jokes. Even tribesmen in the deepest sleep wake to enjoy the laugh and then return to their state of slumber in seconds.

6. Associate only with positive, focused people from whom you can learn and who will not drain your valuable energy with complaining and uninspiring attitudes. By developing relationships with those committed to constant improvement and the pursuit of the best that life has to offer, you will have plenty of company on your path to the top of whatever mountain you seek to climb.

7. No one can insult or hurt you without your permission. One of the golden keys to happiness and great success is the way you interpret events that unfold before you. Highly successful people are master interpreters. People who have attained greatness have an ability that they have developed to interpret negative or disempowering events as positive challenges that will assist them in growing and moving even farther up the ladder of success. There are no negative experiences, only experiences that aid in your development and toughen your character so that you may soar to new heights. There are no failures, only lessons.

8. Treat everyone well. This habit, along with enthusiasm, is one of the great success secrets. Everyone in this world wears an imaginary button that screams out: *"I want to feel important and appreciated!"*

9. Be truthful, patient, persevering, modest and generous.

10. Soak in a warm bath at the end of a long, productive day. Reward yourself for even the smallest of achievement. Take time out for renewal of your mind, body and spirit. Soon all your more important goals will be met and you will move to the next level of peak performance.

11. Learn the power of breathing and its relationship with your energy source. The mind is intimately connected with your breathing. For example, when the mind is agitated, your breathing becomes quick and shallow. When you are relaxed and focused, your breathing is deep and calm. By practicing deep, abdominal breathing, you will develop a calm, serene demeanor that will remain cool in the hottest of circumstances. Remember the rule of the Eastern mountain men: "To breathe properly is to live properly."

12. Recognize and cultivate the power of autosuggestion. We are all performers in one way or another and it is particularly valuable to use such techniques of athletes and public figures for our own enhancement. If you want to become more enthusiastic,

repeat: *"I am more enthusiastic today and am improving this trait daily."* **Repeat it over and over.** Purchase a legal notepad and write out this mantra 500 times. Do it for three weeks with regular practice and feel that this quality is developing.

13. Remember that forgiveness is a virtue that few develop, but one that is most important to maintaining peace of mind. Mark Twain wrote that forgiveness is the fragrance the violet sheds on the heel that has crushed it. Practice forgiveness especially in those situations where it is seemingly difficult. By using your emotional forgiveness muscles more regularly, petty wrongs, remarks and slights will not touch you and nothing will penetrate your concentrated, serene mindset.

14. Once a week, arise at dawn. It is a magical time of day. Be still, go for a walk or simply listen to an old Ella Fitzgerald recording. Take a long, hot shower and do 100 pushups. Read one of the classics. You will feel alive and invigorated.

15. Regularly send handwritten notes to your spouse and kids. Send them postcards. There does not have to be a reason.

16. Become an adventurer. Revitalize your spirit and sense of playfulness. Become a kid again. Once every few months, plan to enjoy a new, thrilling activity such as whitewater rafting, scuba diving, windsurfing, rock-climbing, joining a martial arts club, sailing, deep sea fishing or camping. This will keep your life in perspective, bring you closer to those you share the activity with and keep you feeling invigorated and young.

17. Spend time with Nature. Natural settings have a powerful effect on your senses that in turn will lead to a sense of renewal, refreshment and peacefulness. Peak performers through the ages have understood the importance of getting back to Nature. Start camping or simply taking quiet walks in the forest. Rest by a sparkling stream. Cultivate your own little garden which will serve as your personal oasis in the middle of a crowded city. By cultivating a friendship with Nature, you will quickly find more serenity, contentment and richness in your life.

18. If you are worrying about something, an excellent visualization technique is to picture the words of your worry on a piece of paper. Now burn the paper and watch the worry dissipate into flames. Bruce Lee, the great martial arts master employed this mental control device regularly.

19. Lao-Tzu prized three essential qualities for a person of greatness: "The first is *gentleness*; the second is *frugality*; the third is *humility*, which keeps me from putting myself before others. Be gentle and you can be bold; be frugal and you can be liberal; avoid putting yourself before others and you can become a leader among men."

20. Become your spouse's number one supporter, the one who is always there supporting and fueling hopes and dreams. Develop together and march confidently through the world as an army of two.

21. Make every one of your days a true masterpiece. Remember the old saying: "It's not who you think you are that holds you back but who you think you're not."

22. A contented mind is a continual feast. Greed and material desires must be curbed to achieve lasting happiness and serenity. Be happy with what you have. Do you really

need all of those material possessions? One can develop contentment just as one develops patience, courage and concentration – with daily practice and sincere desire.

23. Place greater importance on staying happy than amassing material possessions. A zest for life is developed and carefully nurtured through thoughtful activities and pursuits.

24. A change is as good as a rest. Whether this change is as major as a change of employment or as minor as a leisure pursuit that occupies your entire attention for an hour three times a week, these changes in routine, and mindset are entirely beneficial. In selecting the activity, try to find something totally engaging which requires deep concentration so that your mind is free from the mundane.

25. Strive to be humble and live a simple life.

26. If you have a choice of taking two paths, always take the more daring of the two. Calculated risk-taking often produces extraordinary results.

27. Develop a sense of wonder about the world. Be an explorer. Find pleasure in the things that others take for granted. Stop and actually listen to that wonderful street musician playing the trumpet. Read that classic book your father loved so much. Plan to get away from the city next week and visit a secluded, powerfully natural place for a few days. Take a mini-retreat and care for your mind, body and spirit. It will profoundly improve the quality of your life.

28. Send cards on birthdays and little notes from time to time showing that you care and were thinking about your relations. We are all busy but if you spend just five minutes a week to send a card to a friend or family member, by the year end you will have sent out 52 cards. This is a small investment for the dividends that are guaranteed to follow.

29. Once every few weeks, leave your watch at home. In this society, we often become bound to the clock and soon it governs our every action like a rigid taskmaster. Go through the day doing precisely what you wish to do and for however long you wish to do it. Spend time with that special person without having to run off to your next appointment. Savor the moments and focus on what is truly important rather than those mundane things that somehow take on a greater importance than they really deserve. Lose the clock and gain some quality time.

30. Use these strategies to improve the quality of your mind-calming meditation: (1). Practice meditation at the same time each day and in the same place so your mind becomes accustomed to entering the desired serene state as soon as you enter the peaceful place. (2). The early morning is undoubtedly the most powerful time to meditate. Indian yogis believe that the pre-dawn time has almost magical qualities that aid in achieving the super-peaceful state so many meditators attempt to attain. (3). Before you start, command your mind to be quiet by using affirmations such as: "I will be focused and very calm now." (4). If thoughts do enter, do not force them out but simply let them pass like clouds making way for the beautiful blue sky. Picture that your mind is like a still lake without even a ripple. (5). Sit for ten minutes

at first and then increase the time every few sittings. After a month or two, you will not be interrupted by any pressing thoughts and will surely feel a sense of peace that you have never felt before.

31. Drown your appetite by drinking more water – ten glasses a day is ideal. It revitalizes the system and purifies the body. Also, get into the habit of eating soups and more complex carbohydrates such as rice, potatoes and pasta, which feed your hunger with far less calories than other less healthy foods. You truly are what you eat and must ensure that your diet is designed to maximize your energy and mental clarity.

32. Confide in your partner. This will strengthen the relationship and allow you both to grow at the same pace. It is also a wonderful tonic to share important or otherwise troubling things with the person you are closest to.

33. Push yourself just a little harder and a little farther each day. Winners on the playing field of life push the envelope of their potential daily. Do the thing you fear and the death of fear is certain. Winners do the things that less developed people don't like doing, even though they also might not enjoy doing them. This is what strength of character and courage are all about. Tackle your weaknesses. Do the thing that you have consistently put off. Write that thank-you note or letter you have neglected for so long. Exercise your discipline muscles and they will rise to the occasion by filling your day with more satisfaction, more effectiveness and far more energy.

34. Learn to laugh at yourself.

35. True happiness comes from only one thing: achievement of goals, whether they are personal, professional or otherwise. You are happiest when you feel you are growing. When you feel that you're contributing and advancing in the direction of your dreams, you will notice that you have boundless energy and vitality. Time spent on activities that offer little reward aside from a fleeting feeling of relaxation (television watching is the best example) is time lost forever. Relaxation is essential but choose the most effective means of renewal and spend your time in productive pursuits that will slowly move you along the path of accomplishment. Happiness comes from doing – not sleeping.

36. It has been said that doing something for others is the highest form of religion. Every week, out of the 168 hours available, spend a few in service to others. Many say that such selfless service soon becomes a key focus within their lives. Give your time at a seniors' home or to needy children. Teach someone how to read or offer to give a public lecture on the subject of your expertise. Simply take action and do something to leave a legacy.

37. Recognize the power of mantras and the repetition of positive, powerful words. Indian yogis have employed this technique for over 4,000 years to live tranquil, productive and focused lives. Create your own personal mantra that you can repeat daily to enhance your character and strengthen your spirit.

38. The mind is like a garden – as you sow, so shall you reap. When you cultivate it and nurture it, it will blossom beyond your wildest expectation. But if you let the weeds

take over, you will never reach your potential. What you put in is what you get out. So avoid violent movies, trashy novels and all other negative influences. Peak performers are meticulous about the thoughts they allow into the gardens of their minds. You truly cannot afford the luxury of a single negative thought.

39. Do a hundred sit ups a day and do not break this habit. Strong abdominal muscles are very helpful to ensuring that you enjoy peak health and injury free days. They also maintain your appearance and confidence level. .

(Taken from 200 Life Lessons – Robin Sharma – 2005)

For any of these that you have chosen to incorporate into your life, please refer to the exercise on *practice* to help you better integrate them.

4. Empowerment and Our Inner Child

Firstly, what is this 'inner child' we are hearing so much about nowadays?

Every child has "a primary need for love, respect, understanding and being taken seriously" (Alice Miller). Whether there was overt abuse or neglect in our childhood or more subtle pressures and expectations, our psyches may bear childhood wounds. Our body and our emotions still hold everything we have ever experienced. Things that happened to us in childhood remain unhealed in most of us, and they contribute to the conflicts and problems we experience as adults.

The inner child represents the nature of emotional life, which can be observed much more clearly in the child than in the adult because the child can experience his feelings much more intensely and, optimally, than an adult. (Alice Miller)

The inner child is about emotions that are rampantly fluid. Other than the need for respect and for the allowance of "let me find my own way," our child just wishes to have fun, explore, play. This is a time for testing out its space, its limits, and its creativity.

As we become adults, veils that we create do not allow ourselves to remember those times. A healthy inner child means to know that, that inner child is always present and that to achieve balance and continued empowerment, we need to have our inner child present with our adult child.

You are miraculous, your children are miraculous, and all you have to do is watch your children as they use their spontaneous creativity to explore their childhood. Here are a few things that may stir up some of those memories:

Be there. Say "Yes" as often as possible, let them run, yell, jump up and down, make lots and lots of noise, play tag, bang on pots and pans. Go to the movies in your pajamas, read stories with fun and glee, with them. Remember what it felt like to be small, with all of their freedom, their innocence, and their purity. Hug a tree together. Find a forest and play hide and seek. Make believe you're a bird and fly, or a dog with its tail wagging, or a cat that loves to cuddle in the middle of the night, or a Kawala bear just being its cute self as it hangs on a branch. Bake a cake and eat it with your hands. Make lots of forts to hide in. Plant jellybeans in your garden. Be free, open up, stop yelling, be free, express your love. Remember, you were able to do it once so why not again?

Remember you are miraculous and, whether you know it or not, this little child will never, ever, ever go away and is just waiting to have fun and be remembered.

We have to ask ourselves how much have we forgotten? Are our children the past or are they our future? Can we be courageous enough to see that our role as a parent and adult is to live our lives, be the best we can be and allow our kids to find out how they can be the best *they* can be.

The question becomes: Can we educate our children to live completely?

This means that we have to help them to be intelligent and make healthy judgments, to help them to be sensitive, because to be able to recognize and practice our sensitivity is the highest form of intelligence.

Therefore when they are not at school, we have to help them at home how to recognize their sensitivity, to look at the trees, the flowers, to listen to the birds, to plant a tree or a garden. To learn what it feels like to cherish and nurture it as it grows up.

We must recognize that schools do not teach sensitivity and intelligence in this way; their role is more mundane as they ask us to study and pass exams so that we may ultimately get a job.

How drab and uninteresting this must be for them.

It makes sense to think that motivation, inspiration and creativity come with asking question after question and exploring the infinite amount of possibilities there are.

For it is our energy, our drive and our passion that lead to an empowered life.

This leads me to tell you about my experience this summer with kids. We can take it for granted that I absolutely am in love with kids. Don't worry, I love you also. I always have been but it is now that I am really getting in touch with my deep connection. I won't go into my childhood too much, because "god" knows that I can write a book about that.

Suffice to say, most of what kids are to experience by being just kids – fun and play and freedom – just wasn't in the cards for me. What I did experience was fear, deep fear. My world was full of mistrust, doubt and quite a bit of failure. I have not shared this with you to ask for any sympathy or anything but to let you know that my inner child has not come from a place of empowerment. Instead, it was covered up with layer upon layer of finding ways to survive.

The thing is, I know that today I am about playing and having fun and just allowing for the kid in me to come out. Consequently, for most of my life, I have been searching for ways to find and heal my inner child. Hence my becoming a teacher and dedicating my life to working with kids and families and, of course, to writing *There Is No Magic* and now *Wisdom in the Family*.

You see, I would never ask you do anything I haven't, so I've done quite a bit of digging for this 'inner child' thing. I can tell you from firsthand experience that he/she does exist and is just waiting to be rediscovered. It is screaming for some recognition. It loves all this adult stuff, but it is just waiting to be part of the mix. We do not have to be ashamed about showing this little plaything. We do not have to cover it up and run away from it. But we do need to see it, to embrace it, to remember it – the good and bad – and make it a full and respected part of who we are.

Getting back to this summer, I was asked by a friend of mine to spend some time in her camp and just to come up and do some activities with the kids. My first inclination was, "Wow, this is great," and I jumped at the opportunity to do this. Then after thinking about it, I asked her what she had in mind. After all, it has been (oh my) 30 years since I have worked in camp. I asked her, "Well, what am I going to do with them? And are you sure you want me to do this?"

In my mind, she seemed to be taking a chance because she really didn't know what I could or would do. I had come up with a few doubts but I just knew I wanted to do it and so I did. We agreed that I would come up and spend 7-10 days.

My next stop was Camp Kawandag, situated on Lake Rousseau, in the Muskoka region about three hours north of Toronto, Ontario. Needless to say it was amazingly beautiful, and I immediately attached myself to this experience.

I had a deep sense that something special was going to happen and it did!

Can you guess?

Yes, Yes, Yes,

I realized that the real reason for being there was just to play and experience with these kids something that up until now I had never experienced in my childhood. Now can you just feel all of those goose-bumps? That is exactly what I did. I became one of them, I did whatever they did, I played with them, I talked with them, I cried with them.

We loved each other and, oh yeah, we did all of those creative things I'd planned and had the greatest time of all. We all felt unconditional love and I healed an aspect of my inner child that was just waiting to happen for 55 years.

This experience transformed my life as it allowed me to find a missing piece. It allowed me to understand, and feel the power of my inner child and the importance of it in being able to live a balanced life. It peeled away a layer of the onion which has shown me how much I can love myself and how much more I have to give others.

I have often said that we cannot teach someone else until we truly know it within ourselves.

There is no doubt in my mind that you can use your creativity, understanding, compassion and love to find a way to empower your inner child for yourself. What do you think?

Exercise 9: Remembering Your Inner Child

Create your own scenario of the things you may do to play and interact with your own inner child.

_____

_____

_____

_____

_____

_____

_____

_____

_____

_____

_____

_____

_____

_____

_____

_____

_____

_____

_____

_____

_____

_____

_____

_____

_____

_____

_____

_____

_____

_____

_____

_____

_____

_____

Exercise 10: Meeting Your Inner Child

Create your own plan on how you can meet your child on its level. To be with it. To play with it. To work with it. To connect with it. To connect with yourself once again.

Don't be afraid to surrender, be free. Watch it as it does things in its most natural way. It will teach you how to do it and at the same time, you will discover something new about yourself.

Surrender to the resistance, to this feeling of being uncomfortable to the judgment.

Suppress the excuses and reasons for not to do it and just "do it."

Walk through this door and just watch and see the Magic,

First build a Daily Plan:

_____
_____
_____
_____
_____
_____
_____
_____
_____

(Note in your journal how you feel while you are finding new connections. Note the new connections you are making. Observe your child, Observe any changes. Write anything that comes into your mind.)

Then, build a weekly plan around personal events that you can participate with your child.

_____
_____
_____
_____
_____
_____
_____
_____
_____

(Note in your journal, all feelings and observations)

What does your inner child now look and feel like?

_____
_____

5. What Does Balance Have to Do with it?

Let us define balance as: "Harmony between what you do and what you think." When there is harmony between, physical health, intellectual capacity and sensory capacity, we can say we are in balance. Don't worry creating balance is a process, you take one step, you find a balance, you take another step you find a place of balance. Do you see this is never ending as there are multi stages of balance? I can guarantee one thing and that as you continue the process up and down and up and down and so on you will grow to be in a place that is more comfortable with yourself (in balance) your surroundings and your family.

Thinking of Having Kids?

Lesson 3
To discover how the nights will feel…
1. Walk around the living room from 5PM to 10PM carrying a wet bag weighing approximately 8-12 pounds, with a radio turned to static (or some other obnoxious sound) playing loudly.
2. At 10 PM, put the bag down, set the alarm for midnight, and go to sleep.
3. Get up at 12 and walk around the living room again, with the bag, until 1AM.
4. Set the alarm for 3AM.
5. As you can't get back to sleep, get up at 2AM and make a drink.
6. Go to bed at 2:45AM.
7. Get up at 3AM when the alarm goes off.
8. Sing songs in the dark until 4AM.
9. Get up. Make breakfast. Keep this up for 5 years. Look cheerful

---

6. The Power of Reflection

When people think of the word 'reflection,' they typically think first of a mirror. After all, we use it as a part of our normal morning routine. We walk to the bathroom and look at ourselves in the mirror. We do that out of habit, to see 'how we look' and to help us improve our appearance for the day ahead.

Mirrors are useful tools in our day. In a short amount of reflection time, we get information about ourselves that helps us have a more successful and enjoyable day. Most of us would miss having a mirror around, and some perhaps wouldn't think they could live without one.

It puzzles me that, while we use the power of reflection with a mirror as our tool; too few of us, far too infrequently, use the greater powers that reflection can bring to our lives for much greater good. In other words, we use a mirror to improve our outward appearance, but may not use the reflection tools that will improve us from the inside – in our minds and behaviors.

As professional and individuals who want to make a difference, reach our goals, achieve more, and unleash our potential, we need to be continuous learners. And to be the most effective continuous learners, we must learn to harness the power of reflection.

Our Experiences with 'Learning'

Most of our deep beliefs and ideas about learning come from our school experiences. In school, for the most part, reflection didn't play much of a role in the learning process. We were always learning the next thing, solving the next kind of problem. Rarely were we asked to look back and review our experiences to help us improve or learn more in the future. We were tested on what we learned – the grade being the outcome – and then we moved on to the next subject.

Because of this training and experience, that is how many people walk through their lives. They do some work, get a result, and move onto the next task or event, without looking back at what they did to see what they learned.

It is this type of reflection that I am speaking of: a process of systematically thinking, and perhaps writing about what happened, with the goal of transforming the experience into knowledge that can be used in all sorts of future situations.

How To Do It

In its simplest form, reflecting is just thinking about what happened. Reflection doesn't mean looking for blame or looking for regrets. It will be most valuable when it is an observation of events and their results. In general, your reflection will be most valuable to you when you think about and answer these types of questions:
- What happened (both the process and the end results)?
- How did I feel about it?
- Why did it happen that way (what contributed to the results)?
- What is it teaching me about me?
- This is an opportunity to grow. What can I now do differently in the future?

Reflecting can be a part of your everyday routine, just like looking in the mirror. You can reflect on the previous day, and see how you can apply the lessons in the coming day. You can take time to reflect on a project or specific event. Once you have the basic pattern of questions in your mind, you can reflect before going to bed, in your car on the way to work, while you exercise, or at some other time when you are doing routine things that don't require your full mental attention.

You might also decide to carve out new time to reflect while sitting with a journal. Writing our observations is a very powerful way to solidify and capture our learning. If this sounds intriguing to you, or you already journal and want to adjust how you use that time, fantastic!

Experience can be our greatest teacher. But it isn't like the teachers we had in school. We have to be our own teacher. We become that teacher when we step back and reflect.

Just like looking in the mirror, reflective thinking can be a habit. It will help you "see yourself better" and, after taking action on what you see (just like we may improve our appearance after what we see in the mirror), you will improve accordingly.

By **PRACTICING** being reflective we improve our skill of reflection.

*************************A Moment of Reflection*************************

A True Story

These moments are magical and can happen at any time. All you need is to be doing the work. In a flash, you are in another place, your body is doing something it never did before, or you just got something where for eons you were stuck. This is a story of one of those moments for me.

I was attending a weeklong workshop where there were 50 other people involved. For me, being with people is lots of fun so I began to intermingle with them, learn about some of them, play with them and allow for them to get to know me. As usual, there were those who I met that I made some quick judgments about and decided we were just not going to make it, or I made this determination that I may not have been good enough to be friends with them. There were also the moments when I had not even talked with a person but just made an arbitrary decision to not approach them. I didn't like them, or I may have been jealous, or whatever. These are thoughts that just flashed by.

Remind you of anything?

After about three days in the workshop, I had a thought that this experience was affording me a great opportunity to examine what these people were mirroring back to me. What were they teaching me, about my interactions with others and the type of judgments that I made for myself? Are these judgments hiding anything (fears, jealousy, etc.) within myself that are preventing me from further growth?

So, I made it into a game and began to question both the positive and negative feelings I was experiencing.

Then, I went up to that person and another and another and spent time with each of them, getting to know them and them me, reflecting on that feeling within me that earlier may have been creating an obstruction.

As I recognized what those feelings were, I pushed myself one step beyond. Not such an easy thing when you think about it, but in this case it was an act of walking through that door I'd never ventured to open before. It opened an entirely new world, new experiences, new interactions, new networking possibilities, greater understandings and clearings for me.

I fell in love with everyone around and, of course, in this moment, I found a piece of self-love that had been undiscoverable to this point.

People began to recognize me; they wanted to talk, play, and know more about me. They saw things in me that I'd not recognized and were my teachers. It was amazing.

This act of reflection allowed for a deep release of myriad emotions that had been blocking my interpersonal and career development for a lifetime.

From this point onward each day represents a further exploration and playing with this new found skill. It also is a great example of the Power of Reflection.

Exercise 11: The Reflection Game

Pretend you are looking in the mirror and your aim is to make yourself look better both inside and outside. On some level, you know you're perceived by the way you present yourself to your environment.

Ask yourself these questions as you place yourself in life situations:

- What is the experience I am in?
- How do I feel about it? What are these feelings?
- How am I reacting to this experience?
- What things are being reflected back to me?
- Traditionally how has this experience ended? Why? (What contributed to the results?)
- What is it teaching me about me?
- How is this an opportunity to grow?
- What can I now do differently in the future?

Reflection Opportunities

1. I own my own business, I have 8 employees working for me and I am looking to increase my bottom line. What can I change about myself to make me a more effective leader?

_____
_____
_____
_____
_____

2. My daughter just broke her curfew for the third time. Each time she has done so, I have grounded her for one week. She has tried to talk to me about it but I won't listen. She is getting more adamant and angry. What is she asking me to do? What can I learn about myself?

_____
_____
_____
_____
_____

---

3. I am driving in the car with my daughter, and thought it would be a good time to talk about our relationship. She says no not now. I ask her why not? She says because she doesn't want to. I get angrier and more defiant with her; Things just build until we have an explosion. What do I need to be aware of my behavior? What do I need to be conscious of my daughters needs?

_____
_____
_____
_____
_____
_____
_____

4. I don't seem to be able to have any patience with my girlfriend. Things had started out so great; for the first 3 months we were really in love, always together, talking, communicating, this relationship seemed to be the one. Now she is not being so attentive, we get into lots of arguments, she is not listening to what I have to say. She is trying to tell me what to do all of the time. What is she mirroring back to me?

_____
_____
_____
_____
_____
_____
_____

5. Now that we had our first baby, I find that my parents are always over. They seem to be wanting to tell me how to be a parent. I feel that they are not allowing me to be a daddy on my own. I want to run away. I can't talk with them because I don't want to cause any problems. I am afraid to hurt their feelings. I am angry, confused and frustrated. What is this experience teaching me about me? What are some of my thoughts that I can change that will shift the way I am feeling about myself? About my parents?

_____
_____
_____
_____
_____
_____

The Power of Choice

Empowerment and the power of choice

We always have a choice. If someone sticks a gun in my face and says, "Your money or your life!" I have a choice. I may not like my choice but I have one. In life we often don't like our choices because we don't know what the outcome is going to be and we are terrified of doing it 'wrong.'

Even with life events that occur in a way that we seemingly don't have a choice over (being laid off work, the car breaking down, a flood, etc.); we still have a choice over how we respond to those events. We can choose to see tragedy as an opportunity for growth. We can choose to focus on the half of the glass that's full and be grateful for it, or to focus on the half that is empty and be the victim of it. We have a choice about where we focus our minds.

"Empowerment is seeing reality as it really is, owning the choices you have, and making the best of it. There is incredible power in the simple words "I choose."

Looking from the outside:

As long as we look outside of Self – with a capital S – to find out who we are, to define ourselves and give us self-worth, we are setting ourselves up to be victims.

We were taught to look outside of ourselves – to people, places, and things; to money, property, and prestige – for fulfillment and happiness. It does not work; it is dysfunctional. We cannot fill the hole within with anything outside of self.

You can get all the money, property, and prestige in the world, and have everyone in the world adore you, but if you are not at peace within; if you don't love and accept yourself, none of it will work to make you truly happy.

When we look outside for self-definition and self-worth, we are giving power away and setting ourselves up to be victims. We are trained to be victims. We are taught to give our power away.

As just one small example of how pervasively we are trained to be victims, consider how often you have said, or heard someone say, "I have to go to work tomorrow." When we say "I *have* to." we are making a victim statement. To say, "I have to get up, and I have to go to work," is a lie. No one forces an adult to get up and go to work. The truth is: "I *choose* to get up and I *choose* to go to work today, because I *choose* to not have the consequences of not working." To say, *"I choose,"* is not only the truth, it is empowering and acknowledges an act of self-love. When we "have to" do something, we feel like a victim. And because we feel victimized, we will then be angry and want to punish whomever we see as forcing us to do something we do not want to do, such as our family, or our boss, or society.

Finding a Balance:

As children, we were taught that it is shamefully bad to make mistakes – that we caused our parents great emotional pain if we were not perfect. So as adults, most of us went to one extreme or the other ... that is we tried to do it perfectly according to the rules we were taught (get married, have a family and career, work hard and you will be rewarded, etc.) or we rebelled and broke the rules (and usually became conformists to the anti-establishment rules). Some of us tried going one way and when that didn't work; we turned around and went the other way.

By going to either extreme, we were giving our power away. We were not choosing our own path but were reacting to their path.

Integrating spiritual truth into our process is vital in order to take the crippling toxic shame about being imperfect humans out of the equation. That toxic shame is what makes it so hard for us to own our right to make choices instead of just reacting to someone else's set of rules.

Recovery from victim hood is about balance and integration. Finding the balance of taking responsibility for our part in things while also holding others responsible for their part. The black and white perspective is never the truth. The truth in human interactions (the horizontal) is always somewhere in the gray area.

In order to become empowered, to become the co-creator in our lives, and to stop giving power to the belief that we are the victim, it is absolutely necessary to own that we have choices. As in the discussion above, if we believe we *have* to do something, then we are buying into the belief that we are the victim and don't have the power to make choices. To say, "I *have* to go to work" is a lie. "I have to go to work if I want to eat" may be the truth but then you are making a choice to eat. The more conscious we get about our choices, the more empowered we become.

We need to take *have to* out of our vocabulary. As long as we are reacting to life unconsciously, we do not have choices. In consciousness, we always have a choice. We do not *have to* do anything.

Until we own that we have a choice, we haven't made one. In other words, if you do not believe you have a choice to leave your job, or relationship, then you have not made a choice to stay in it. You can only truly commit yourself to something if you are consciously choosing to do it. This includes the area that is probably the single hardest job in our society today, the area that it is almost impossible not to feel trapped in some of the time – being a single parent. A single parent has the choice of giving their children up for adoption, or abandoning them. That is a choice! If a single parent believes that he/she has no choice, then they will feel trapped and resentful and will end up taking it out on their children.

Empowerment is seeing reality as it really is, owning the choices you have, and making the best of it with the support of a loving God-Force. There is incredible power in the simple words, "I choose."

2. The Power of Practice

I have saved the best for last because, even though I have not spoken of this word practice so much, *Wisdom in the Family* is all about *practice*. If we look at any aspect of our life, whether we are an athlete, a businessman, an actor, an artist, a speaker, we use "practice" to develop our skill.

The job of parenting is no different. To develop our skill, we must practice the skills of observation, listening, communication, planning, discipline, motivation, introspection, compassion, understanding, research, advocacy, homemaking, art, discernment, exercise and so on … the list is endless. Are you getting the picture? Parenting, in fact, is a conglomeration of every job that exists in the universe.

The most important aspect of it all (and this may sound repetitive) but the overall theme of this piece of work, of your piece of work, is that parenting is all about 'life.' That life is all about playing this game, making changes and playing some more.

In actual fact, to be a 'parent' means to be in the practice of bringing up the next generation. This is 'The Forever Game.' So wouldn't it behoove us to learn, develop and practice the skills that will allow us to be exemplary players of this game?

I was driving in my car when my spouse first told me we were expecting to have a child. I'm not kidding. My first thought and almost reflex action at that moment was to put on my seat belt. From that time on, I have never been in my car without my seatbelt buckled. For the first time in my life, I felt mortal. I knew that 'The Forever Game' had begun. I was happy, afraid, confused, consumed by it all.

So lets all of us make it our passion to play this game of "Parenting"

WE DO HAVE A CHOICE!

To play this game, to get ahead in this game, to find your balance in this game,
The answer is simple:
Create a plan and
PRACTICE, PRACTICE, PRACTICE

Game Plan

Use your new found knowledge of how you may manifest your life's passion knowing your impediments, knowing where you manifest your, "Thunder and Lightning", rediscovering your inner child and all of the new powers which you can test out and using these awareness's to create something you have wanted for a long time.

Exercise 12: The Game Plan

The process looks like this:

- We must understand what our impediments are that are not allowing us to create positive change.
- We must really understand our behaviors, our roles and how we fit into the mix. We need to be open and accept responsibility that we are the creators of our Magic.
- What are the things that empower us? Are we ready to incorporate into our lives what is necessary to remove these obstructions? Are we ready to feel better about ourselves? Do we really understand the implications of empowerment for ourselves, for our relationships, for our families?
- We have spoken about changing attitudes? To do this, we must first recognize our thought patterns.
- These thought patterns directly translate into how we behave.
- So we can logically say, to change our behavior, we must change our thoughts. There is only one way to do this and that is to *practice*.

_____

_____

_____

_____

_____

_____

_____

_____

_____

_____

_____

_____

_____

_____

_____

_____

_____

_____

_____

_____

_____

_____

_____

Chapter 3

The Empowered Family:

Understanding Our Children

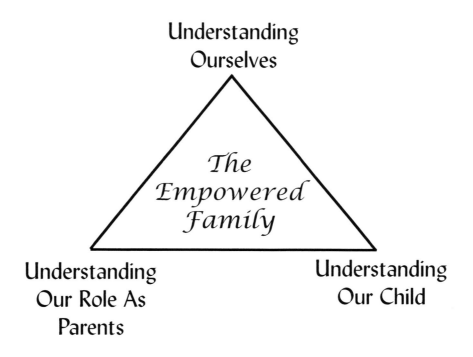

Understanding
Ourselves

The
Empowered
Family

Understanding
Our Role As
Parents

Understanding
Our Child

The first step in understanding who our kids are is to get to know ourselves a little more. The best way to do this is to see how we are interfacing with our kids and, very specifically, to see how that is directly affecting the relationship we are having with them. To do this, it is important to realize the style of parenting you are using and the impact that style is having on the social and emotional development of your child.

The Four Parenting Styles

There are held to be four main styles of parenting: indulgent, authoritarian, authoritative and laissez-faire. Each of these parenting styles reflects naturally learned patterns of parental values, practices and behaviors.

We'll briefly examine each style.

1. **Indulgent parents** (may also be classified as 'permissive' or 'non-directive') are more responsive than they are demanding. They are non-traditional and lenient, do not require mature behavior, and they allow considerable self-regulation and avoid confrontation.

2. **Authoritarian Parents** - are highly demanding and directive, but non-responsive. They are obedience- and status-oriented and expect their orders to be obeyed without explanation or questioning. These parents provide well-ordered and structured environments with clearly stated rules and limits. Authoritarian parents can be divided into two types: non-authoritarian-directive, who are directive, but not intrusive or autocratic in their use of power; and authoritarian-directive, who are highly intrusive and controlling with their demands.

3. **Authoritative parents** can be both demanding and responsive. They monitor and impart clear standards for their child's behavior. They are assertive, but not intrusive and restrictive. Their disciplinary methods are supportive, rather than punitive. They want their children to be assertive as well as socially responsible, and self-regulated as well as cooperative.

4. **Laissez-faire Parents** are low in both responsiveness and making demands. They are passive and may have difficulty accepting responsibility for their behavior in the full parenting of their child.

To clarify some differences between the Authoritarian and the Authoritative parenting styles, both Authoritarian and Authoritative parents place high demands on their children and expect their children to behave 'appropriately' and obey parental rules. Authoritarian parents, however, also expect their children to accept their judgments, values and goals without questioning. In contrast, authoritative parents are more open to give-and-take with their children and make greater use of explanations. Thus, although authoritative and authoritarian parents are equally high in behavioral control, authoritative parents tend to be low in psychological control, while authoritarian parents tend to be high.

As I was researching parenting styles, a few very interesting facts stuck out: I observed that:

- Parenting style has been found to predict the child's well-being in the areas of social competence, academic performance, as well as psychological development and problem behavior.
- Children and adolescents whose parents are consistently authoritative are more socially and psychologically competent than those whose parents are non-authoritative. It was found that the more responsive a parent is, the more socially and psychologically balanced the child is, while parental demands are associated with how the child may do academically and behaviorally.
- Children and adolescents from authoritarian families (high in demands, but low in responsiveness) tend to perform moderately well academically and be disinterested in their problem behavior. They have poor social skills, lower self-esteem and higher levels of depression.
- Children and adolescents from indulgent homes (high in responsiveness, low in demands) are more likely to be involved in their behavior and perform less well in school. That they have a higher self-esteem, better social skills and lower levels of depression.

It's interesting to note that children who have parents who exhibit an authoritative style of parenting exhibit lower levels of acting out (problem behavior), are better socially adjusted and do better academically.

Since there are several types of temperaments your child may have, your parenting style may be influenced by your child's personality characteristics. The next section discusses these different temperaments and how you may best adjust your parenting style accordingly.

Are we ready to see our children as feeling better about themselves, safer and more confident? Are we ready to experience a higher degree of success as parents? Are we really ready to bridge the widening gap and create a more harmonious family unit? Are we ready to take what we know about ourselves and our children and to take a stand and follow through on the "Big Three" keys to successful parenting?

The three keys to successful parenting are:

1. **Be CONSISTENT**
2. **Be FIRM**
3. **Be LOVING**

In adapting this to our parenting style, we can empower our child to be the very best they can be!

DISCLAIMER

It must be emphasized, and you can use this as a *mantra:*

"Any one of the above parenting styles is not to be seen as BAD. Just like my kids, I have my own unique styles."

(Say this 108 times every day for 3 weeks or until it is ingrained in your memory)

The lesson here is to understand that we may use any and all of these styles at different times. They depend on:

Ø The situation which you may be in.

Ø The developmental stage which your child is in. For example, if your sole parenting style is Authoritarian and you have a teenager, it is guaranteed that you will be butting heads and probably be in chaos for 5 to 6 years. You have a choice and judgment as to how you want to respond to certain situations.

Ø The temperament of your child.

Ø The learning style of your child.

Ø Your own unique temperament.

Exercise: Parenting Style

<u>Parenting Style Inventory</u>

Please remember that the situation, the age, the temperament and the developmental stage of your child will dictate what type of parenting style you will use. So the characteristics below are not *bad* or *good*.

Please be as accurate as you can when filling out this inventory.

Place a check mark to as many characteristics that describes your dominant Parenting Style.

After you are done you will see a symbol next to those lines that you checked, count each symbol separately and the symbol that you have most of represents your dominant parenting style.

- ❑   Highly demanding *
- ❑   Permissive ^
- ❑   Highly Responsive > ^
- ❑   Low Responsive #
- ❑   Not Demanding ^
- ❑   Proactive * >
- ❑   Passive # ^
- ❑   Accepts Responsibility >
- ❑   Does not Accept Responsibility #
- ❑   Set clear standards * >
- ❑   Monitor behavior *>
- ❑   Assertive * >
- ❑   Highly restrictive *
- ❑   Low restrictive ^ # >
- ❑   Disciplinary methods are supportive > ^ #
- ❑   Disciplinary methods are punitive *
- ❑   Tend to be non-directive ^ #
- ❑   Lenient when it comes to discipline ^ #
- ❑   You allow your children to regulate themselves > ^ #
- ❑   You avoid confrontation ^ # *
- ❑   You promote confrontation >
- ❑   You are non-responsive # *
- ❑   You require obedience * >
- ❑   You are highly Directive *
- ❑   You provide a well ordered, structured environment * >
- ❑   You provide clearly stated rules and Limits * >

<u>Key:</u>

(*) Authoritarian
(^) Indulgent
(>) Authoritative
(#) Laissez-faire

Traits of Children

Earlier in this chapter, we were discussing different aspects of ways that we may be able to better understand our child. What follows is some excellent information as to the type of temperament your child may have. It provides descriptions of each, and gives some suggestions as to how to adapt your parenting style and the optimum learning strategies for each temperament in the hope that it will assist you in making parental and educational decisions.

An infamous psychiatrist named Carl Jung did extensive research on the differences and temperaments of children in an effort to familiarize parents with their child's needs.

He classified four differences that exist:

1. Introversion vs. Extroversion
2. Sensation vs. Intuition
3. Thinking vs. Feeling
4. Judgment vs. Perception

We will look at these four temperaments as they present themselves in childhood and then examine how they affect the teaching of, and learning ability, of a child.

Extroversion vs. Introversion

An Observation: Does the child show hesitation in approaching a stranger, teacher, an event, or does the child approach a stranger, teacher or event with enthusiasm and without apparent reserve?

The introverted child is likely to hold back when faced with something or someone unfamiliar, while the extroverted child is more likely to approach the situation without hesitation. The introverted child tends to be shy, quiet and less intrusive than the extroverted child. The introverted child is apt to take their time about a decision and be slower to respond, seeming to absorb the information before communicating. Because of this, the introverted child may appear to be less intellectually capable than he/she actually is. The introvert reserves from 'public view' aspects of their temperament, which are in the process of developing. What is presented to the public are those qualities already developed. There are parts of their real selves, which are not available to their teachers, parents and friends. They are sometimes seen as a puzzle waiting to unfold. They may be judged as being stubborn or lack self-esteem because of their desire to hold back until they are surer of what they wish to present of themselves. It is the introverted child who is most often misunderstood and pressured to change. Their tendency to be retiring and shy, their slower development of social skills, their tendency to draw back when confronted by a more assertive person, their slowness to interact in the classroom and their need for privacy are all behaviors that parents and teachers may attempt to correct. In the process of doing this, they may be communicating to this child that its natural ways are wrong. How often have you heard someone say to a shy child, "Is there anything wrong? You're being so quiet." Quite often this just causes the introverted child to become even more withdrawn. For some reason, we as adults become uncomfortable, or maybe personally threatened, when we encounter a being who operates more from within.

On the other hand, the extroverted child is usually better understood and relates well to others. They are at home in their social environment and tend to be responsive, expressive and enthusiastic. They more readily enter into group activities. They seem to adjust better to changes in their lives and tolerate negative interactions better than the introverted child does. They tend to approach new situations quickly, to verbalize and act quickly. They exhibit a certainty in making decisions, giving the impression of self-confidence. The extroverted child gets considerably more confirmation of their behavior and attitude, both from adults and other children, than does the introverted child. The consequence of this is that extroverts grow up with fewer doubts about themselves than their counterparts.

Sensation vs. Intuition

An Observation: Does the child daydream frequently and seem hungry for fantastic tales, even wanting them repeated over and over, or is the child more bent on action, getting involved in games and liking more factual stories?

According to research, the intuitive child is likely to ask for repetition of stories and likes stories that are fantasy-related. The sensitive child likes the adventure story that is familiar and factual in nature. They want the story to make sense. They like stories with lots of detail. The sensation child likes to engage in playing games or activities that involve some form of action.

The intuitive child is likely to anticipate future events. Also, if a promise is made to the intuitive child, breaking that promise will result in major upset, where the sensitive child may take the change more in stride. The intuitive child may pose a behavior problem because they want to 'do their own thing' or 'are their own person.' If they do not believe that someone is speaking the truth, they will challenge their authority. They seem confident as to their intents and purposes as if they know what they are supposed to be doing. Adults may interpret this behavior as being defiant and this will often lead to discipline and conflict if one is not aware. In addition, because the intuitive child is often looking ahead, they may seem preoccupied and inattentive. Some of these qualities are associated with Attention Deficit and Hyperactive Disorder (ADHD). Both educators and parents need to be cautious because there are many cases where these children are identified and labeled with ADHD when such is not the case.

In addition, intuitive children are passionate about their beliefs and if their trust is violated, their feelings are likely to be hurt. They are honest and direct in their relationships with their peers and authority figures. They speak their mind, which they know to be the truth. As their parents and teachers, we often tend to think that these children are eccentric, live a life of their own or are troublemakers. This type of reaction to them creates a block in their creative processes and they can suffer considerable damage to their self-esteem.

Where the intuitive child may be daydreaming away the hours, the sensitive child is animated and very involved with their activities and relationships. The sensitive child responds well to details and loves to engage with those that are around him. Toys, for a sensitive child, will retain their character. For example, a truck remains a truck to be used for hauling or storing, whereas for the intuitive child, that same truck might be turned into a submarine or a monster that is able to fly.

Understanding these differences of both the intuitive child and the sensitive child can be vital to the academic and social development of both of these types of children. It is, however, the intuitive child who is most likely to be the one who seems 'odd.'

Thinking vs. Feeling

An Observation: When asked to obey in a situation he does not quite understand, does the child tend to ask for reasons (thinking) or does the child tend to seek to please (feeling)?

The child who prefers the 'thinking' way is likely to want an explanation for being asked to do something, while the child who chooses the 'feeling' way will want some confirmation that he/she is pleasing the other person by his good deed. The feeling child is likely to be more sensitive to the feelings of others and is likely to want to do little things to help out and then be recognized for their accomplishments.

The feeling child is very sensitive to the emotional climate of their home and will react to the conflict and stress they are feeling around them. On the other hand, the thinking child seems to find it easy to detach himself from the disharmony happening around him. The thinking child may not want to be touched and may have difficulty in approaching a parent with affection while the feeling child responds easily with physical affection. The feeling child is likely to cry more easily than the thinking child is. Although the feeling child seems more vulnerable than does the thinking child to the approval or disapproval of a parent or teacher, this is usually a front or defensive reaction. The thinking child may seem to be indifferent and unresponsive, but inside may be hurting or desiring just as much as the more expressive and open feeling child.

Perceiving vs. Judging

An Observation: *Does the child seem to want things settled, decided and chosen, or does he want to be surprised and have choices at all times?*

The judging child, who seems to want things established and in order, probably has a tendency to be calculating and will, more often than not, weigh things before making decisions. The child who seems indifferent to authority figures, the perceiving child, may be the one who is reacting to his perceptions and his environment. It is the judging child who is likely to be ready and on time for appointments and tends to be neat and organized. The perceiving child may seem unconcerned about being on time, his room or desk may be a mess and he may have difficulty understanding why this type of behavior causes discomfort with teachers or parents.

The judging child is apt to be more of a leader within his peer group. The perceiving child often needs to be reminded to get dressed, to come to dinner, to do homework or chores, etc.

The judging child is more the more assertive one and initiates carrying out his/her daily routines. The judging child seems surer of himself whereas the perceiving child may be more tentative and laid back.

Thinking of Having Kids?

<u>Lesson 4</u>
Can you stand the mess children make? To find out...
1. **Smear peanut butter onto the sofa and jam onto the curtains.**
2. **Hide a piece of raw chicken behind the stereo and leave it there all summer.**
3. **Stick your fingers in the flower bed.**
4. **Then rub them on the clean walls.**
5. **Cover the stains with crayons. How does that look?**

The Four Temperaments in Children

In his research, Jung broke up the temperaments of children into four categories. If you can identify your child, it may help when making some decisions about educational, social and emotional needs.

1.   The Sensible Playful Temperament

This child is likely to be active. They love to eat and love to get 'down and dirty.' Leave them in the sandbox or backyard and they will find the nearest mud puddle to roll around in. This will undoubtedly lead to many reprimands, but as a parent, we should be cautious about discouraging this behavior. After a while, your child will be indifferent to the scolding. If you can treat it with lightness and humor, you will see that you will be positively reinforcing this natural behavior in them. As they grow up, they are more likely to approach their lives with a sense of being able to get right into the fray of things. Their rooms are likely to be a jumble of toys, clothes and assorted objects, all in apparent disarray but absolutely perfect for the sensible playful child. I was witness to my brother displaying all of these characteristics, and today he has turned out to be quite the successful businessman.

This child is really in a different zone from the one we operate in. Their attitude is "What difference does it make?" They would rather be off doing something that makes sense to them, like having fun.

Yet the Sensible Playful Child can get really involved in an activity and stay there for hours at a time. He can spend hours with a musical instrument, only to lose interest the next day. Those who do not lose interest, and are adequately reinforced by their parents, become the outstanding performing artists, graphic artists and artists of all types. The sensible playful child needs movement and excitement and they thirst for competition.

This is a very upbeat child and really cheerful. They can bring fun and laughter into the home and classroom. They love to participate in activities, and they throw themselves wholeheartedly into instrumental play, musical performances, art activities and games. They may enjoy working with a variety of tools rather than the actual product they make. The more game-like the task, the better it is for them. They love the ages of 3 – 6 because it is all fun and play and exploration, but as they move up through the grades and schoolwork becomes more a matter of following a specific curriculum and structure, they often become disinterested. They do not like to prepare or 'get ready' for anything and, as the demand for concentration grows, so does their restlessness. The result may be in the form of disruption of their class or acting out at home. They may be seen as very jittery, bored and not being able to focus well. At times, they have been labeled as hyperactive or as having Attention Deficit Disorder. This brings on a panacea of negative behaviors, which include a low self-esteem and poor academic and social performances.

It is important that the sensible playful child be provided periods of quiet activities and training in relaxation such as Yoga, meditation, breathing and visualization exercises. They need space in which they can be active, but they also require their own private space. A learning carrel (desk with three sides to cut down on external stimuli) proves effective in facilitating the completion of their schoolwork.

Sensible Playful Children are likely to feel good about themselves and about those who have control over them if they are provided a great deal of room to move around. Lecture type presentations should be short, as should their reading activities. Quiet, learning activities are best mixed in with opportunities for the child to be active with some area of personal interest. Frequent change from individual work space to a small group and then to large group activities will also help to better meet the sensible playful child's educational and social needs.

All of this is not to imply that they should not be given practice in concentration and limit-setting. Of course, they must also develop these abilities, but the first step to this development is to legitimize and recognize their natural preferences and their acute nature to be impulsive and to become easily frustrated.

Needless to say,. The Sensible Playful Child can be a behavioral problem in school and at home. They do not respond well to our traditional ways of discipline. These are the children that are labeled as combative and defiant. Because they do not conform, they learn to seek attention in very negative ways. An alternative to this is to recognize them for who they are and what they need in order to be successful.

Learning Style

These children require the freedom to get involved in physical activities, to learn in an environment of excitement, where adventure and competition are part of the curriculum. Where sound, color and motions are plentiful. They love to get involved with musical instruments because this provides both hands-on activity and performing in front of groups.

They can be excellent team members if there is a competition. They gravitate towards music, drama, art, crafts, mechanics and construction. Anything that requires hands-on activity is a valuable learning tool for this child.

They are quite visual and kinesthetic in their learning styles and their curriculums should reflect and take advantage of these strengths.

If these kinds of activities are not provided, this child will most likely find other outlets, which may be disruptive. If they are forced to conform by being made to stand in line, waiting, routines, "Wait for tomorrow," they will find this task less and less appealing. For the most part, this child does far less in school than they could do had they been given sufficient incentive. This child will be a source of frustration to parents, teachers and administrators, as these people will be trying to project their own desires and controls on them. The sensible playful child will have none of this. Their goals are to find out 'who they are' and to be more in the moment.

2.   The Sensible Judicious Temperament

The Sensible Judicious Child is more sensitive and vulnerable to instabilities within their environment. They find security in knowing that their parents are unified and in control. If there are inconsistencies from one parent to the other regarding discipline and family policies, this will create disharmony in this child's life. It should be noted that this statement is true for almost any child and is not just specific to the sensible judicious personality.

The Sensible Judicious Child does best when their surroundings are familiar to them. Growing up with the same friends, in the same neighborhood and school system, suits them best. They love to share with the extended family such as grandparents, uncles, aunts and cousins.

The Sensible Judicious Child works best when there are established routines in place and they know what their responsibilities are. Their great source of pleasure is the approval they are given by adults as they go about their activities. As a matter of fact, this reinforcement is vital to the development of their healthy self-esteem. They tend to adjust well to their school environment and daily routines. Since they flourish with structure, they thrive on activities such as workbook activities, repetition, reading aloud, spelling, factual aspects of social studies, science and history and any activity that requires drill. They pay attention to details and hold high standards of achievement for themselves and others. Good study habits are important and they learn best when kept on a schedule. They will try in earnest to please their teacher and will respond negatively to criticism. In college the Sensible Judicious Child tends to focus on careers such as business, accounting, and teaching.

Learning Style

This child desires to belong within the family unit and later, when they enter school, to the classroom group. Responsibility, dependability, duty and service are words that are strongly associated with this child. This child thrives in the traditional classroom setting. They have a strong wish to please their teacher, basically because they mirror the teacher, this authority figure who sets structure and limits and where a sense of security is felt and developed. The values of the teacher are compatible with their own. Good study habits, doing homework as assigned and on time, and following the assigned rules as directed, are seen as worthwhile. They are conscientious and will attempt to do their best as long as they receive clear directions so they know how to proceed with the activity.

The Sensible Judicious Child acquires knowledge through searching for facts; through frequent review and traditional teaching materials (textbook and workbook) Programmed-learning materials are very effective tools for this child.

They are auditory and tactile, kinesthetic learners. That is to say, they learn best when they hear the information and write or say the response. They also do best with "hands-on" materials.

3.   The Intuitive Thinking Temperament

The Intuitive Thinking Child will tend to be a puzzle to those people around them. They may be classified as precocious; they tend talk at an early age and learn to read before going to elementary school. The Intuitive Thinking Child is likely to ask a lot of "why" questions. "Why do the stars come out at night?" "Why does a bird fly?" "Why can't I fly like a bird?" "Why do I have to go to school when I can learn at home?"

They are usually very independent children and are seen as nonconformists. They are extremely curious and learn best when given the freedom to explore. They will ask themselves, "What would happen if...?" and then proceed to attempt to find the answer, sometimes resulting in getting themselves into trouble. For example, even though you may have told them a dozen times that the stove is hot and not to touch, they may have to see for themselves before believing you. Despite this, they tend to be obedient and compliant with issues they are indifferent to. They tend not to be interested in coming into conflict with those around them. If punishment is administered as a result of their curiosity and investigations, they are apt to accept the consequences impersonally. They can be a frustration to their teachers and other authoritative figures because they stay somewhat detached in their reactions to discipline. The Intuitive Thinking Child will quickly lose respect and ignore those who are not consistent and logical in their style of discipline. Sometimes, as parents and teachers, we say things or threaten with things that we cannot follow through on. This child learns quickly not to respond to these tactics.

Any physical punishment is deeply violating to the Intuitive Thinking Child. His body is a source of endless exploration, as is his external environment. Because of this, they may overreact to discipline in the physical sense. They see this as a violation to their mind, body and spirit.

They are seen as full of pride and dignified and they expect the same in others.

Parenting the intuitive thinking child mainly means *hands off*. The Intuitive Thinking Child needs an abundance of opportunities to experiment, find out and get the answers. Attempting to shut off this experimental and exploration avenue will cause this child to act out, seek attention in negative ways and be disruptive.

Learning Style

The Intuitive Thinking Child usually enjoys reading books and being read to. Their enjoyment in being read to is a function of their curiosity and, through stories; they encounter complexities and learning that they cannot gain through their own reading. They can get deeply engrossed with a new toy or activity and play for hours at a time on their own. On the other hand, they may lose interest in this toy just as fast and never go back to it again. Providing them with help and guidance when they ask for it, being patient with their endless questioning, and allowing them the freedom and space they require in order to function within their world will ultimately allow for them to grow up with a healthy and self-confident feeling about themselves.

They have a great hunger to learn and these desires are directly linked to their levels of ability and their self-confidence. They have difficulty is setting priorities and often need help with their organizational skills.

Intuitive Thinking Children are devastated by criticism of their skill and ability levels. They can be self-doubting and require vast amounts of positive reinforcement to develop a healthy sense of self. Sometimes, because of their early interest in the sciences, well-meaning parents and teachers may expect too much from them, resulting in failure and withdrawal.

4.   The Intuitive Feeling Temperament

At a very early age, these children display a gift for language. They are early talkers and love to partake in conversation. They can be very charming and love to play as they express their creativity through their talking. Because of this heightened degree of sociability, they frequently will draw both their peers and adults around them. It is important to note that they are highly imaginative, and that it's important for this quality to be reinforced. In addition, it is important to note that the Intuitive Feeling Child may be hypersensitive emotionally to rejection and conflict, so they require reassurance that those around them are feeling good about themselves and in control.

The Intuitive Feeling Child enjoys being read to, especially highly imaginative stories, and may ask you to repeat the same story over again several times. They love to play with toys and can identify with their characters. It is common for this child to have and play with an imaginary friend. As a parent, it is important to recognize and support your child and their character. This will help to develop self-esteem and will nurture their creativity, spirituality and ability to relate to others in later life. If the child's fantasies are rejected, the child may withdraw, become more fearful and less trusting of their world and the people in it.

Because Intuitive Feeling Children are quite sensitive, they need to be gently guided through their successes and failures as they learn to stand up for themselves and fully walk with a sense of confidence through the complexities of life. A harsh and authoritative approach will again cause withdrawal and the seeking of attention in negative ways. A common form used is passive aggression.

Learning Style

Because of their outstanding linguistic abilities, the Intuitive Feeling Child will tend to do well academically. They are good readers with good comprehension skills. They are good communicators. They like to work in small groups and are very democratic and introspective by nature. They activities that involve research, history and social studies. They use their perceptive skills to study people's attitudes and values. They can quickly discern in people what they like and dislike, how they behave, why they behave the way they do. All of this fascinates this child.

They are kinesthetic and visual learners. That is, they learn best when interaction occurs both visually and by touch in their world.

It would seem that they would choose careers that involve liberal arts, psychology and teaching.

We are all different. We want different things; have different goals and objectives, values, ethics, drives and impulses. Nothing is more obvious than this. We think, perceive, understand, and comprehend differently. As parents, it is important to understand this about ourselves as well as our children. To explore new ways of looking at ourselves and the people in our lives. Not only are we what we have learned from our role models but, as unique individuals and spirits, we all deserve the opportunity to be recognized individually and to be treated in the same manner. We deserve the opportunity to learn and explore our world as unique and gentle beings in order to walk through our lives feeling good about who we are and ultimately to be exemplary contributors to our communities. It is our birthright to experience growth and to recognize our responsibility to then pass it on to our loved ones.

Exercise: Child Temperament Inventory
Please read this whole chapter prior to doing this exercise

After you are done you will see a symbol next to those lines that you checked, count each symbol separately and the symbol that you have most of represents your Child's unique Temperament.

Child Temperament Inventory

- ❑ Active – get down & dirty *
- ❑ More Sensitive – Vulnerable to change >
- ❑ Are your children a puzzle? ^ #
- ❑ Displays a gift for language # ^
- ❑ Precocious – they talk / learn to read early ^ #
- ❑ They like to get involved in activities *
- ❑ Assertive, go getter *
- ❑ Feelings of safety hinges upon consistency with parents /environment >
- ❑ Respond best with immediate reinforcement >
- ❑ Lots of "Why" questions ^
- ❑ Early talkers # ^
- ❑ Independent ^
- ❑ Love conversation #
- ❑ Non-Conformist ^
- ❑ They love movement & excitement. *
- ❑ Do best with structure *
- ❑ Very social #
- ❑ Require freedom to explore ^
- ❑ Highly imaginative #
- ❑ Very sensitive # ^
- ❑ Highly creative # * ^
- ❑ Require quiet time / private time * ^ #
- ❑ They try very hard to please >
- ❑ They require gentle parenting # ^ >

Key

* The Sensible Playful child.
\> The Sensible Judicious child.
^ The Intuitive Thinking child.
\# The Intuitive Feeling child.

After you are done you will see a symbol next to those lines that you checked, count each symbol separately and the symbol that you have most of represents your Child's dominant Learning Style

<u>Learning Style Inventory</u>
- ❑ They love to learn through fun *
- ❑ Require freedom to get involved in physical Activities *
- ❑ Auditory / Tactile learners >
- ❑ Thrives in traditional classroom setting >
- ❑ Visual / Auditory / Kinesthetic Learners ^
- ❑ Excellent Reading / Comprehension skills #
- ❑ Good listeners #
- ❑ Extremely Curious ^
- ❑ Love to read and be read to ^ #
- ❑ Feels safe & secure when structure is imposed >
- ❑ Learns best with highly creative curriculum *
- ❑ Very perceptive #
- ❑ Needs help with organization ^
- ❑ Lots of sound & color & motion *
- ❑ Likes to work in small groups #
- ❑ Requires patience ^ # >
- ❑ Likes to get involved with musical instruments *
- ❑ Frequent change- Individual work / small group/ larger group *
- ❑ Conscientious – does best when instructions are clear >
- ❑ Does not react well to harsh criticism ^ >
- ❑ Programmed learning materials are effective >
- ❑ Can withdraw or act out * ^ # >
- ❑ Loves to do research #
- ❑ Introspective # ^
- ❑ Loves to practice and repetitive exercises >

<u>Key</u>
* The Sensible Playful child.
> The Sensible Judicious child.
^ The Intuitive thinking child.
# The Intuitive Feel child.

<u>Results:</u>
1. What is your dominant Parenting style? _____.
2. What is your child's Temperament? _____.
3. What is your child's learning style? _____.

Based on the above information you can now begin to draw some conclusions and develop a picture of your own child. Remember, each child is different so each picture will be different and your way for each child will be different as

well. This information will allow for you to be better managers of your child. It will also allow for you to supply important information to your teacher about the nature of your child.

As a preliminary exercise you can practice with any one of the case studies you find below.

Name:_____

_____
_____
_____
_____
_____
_____ .

Case Studies

The Dover Family

History

Recently an acquaintance dropped by my office to ask my advice about a problem he was having with his son. Charles was saying he was feeling frustrated because his twelve-year-old son, Arlen, was not listening to him. Although the boy was a good student, he hated to do homework. When inquiring about changes in his behavior during class time, no notable behavioral problems appeared to exist but Arlen was clearly being defiant at home.

We spent a few minutes talking and I suggested to him that I spend some time observing the family. He agreed and we set up a time where I could casually join the family for dinner one evening.

Prior to doing so, I met with Charles and his wife to get a more informed picture of what their concerns for Arlen were. Charles' parenting style was authoritarian; he is highly demanding, directive and expects all orders to be obeyed without explanation. His wife is more lenient she is assertive but not restrictive, and attempts to be more supportive than punitive.

They explained that Arlen, whose biological mother lives overseas, is torn as to whom to choose to live with. Neither parent wished to impose their will on him, but at the same time, both were making their wishes very clear. He had already tested living within both households and found it difficult to make any kind of final decision on his own.

They continued by saying that although Arlen did not exhibit any outward anger, he chose to do it in passive ways. They were tired of the continuous discipline they needed to give.

They described Arlen as a good child but one that was lazy, unmotivated and not responsible.

I then spent some time interviewing Arlen. My initial observations were that he was very intelligent, and quite articulate. In addition, I found him to be a warm, sensitive and quite compassionate person. He seemed ahead of his years in terms of emotional development.

My impressions were that this was a loving family who were very eager to find away to create a more harmonious flow to relating to one another.

Desired outcomes:

1. For both Mom and Dad to be one with their expectations and delivery to Arlen.
2. To be able to be consistent when setting limits for him and to be able to carry through with the consequences when setting limits.
3. To do it in a loving and caring way without any loss of composure.
4. To come to a decision as to what is in Arlen's best interest as to where he should reside.

My observations:

I determined that parenting Arlen in a consistent but gentle way would be supportive for this very sensitive and gentle boy. This would help to eliminate the minor acting out they were experiencing from him. It was important that all avenues of communication be open between everyone involved so that Arlen felt comfortable to discuss his confused emotions around his living situation. It was also very clear that this decision was too enormous and impactful for Arlen to make on his own. Making this decision was challenging his safety and security. In this case, my feeling was that all parenting authorities should take it upon themselves to come to an equitable solution to the situation and create as much of a harmonious resolve as possible.

Results:

Initially there was a considerable power struggle between Charles and his new wife and Arlen's biological mother. Each felt confident in their ability to provide a nurturing and stable environment for raising their child.

Within Arlen's current home structure, things took on a new light. Expectations and limits for Arlen's behavior were clearly set out. Consequences for inappropriate behaviors and rewards for achievement were determined.

At the beginning of this new management plan, there was considerable upheaval. Arlen was not happy to be under such a strict regime and acted out. All consequences were enforced and he was reminded at the same time that the alternative behavior had a far more enjoyable result. Within a short time, desired behavior was the norm.

Arlen's father and stepmother made it clear to Arlen that he would not be the one making a decision as to where he lived. They had decided that if a compromise could not be made between the adults, a court would have to make the decision for them. The biological mother was informed and, after lengthy discussions, an amicable plan was decided on. Because it would mean a complete life-style change not only in the home but in schooling and culture as well if he were to move overseas, it was thought best for Arlen to remain in his father's home. Summers would be spent with Mom, getting to know her home, lifestyle and culture and, if at a later date, Arlen were to show interest in a move, the situation would be reconsidered. Holidays were to be split between the two homes.

Note:

At times without knowing it, our parenting style can place undue pressure on our child. This may cause acting out in ways, which we do not understand. In this case, it was Arlen's sense of relief at the shift he sensed in parenting style that allowed him to relax and change his behavior.

Tommy's Story

History

The following is a description of Tommy given by his parents. Tommy was a bright, sensitive and honorable 12-year-old child.

He was quite smart, always achieving As and Bs. Although he was good at reading, he never liked to sit down to do it and reading out loud was something he wouldn't ever talk about. It wasn't until the eighth grade that he began to display academic problems.

It was then that his general attitude changed. He became more somber and withdrawn. During puberty, he developed some acne and became quite self-conscious about his appearance. Although he continued to get passing grades, it was evident that he was underachieving.

His behavior worsened through high school but even though he was underachieving, Tommy still managed to finish 11th grade with passing scores.

During his last year of high school, Tommy fell apart. There was a period of a month where he refused to go to school and just stayed at home. He only went to class about 70% of the time, he refused to do any of the work that was sent home for him and this resulted in him failing all of his classes.

Although he still played tennis, he seemed to have lost his competitive edge.

My Observations

After meeting with him, the picture I had of this child was that:

- He is not capable of communicating with his parents or perhaps even recognizing himself what the issues were.
- He repressed much of his feelings and anger.
- He felt lonely, unsupported as well as a deep sense of loss.

Evidently Mom and Dad had very high expectations that he had the ability to, and would become, a professional tennis player. For many years, he worked very hard to achieve this goal for them. Until the age of approximately 16, he did everything in his power to make it happen for them. Then, one day he realized what it would take to pursue his tennis career. He didn't believe in himself enough to think he had what it took. At this point, he gave up, got very angry and self-destructed. Tommy had poor self-esteem and lacked confidence. It seemed to him that his life was one-dimensional and, even though he wanted to find a way back, he didn't know how or where to start.

Desired Outcomes:

Tommy and I had several private sessions together with the purpose of allowing him to unwind and just talk about what was going on in his life. We worked on creating a picture of who 'Tommy' really was. This personable, sensitive sometimes shy person who was gentle functioned best when treated in a gentle way. As the pressures were released, he became more comfortable with himself. He did not hammer himself so much with the thought that he wasn't good enough. Our focus was on allowing him to re-empower himself, and eventually he took complete control of the sessions. Once he became comfortable with the self-discoveries he had made, we decided it was time to bring the whole family into the meetings to discuss some of the issues that helped to create some of these feelings of inadequacy he had had. Some of these things blocked his ability to perform and show everyone who he really was.

Results:

The family meeting allowed Tommy to comfortably speak to his parents about some of the things that had taken place to create such high demands on what he was to do with his life. It also allowed him to see how open they were to listen to what he had to say and what he thought. They talked and responded with him in an open and honest manner. Everyone felt safe to discuss what their feelings were.

For Mom and Dad, the meeting allowed them to take a step back and see what they were doing that contributed to Tommy's self-destructive behaviors. It also empowered them to see the changes in their son and the family due to some very simple adjustments to their parenting style.

Note:

As parents, we all have the best intentions for our children but, at times, we may allow our personal expectations to interfere with the natural development of our children. It is important not to lose sight of the fact that they have their own unique journey. This journey allows for them to explore who they are, but not what we desire them to be. In this case, Tommy's parents had lost sight of what they were doing. They really did not understand how their aggressive style of parenting was actually moving their son further away from the desired result as well as from the family as a whole.

Thinking of Having Kids?

Lesson 5
Dressing small children is not as easy as it seems.
1. Buy an octopus and a small bag made out of loose mesh.
2. Attempt to put the octopus into the bag so that none of the arms hang out.
Time allowed for this – all morning.

The Keys to a Better Understanding of Your Child

Understanding the Purpose of Your Child's Behavior

Try to discern the underlying reason for your child's behavior. Ask the who, what, when, where, how and why questions regarding whatever is going on at the time. Many times, the responsibility for the behavior is incorrectly left with the child.

The undesirable behavior may be caused by some physical or chemical imbalance. It may be caused from some side-effect of medication or from conflict between them and a teacher or friend. Even an upset with you may be the cause of the problem.

It is important for all of us to know that behavior is a form of communication, even bad behavior. It becomes our responsibility to try to comprehend what it is our child is really trying to communicate to us, and then make any necessary changes to affect the appropriate solution.

Asking yourself some of the following questions will help you with this task.

Is your child asking for?

- A different type of structure. It may be more or less than is currently being applied. Sometimes your child needs more freedom than what is being given to them, and the opposite is true as well.
- More emotional support and reassurance.
- More movement and exercise.
- More (or less) stimulation, challenging work and experiences.

Could the behavior be in response to?

- Undue expectations, which cannot be met.
- Our style of dealing with the child. Maybe we are being too authoritative; maybe we are not listening carefully enough. Maybe we are not paying enough attention.
- A change within the family. Has there been a newborn? Are there marital problems going on. Has there been a move from one location to another.
- Could the behavior be due to an allergy? Our physical environment is changing very rapidly and our sensitive bodies are reacting to these changes. It is critical that you have both yourself and your child checked for allergies.
- Also have comprehensive blood tests done to see if there is some sort of chemical imbalance.
- Foods play a huge role on our physical and emotional balance, so we must constantly assess our diet to make sure our body is receiving the proper nutrients and exercise as well.

Could the behavior be in reaction to?

- Criticizing the child in front of their friends.
- Insisting on a response before your child has the time to access the information or perform the activity.
- Teasing by friends or siblings.
- Being reprimanded for poor organization.
- Assigning a task that is too difficult.
- Assigning a task that is too repetitive and boring.
- Being given unclear directions.

As a parent, it is paramount that we become good listeners and observers, and that we are cautious not to react too quickly, or before we know all of the underlying factors of a certain situation. We must practice first being introspective and then reacting on what it is our children are showing us that they really need.

First and foremost, we must remember that each child comes into this world as a unique individual. They are born as pure, unconditional loving, honest, trusting, and open to the world and what it has to offer. Their uniqueness is further established through their interactions within the family and outside social issues.

There are, however, some common elements in their humanness that they share with others. Among the most important of these is the characteristic of being a social animal with a strong desire to have acceptance, to find their place in life, and to have a relationship with others that gives them a sense of identity and security.

Children's needs are very basic. They need to:

- Have a sense of physical and economic security.
- Love others and to be loved.
- Have a sense of personal worth.
- Experience life through their own mind, body and spirit.

We sometimes ask ourselves why our child does a certain thing. It is important to recognize that children do most of what they do to achieve social acceptance. Their desire is to be respected by, and to respect others. Accomplishing this creates a strong sense of self. Their behaviors are experiments in trying to discover what will bring recognition, acceptance and success. These are basic human needs and if we keep in mind they are just trying to fulfill these needs, we will realize the "why" of most of the behaviors our children display. They do what they do for the same reasons that we do. They want, need and indeed must have, recognition, love and feelings of self-worth.

We can see in ourselves some of the ways in which we seek to satisfy these basic needs. We may recall, for example, a time when we went out of our way to make sure someone knew of an accomplishment, actually seeking to be complimented. Or, we may remember a time when we felt alone or depressed and sought reassurance from a friend or family member. Children also have a need to engage in behaviors that assure them they have a place or identity in their world. Children need this reassurance much more often than we think. Without us knowing it, much of a child's actions during the course of a day are aimed at satisfying these basic needs.

These feelings of love and worthiness give children their sense of self and well being we all aspire to attain in life. This basic identity is either positive – feeling a sense of success within oneself – or negative, which is, feeling a sense of failure. Whether a child is gifted, ADHD or anywhere in between, to overcome a negative self-image or enhance a positive one, you must radiate unconditional love by showing acceptance, interest, being nonjudgmental and constantly encouraging them.

Characteristics that Grow Relationships

Genuineness

The ability to be open and honest is essential in the development of any relationship. It nurtures trust and a general feeling of well being within us. Try to recognize those times that you are being honest with yourselves. You should also recognize a feeling of satisfaction. This is very healing both for yourself and your child. Make this the only acceptable way in which you and your child communicate with each other.

Understanding

How much you are aware of and understand your own feelings can be determinative of your capacity for understanding what another person is going through and how you choose to respond to them under that particular circumstance. Compassion and empathy are learned behaviors, usually resulting from how we were treated, or wished to be treated, under tumultuous circumstances.

Valuing

To what extent do we see others and ourselves as being worthy of respect as human beings? How much do we value who we really are? Very often we will allow for our expectations to interfere with this, resulting in our being disappointed and angry.

Observe how you interact with pets. With them, we are open, accepting and have very few expectations of them. You respect them for who they are. What you give them, you get back. The same can be said for the way we treat our children, our neighbors and ourselves.

Acceptance

This is the degree to which you allow yourself, or other people to be themselves, to have their own opinions, ideas and feelings and the extent to which you allow them to express their own individuality. This has to be done unconditionally and without any expectations. This is where we explore the degree of freedom we give to ourselves as well. Make a list of all of the guidelines and limits that you place on yourself, on your emotions, on your ability to express your own creativity. Each new rule creates another layer or wall that we choose to hide behind rather than allowing it to come out in our character. Each layer removes a tiny bit of the *true* freedom we have. The *true* freedom we have taken away from ourselves and then cannot pass on to others.

The communication of love, genuineness, understanding, and acceptance can be done in many ways. We do it with words, tone of voice, body language, but mostly thorough our attitude. More important than anything else is the basic attitude that you bring to the interaction you have with your child. If you recognize that children need only the proper guidance to develop into successful adults, then this is what will be communicated to the child. Your positive attitude will enable you to have a strong and positive relationship with your child.

Game Plan

Create an action plan of a current event or situation that you are having with your child. Using the information that you know about your Parent / Life style and also the temperament and learning styles of your child.
How would you now deal with this?

_____
_____
_____
_____
_____
_____
_____
_____
_____
_____
_____
_____
_____
_____
_____
_____
_____
_____
_____
_____
_____
_____
_____
_____
_____
_____
_____
_____
_____
_____
_____
_____
_____

Chapter 4

The Roles Parents Play

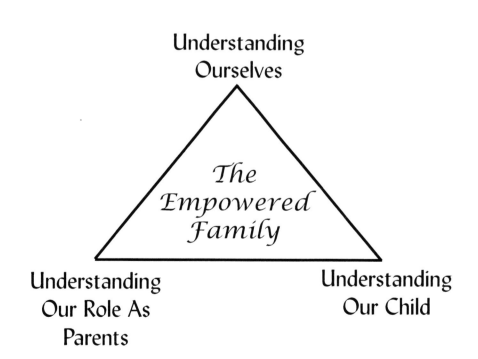

Understanding
Ourselves

The
Empowered
Family

Understanding
Our Role As
Parents

Understanding
Our Child

> In every child who is born,
> Under no matter what circumstances,
> and of no matter what parents,
> the potentiality of the
> Human race is born again.
>
> *— James Agee*

Your Role in Parenting Your Child

Even though we will talk predominantly about the child who has various learning challenges, the information here can and does apply to anyone who is raising a family.

Normal parenting styles would have us either bringing up our children in the same way that we were raised or more probably by the 'trial and error' method. There are many books, this one included, on the subject of parenting and enough counselors and coaches who would make it seem like they have all of the answers. It is very simple really. That is, once you realize that there is no one book, nor is there any one all-knowing person better than yourself to decide how best to raise your child.

Books and counselors can only be used as guidelines. They are tools to be used to provoke thoughts or bring you new ideas that you may not have thought of, or perhaps be the support you may look for when you are faced with difficult times. You are in charge of parenting your child for better or worse.

Where Do We Start

I remember when my wife and I brought home our first child, an absolutely adorable daughter we named Jenna. Three days later, we were walking through the front door of our home with her in one of those carryalls that convert into a hundred different things. We were filled with love and pride for her and so much apprehension about being the perfect parents. We put her down on the kitchen table and stared in amazement. We looked at her and then at each other, and both said simultaneously, "Well, now what do we do?" and burst into laughter. I can honestly say that at that time, I knew more about taking that carryall and making it into all of the things it could become than I did about raising this beautiful, little girl. What were we to do?

As a parent, we can honestly, and in some cases painfully, say that each and every moment of child rearing comes with that exact question: WHAT DO WE DO NEXT?

People plan for their careers, their financial future, vacations and details about life both at home and on the job, but how much real consideration is given to parenthood? Sure, there is thought given to the preparation of the baby's room, what the child's name will be and who will be the one to take time off to care for the child and that sort of thing. How many parents sit down and work out a parenting plan? Do many speak to their significant other in order to determine their points of view on parenting?

I'm no exception. I went into parenthood blindly, just hoping for the best. In hindsight, I now see how things could have come about much simpler and with a lot less misunderstandings had my wife and I set out with a plan, or at the very least, knew what each other's philosophies were. How can we leave something so important to chance? Yet when it comes to parenting we seem to have this void, we take so much for granted and generally feel that everything will just fall into place.

You won't be capable of planning for everything that will come up in your parenting careers, but having an idea of where each other stands on certain issues and having a general game plan set up for the overall upbringing of your child will make parenting a lot less stressful. Know your plans for schooling, for childcare, nutrition and healthcare, the budget restrictions that will have to be considered.

The world today is fast-paced and full of expectation. Our days are filled with organizing, managing and making sure that things flow smoothly for everyone. Sometimes motivating ourselves to even get up in the morning to face the day can be a challenge. Go easy on yourselves. Being a burned out super-mom/dad is not what your children really want. They're looking for someone who is human; someone who is "okay" with making a mistake. This sets a safe space for them to experiment and be all right when things don't quite go as they had planned. There is no failure, except for not trying in the first place.

We are looking to teach our children discipline, self-esteem (for themselves as well as others), courage, compassion, understanding and a sense of responsibility. We are looking to build a core for our children that will allow them to proceed into this world as strong, knowing and confident individuals. This is not something that can be taught from any manual, course or lecture. It is something we show our children through example. You are their teacher, mentor and advocate.

We teach this through offering a caring, firm, supportive and consistent environment. We make ourselves accessible and are there emotionally and spiritually for them to provide for a healthier, happier and solid family unit.

Your Role in Teaching Positive Discipline

Do you know the difference between punishment and discipline?

Punishment: To inflict pain or loss. To cause pain, loss or some discomfort to a person because of some fault or offence.

Discipline: The training, especially of the mind or character. The ultimate training effect of experience. We often confuse the words *discipline* with *punishment*. It is through disciplining our children that we will teach them values and setting their boundaries. This can, and should, always be done in a constructive, nurturing and caring, but firm manner. Through this, self-control, self-esteem and responsibility are manifested and ingrained in your child.

Effective strategies that can provide discipline while nurturing the dignity and grace within your child are through:

Setting limits: Parents must set limits for their children. No one else can discipline with the same love and affection and caring as a parent. Knowing where their boundaries are allows children a sense of safety and security. They are naturally more comfortable with regular routines where they know what is expected of them. Sit with your child and decide certain consequences for negative behaviors. Allow them to be aware of the consequence that will occur if they go beyond the set limit prior to them finding themselves in the situation.

Discipline: It is the parent's gift to their children to see that they experience the consequence of their own behavior. Consequence is one of the best teaching methods available. Allow your children to see that they are in control of their own outcomes. Giving children choices while letting them know what the outcome will be will provide them with experience in good decision-making vs. poor decision-making.

Remember to acknowledge when your child makes a good choice, and praise them for it. Positive reinforcement is so important to the esteem of everyone and I cannot stress enough how important I find it to be in the parenting of a child. Find something to praise in your child at least three times during the day. In fact, find something to praise yourself for. Yes, pat yourself on the back. You are doing a wonderful job at parenting this amazing child you have. Feeling good about yourself? This is exactly how your child will feel from the praise they receive from you. It may be all the encouragement they need.

Avoid power struggles with a child; for this just shows your child that you are not in control of the situation. Power struggles are just another way for us to exert control, and control is exactly what we are trying to not teach here. We want them to learn from the outcomes and consequences of their decisions. We want to reinforce the situation where our children can learn more about themselves from their own experiences and through good decision-making.

Empty threats: We've all done this. If we allowed ourselves to look, we'd see how foolish we are for doing it. We could actually have a good laugh at our own expense when we look back at some of the outrageous, emotionally charged and frustrating, empty threats we've made.

Making threats that cannot be carried out is worse than futile. At best, threats just show our kids that we are feeling helpless and hopeless. Kids will become defiant to worthless threats because they already know the truth, which is that we have no intention of carrying them out in the first place. We've lost composure and control of the situation. The child can then challenge the threat and show us who is really in control. Is this what we want? A wise parent will not make any statements that cannot be followed through. I wish you good luck with this one because once again, for some of us it may be easier said than practiced.

Children may not believe what we say,
but will always believe everything we do!

— Elaine Gibson

The key to it is to take the emotion out of discipline by not lecturing, arguing, or raising your voice. Your job is to set the limits, the consequences and then ***follow through!*** Punishment will not work but ***discipline*** will!

Your Role - Parental Authority

If at all, we wish to convey a sense of authority in a positive way. To be authoritative is to show through our attitude, body language, our tone of voice and the volume with which we speak what it is that we wish from our child. My suggestion is that it be done in a consistent, firm, and loving manner. These are the qualities we wish to use when conveying authority to our child.

If there is a hint of fear, tentativeness, confusion, begging, pleading or anger in our voice, then our authority is lost as the child can clearly see that we have lost our composure. I have seen countless times where children as young as a year old are literally running their families because the parent was afraid to assert their authority. In this case the child will seize control because he or she knows the adult is obviously not the one in charge.

We can be kind to children and still be firm, but our expectations must be clear right from the beginning. When a child has no choice, then no options should be given to them.

An example of this is when it's time for supper and Jackie is called to come to sit down at the table and Jackie says, "I'll be there in one second," and keeps on playing. Five minutes later, Jackie is called once again, and again Jackie says, "I'll be right there." The parent then tries to convince Jackie to come to the table and a confrontation occurs.

When it is time to eat, the parent must let the child know what the expectations and consequences are.

What we are not realizing in this situation is that by allowing this situation to occur, we are sending out the message that this is acceptable behavior. We are teaching our children how to be defiant. The term that is used to describe the behavior is "opposition defiance."

We know that parenting is never simple, but perhaps these suggestions will assist you in making your wishes known to your child:

- Make your expectations clear;
- Talk and act like a parent who is in control and has self-control;
- Believe in and institute a gentle but firm way of delivering your authority;
- Help the child follow through with your expectation of them;
- Be prepared to carry out the consequence if they don't.

This is a time when your child is learning from you. Remember to be consistent, firm and loving. Your patience in this will work miracles in the raising of your child.

Don't be afraid to be boss
Children are constantly testing, attempting to see
How much they can get away with - how far you will let them go.
And they secretly hope you will not let them go far.

— *Ann Landers*

Thinking of Having Kids?

Lesson 6
1. Take an egg carton. Using a pair of scissors and a jar of paint, turn it into an alligator.
2. Now take the tube from a roll of toilet paper. Using only Scotch tape and a piece of aluminum foil, turn it into an attractive Christmas candle.
3. Last, take a milk carton, a ping-pong ball, and an empty packet of Cocoa Puffs.
4. Make an exact replica of the Eiffel Tower.

Your Role in Establishing Discipline

I. Justifying the Aspects Needed for Your Own Behavioral Plan

You will initially want to identify what the behavior problems are and then start working on them, one behavior at a time.

Identify those behavior cycles that your child is displaying on a continuing basis. Prior to initiating a change, you will need to understand that you play a part in precipitating this behavior. Know what your role in it is and be open to the possibility of making a change within yourself in order to alter your child's behavior. Sometimes simply in shifting your reaction, you create the desired shift within your child.

What is it exactly that you wish to change? Setting boundaries that show clear limits will encourage self-control within your child. Allow them to participate in the process of determining appropriate consequences. Giving your child an explanation of the consequences helps for them to make conscious choices and it hones in on developing their decision-making skills.

Empower children by encouraging them to realize they are in control of their own outcomes.

Any behavioral plan is based on two important concepts. First, you are more likely to succeed in changing behavior by rewarding what is desired than by punishing what is undesired. Secondly, for a plan to work, your responses to acceptable and unacceptable behaviors must be consistent. You must continue the program until you are absolutely certain that the unacceptable behavior is gone. Inconsistencies in your responses will actually increase the behavior you wish to stop. As you know, there is no right or wrong here; what is important is to work together with other parenting authorities in the home to develop this plan.

None of the above can be accomplished through *reasoning, bargaining, bribing, threatening* or *trying to provoke guilt*. You must already know that if you "step into the arena," play your child's game and agree to debate or argue with your child, you lose.

If you say, "It's time to go to sleep," and your child says, "But just another fifteen minutes, please, pretty please," the answer must be, "I said that now is the time for bed." If you argue or relent about the 15 minutes, then it will soon become much more than just an additional 15 minutes, and soon your frustration and anger will result in additional confrontations and defiance. Now is not the time to be building in flexibility.

2. Planning Your Intervention Strategies

Overwhelmed? Are you confused, exhausted and frustrated as to why nothing has worked and that things seem to be getting worse?

Knowing that action needs to be taken but not quite knowing what to do can create stress and tension between you and your spouse. You may not quite agree as to what strategies should be used or what will work given the situation. When this happens, stop for a moment; literally take a breath and a break.

The first step is to collect data on your observations of the behavior. Each of the parenting figures should collect data separately so you can compare. It is important to do this baseline so you may begin to change things from the way you see them as having happened.

To collate the data, you may wish to develop a chart. This chart will be used to record the particular behavior, the antecedent (what happened just before the behavior occurred) and the resulting consequence for the inappropriate behavior.

Date and Time:_____, ___ at __:__ am/pm

Antecedent: _____

Behavior: _____

Consequence: _____

Everyone involved will have different lists that will reflect the different parenting styles you use. For example, one may be a disciplinarian and the other maybe more laid-back. Whichever way you deal with it is neither right nor wrong. The important goal is that each of you agrees on what the expectations are for the child and that the both of you are being consistent in asking that they be met.

Inconsistency reinforces the poor behavior,
Consistency stops it.

In keeping track of your child's cycles, you will begin to see a pattern of that specific behavior.

- *Physical* - (hitting or throwing)
- *Verbal* - (yelling, teasing, cursing, threatening)
- *Noncompliance* - (not listening to what is said, not doing what is requested, being openly defiant)

Once the cycle is identified, it is useful to recognize the patterns. For example, does the behavior occur when the child is hungry, not feeling well or tired? Is the behavior occurring when the child comes from school, when he/she has missed their medication or when they are around a certain person? Is it related to academic performance or possibly the type of parenting style?

3. Setting Up the Plan

At this stage, define the behavior as clearly as possible and work out a consequence that will be carried out in a consistent fashion. Once the plan is put on paper, introduce it to the family. The plan should be consistent among all siblings. Even if the behavior pattern is not for all the children, it will benefit them to be aware of consequences and/or the reward for their behavior.

The plan you create should be divided into 3 steps:

1. Create a schedule and divide the day into intervals. Wake-up time until departure for school, arrival from school until after supper, and after supper to bedtime. Weekends can be divided into 4 parts with the meals as the dividers.
2. List the behavior(s) that you are focusing on.
3. The purpose of the plan is to reinforce positive behaviors, which can be done in several ways. You can set up a point system, whereby if the behavior does not occur during a specific interval, then the child will receive a point, or a sticker. It can be anything that will motivate the child to want to receive the reward. You can also use verbal praise and in most cases will use both together, which of course works best.

A scenario that implements this practice could be:

Elliott gets up in the morning, completes all of his responsibilities, but calls his sister, "stupid." So Elliot gets his points for completing his tasks and for not hitting. You may say "Elliott, I am pleased that you earned two points for following the rules, tidying up and for not hitting this morning. I wish I could have given you your third point, but you did call your sister a name."

You may also say to Cathy, "Cathy, I'm happy that you earned all three of your points. Thank you for not calling your brother a name, after he called you one."

Can you see here that behavior is being changed by rewarding appropriate behavior from the child and not by punishing their wrongdoing?

A system is set up where the points are counted daily and recorded on a chart. The points can be used either daily, weekly or even a special reward for a major accomplishment.

Having the child participate in developing the rewards will create the excitement to then accomplish the task, but, all final decisions on the type of reward and whether or not the child has earned the reward will be made by you. There will be those children who will say, "This is stupid and I'm not doing it." You will need to respond to this firmly and let them know that the system is going ahead, and if they would like an input on the reward for proper behavior, they will need to participate or have you make the final decision without their input.

Each reward is individualized to the specific child's likes and desires.

4. Setting Time Out Procedures

Before starting this plan, define which behaviors will be considered so unacceptable to the family that the result will not only be not earning a point, but also being removed from the family for a limited time. The "Time Out" strategy, one that you have probably used many times over already, is one of the best. It provides time for everyone involved to cool down and rethink things. Be sure to designate a specific room that is not equipped with a television, stereo, games or other pleasurable distractions. The door should remain closed and the child quiet. Make the period of time for the time out fit the misbehavior – longer times for more serious situations and shorter for minor infractions. Each time the door is opened, the child yells, screams, or has a tantrum, the clock should start over.

For the plan to work, communication must be clear, consistent and absolutely firm.

It is important to realize that, while implementing any new behavioral management system, initially, there will probably be an increase in the unacceptable behavior. This may make things seem hopeless and futile. You will probably feel that you are in a war and the reality is that you are in a battle, not only with your child but likely with yourselves as well. This is one time you must take a stand if you wish to create positive change.

You may want to reassure your child by saying, "I will always be here to support you and love you, but when you choose this behavior I will not choose to participate with you."

Although it may interfere with family plans and routines, it is very important to maintain no interaction or communication with the child in any way until after the time out. At that point, it will be very beneficial for them to be able to express, quietly and calmly what brought on the behavior, how they felt before during and after, and most importantly, how they intend to deal with the situation the next time it crops up.

While continuing to do external reinforcing through time outs and reward systems, at some point you will wish to combine it with a more interactive relationship between the child and yourself. Begin talking about the behaviors and the progress in their ability to make the necessary behavior modifications. A good time to do this is at the end of the day, just before bedtime. You can use this period to reflect on the day and teach better self-management and decision-making skills. Your child will learn from hearing you openly discuss how you feel about things and what your thoughts are on how things are going. Make a point of broaching the topic from a removed point of view, rather than from the drama of the day.

You are now becoming the role model, teaching alternative ways for your son/daughter on how to deal with their actions and feelings. We are sometimes quick to tell our children not to show anger or disappointment. "Anger is a normal feeling, yes you may want to yell, but don't abuse anyone; you might stamp your feet, but do not break anything." We exhibit these behaviors during frustrating times and children need to know they can do it as well, provided it is done in an appropriate way.

Your Role as a Guide

Guidelines will help your child understand the process and follow through on instructions, thereby empowering them and teaching them better self-management skills.

Try any or all of the following and see which work best for you and your child.

- It is important to get your child's complete attention.
- Touching or cueing them, bring them into direct focus with you.
- Do not compete with distractions such as television, stereo, computer, telephones or anything else that will distract the child from completely understanding your directions.
- Show your child what you want them to do, and role-play it if necessary so they know exactly what is expected of them.
- If required, break down tasks into smaller steps. Remember, you want to guarantee success.
- Know your child and the number of directions they can take at one time.
- Try putting down on flash cards, what you want done, use pictures if necessary.
- Color code directions in order of priority.

- Keep all directions very brief and to the point.
- For young children, draw pictures that show the sequence of events.
- Always check whether the instructions have been understood. Many of these children have short-term memory difficulties.
- Provide follow-up and give frequent praise.

Don't show frustration when directions are not fully followed. Remember that many ADHD children have difficulty in disengaging from activities. They do not do well with transitioning and changes in their routine and they have poor memory recall.

Once you have provided the necessary structure, support and guidance, it is important that your child work independently to the best of their ability and that they are recognized for that. Remember, practice is always the key to anything when we want to see improvement.

Your Role as a Motivator

Bringing out the best in your child

Let's not underestimate ourselves. We can and do play crucial roles in awakening or developing the strengths within our children through the experiences you provide your child at home. Included here are some ways for you to bring out the best in your child, regardless of how he/she is packaged.

- Allow for your child to discover his/her own interests. Pay attention to the activities that they choose. There is a lot you can learn from this. Expose your child to a broad spectrum of experiences. This will activate skills, which perhaps neither you, nor they, knew about.
- Give permission for them to make mistakes. If they have to do things perfectly, they'll never take the risks necessary to make new discoveries about their world. Allow them to see that they are in control of the outcomes of their decisions.
- Allow them to see that they are in control of their behavior and that appropriate behaviors are rewarded and poor behavior is disciplined. Teach them that they are not victims. Through this, they learn the consequences of their decision-making. THESE ARE LIFE LESSONS!
- Plan special family projects. Shared creativity is known to awaken many new ideas and positive changes.
- Don't compare your child to anyone else and don't pressure them to be someone they are not. They will become inhibited, stressed and literally to exhausted to perform to your expectations. Allow your standards to be realistic.
- Keep your passions for learning and life ALIVE. Your child will learn from this.
- Don't criticize or judge the things that your child does. This destroys confidence and self-esteem.

- Share your success as a family, talk about good things that happened during the day, play with your child; show your sense of humor.
- Allow for your child to have a special place at home for them to play, work, dream and cry.
- Praise them... All the time and every day.
- Don't bribe your child.
- Teach your child to trust their intuition and believe in their abilities. Encourage them to try things that are different and maybe more difficult. Help them to confront their limitations with no shame. Help them confront their fears. Encourage them to keep on moving forward no matter what happens.
- ACCEPT YOUR CHILDREN FOR WHO THEY ARE!

Case Study 1

History - Alex is 9½ years old and was professionally diagnosed as ADHD as well as opposition defiance. He was referred as a result of his mother's concern over poor school performance. He was extremely oppositional in the home setting and had difficulty with organizing himself.

His mother had a problem with structuring homework time for him. He was confused and angry due to his parents' marital separation and was plagued with an extremely poor self-esteem.

The first four years of his life were spent in day care, where he experienced difficulty with change. He did not relate well to authority, did not listen and when he did not get his way, he went into tantrums. In his first grade, which was a dual language program, he was overwhelmed with the work and academic expectations and had just gone through a move when his parents separated. He had difficulty focusing and very often out of fear that he would not succeed, he withdrew by running away and hiding in closets, under tables and desks.

He was placed on Ritalin by the pediatrician who diagnosed him as ADHD. On this medication, he was less anxious, focused better and showed some improvement in school. Although he scored above average in intelligence, he was an underachiever.

Second and third grades were average, but difficulty with structure was exhibited during the fourth grade.

He became more defiant, angry, withdrawn and non-compliant. His grades went below passing.

At that time, the home was in chaos and very little control could be exerted by Mom or even Dad when he visited.

There was limited school support as they were not sure how to handle his behavior. The school was about to make the recommendation that he be retained in fourth grade.

Goals

- Defuse his defiant behavior.
- Increase level of success in school.
- Set limits for homework time, bedtime and argumentative behavior.
- Empower him by allowing him to see the results of his own decisions.
- Create a more positive relationship with his father.
- Show how Mom could empower herself through a greater awareness and shift of her parenting techniques.

Behavior Cycle

As an example, Alex would be watching television and Mom would ask him to turn it off and come to dinner. Alex would say, "Okay. Mom, in two minutes." Mom would let it go and then ask again. Alex would repeat, "Okay mom, right away." This would go back and forth until mom would blow.

Alex learned that being defiant was the way he could get attention from mom.

Strategies

- Mom set up a behavior plan where she would give Alex one reminder. After that if he did not listen, he would have the consequence of losing a privilege. This was discussed with Alex beforehand so he was able to participate in the plan. The key here was Mom needed to take a stand, be consistent and follow through. This in effect was her major parenting shift.
- Mom met with the teacher to discuss strategies on how the curriculum could be modified for Alex to ensure greater success.
- Mom set up a communication system with Alex's teacher whereby they used his agenda book to pass notes back and forth.
- Mom set up a specific homework area for Alex. She specified what time he had to begin and that he had to complete his homework with 90% accuracy.
- Mom allowed Alex to make his behavioral decisions so that he would see that he was responsible for his own behavior or consequences and not be able to blame someone else.
- Mom set up regular family meetings between Dad, Alex and herself thereby allowing for Dad to participate in the process and showing Alex that Dad did have a stake in the outcome. This provided consistency throughout the family.

Results

- Alex's oppositional behavior was gone within three weeks.
- He became more compliant and more responsible for his behavior.
- He began to open up and was able to communicate his needs.
- He was generally less anxious and spent more quality time with Mom and Dad.
- The family was more supportive of one another.
- Alex proceeded to get better grades; he made new friends, was happier and had an increased self-esteem.
- Eventually he was taken off Ritalin and was retested and found to be misdiagnosed as ADHD.

In this case, we see that Alex's ADHD was confused with emotional issues that created the same symptoms.

Thinking of Having Kids?

Lesson 7

Forget the BMW and buy a mini-van. And don't think that you can leave it out in the driveway spotless and shining. Family cars don't look like that.
1. Buy a chocolate ice cream cone and put it in the glove compartment. Leave it there.
2. Get a dime. Stick it in the cassette player.
3. Take a family size package of chocolate cookies. Mash them into the back seat.
4. Run a garden rake along both sides of the car.
There. Perfect

Your Role in:

Managing Homework Time

I believe every parent will agree that family stress levels increase during homework time and continue as the dinner and then bedtime hour approaches. Does it feel at times that you are preparing to do battle with seemingly no ammunition! Homework is often the major cause of family battles – not to be won – but the cause of tremendous chaos.

Homework should be a means of practicing previously taught material, so if your children cannot do it, this may be an indication that something is going wrong and it would be a good time to set up a meeting with their teacher.

The following recommendations will minimize some of the stress associated with homework time:

Exercise will assist your child in his ability to stay focused. Have them engage in some form of challenging exercise program approximately 20 minutes prior to starting their homework.

At the elementary level, it should be completed before dinner. Allow for a 30-minute break after school as snack time and a winding down period before getting started. Following the same routine and time pattern everyday is important.

Designate specific areas for homework and studying. Possibilities include the child's room or the kitchen or dining room table. If you have a basement, you may want to create a special work area. Eliminate as much distraction as possible. Be sure there is sufficient space to spread out materials. A table that allows for all necessary supplies such as pencils, pens, paper and books works well. Place a bulletin board in your child's workspace. Keeping supplies on hand is important. Check with your child and teacher about their needs.

Try to ignore off-task behavior. Sit down with your child and set up goals outlining your expectations and the consequences. Then remember to follow through. Inconsistencies in following the plan will just increase the exact behaviors that you are trying to eliminate.

If your child maintains an agenda book, have the teacher initial it upon satisfactory completion. You initial it as well. Call the teacher every two weeks or so to make sure things are on track. If assignments are too difficult, write notes to the teacher. Keep an extra set of schoolbooks on hand to be prepared for the times when they are forgotten.

Get a large calendar, one that allows space for jotting down notes and reminders in the daily boxes. Tear off two or three months at a time and post them in your child's work area. Mark in test dates, projects and reports that are due. Once your child gets into a routine to check the calendar this will be an excellent reminder and help him with time management.

Check to make sure that your child understands the assignments. Keep a record as to when your child begins; the actual time spent doing it and the time of completion. These 3 things will provide a good indicator if problems do exist and if things are improving or not.

The key to success is to follow your management system. Your caring, firm, gentle and consistent attitude will play an important role in determining the results.

Homework Environment Checklist

Summary of Helpful hints

- Slow down, step back and take a long look at your world.
- Look at yourselves and the role that you are playing in the life of your child.
- Include yourselves in the plan. Observe necessary changes and make the adjustments.

- Allow your child to see that they are in control of their outcomes. From this they will learn the consequences of their good decision making vs. poor decision making. They are learning life's lessons.
- Teach them that they are not victims, and that they are responsible for their own behavior.
- It is the role of a parent to allow their child to learn from within and not be afraid to assert themselves. Help and encourage them to feel confident and secure.
- Be involved and aware of what is going on in your child's head, heart and school.
- Praise their efforts.
- Remember that mistakes are opportunities for growth and learning.
- Be consistent, be firm and be caring.

Teenagers

After all of this talk on behavior management techniques, role-playing and token reinforcements for your elementary age child, I bet you were asking when we would get to your teenager. Teenagers are a special entity on to themselves so we are about to give them their due.

While hormones, the struggle for independence and an emerging identity are wreaking havoc both on you and your teenager, the main issue is how much freedom to give, how much 'attitude' to take, what kind of disciplines to use and what issues are worth fighting about. But even with all of this, setting up behavior plans, being consistent and firm remains the focus of your relationship.

Guiding your teenager to adulthood and help negotiate relationships, setting goals and supporting values is quite a journey. You may not be able to anticipate some of the landmines, but the trick is to learn and see what works best for both your child and yourself. One of the challenges is to find a way to keep the road open between you and them so that as those landmines erupt, you will be in a better position to 'chill' until cooler heads prevail.

For teenagers, this is a time to test out their independence, to take risks, to be extremely self-centered and self-focused. They know everything and do not want to hear any advice coming from your direction. Lectures in many cases are just a waste of time and energy. They are beginning to make decisions on their own and these decisions are indications of the path they are choosing. Now, no matter what the results of these decisions (excluding the cases where they can get themselves into some serious trouble) they should be encouraged to think for themselves. They are in the process of fine-tuning the skills, which you have guided them by, and preparing for adulthood. So even though the changes that are occurring often seem confusing and challenging, it can also be a very rewarding experience as you have a front seat view of your child going out into the world and becoming who they really are.

Although teenagers will make their own choices, a good home life can increase the odds that kids will avoid some of the pitfalls of adolescence. Passive listening works well. A kind warm and open relationship, one that demonstrates respect for one another, will set a reassuring tone and at the same time, you will be teaching them to be understanding, open and caring. The key here is to balance this with setting firm boundaries.

Three major areas are important to the development of your relationship with your teenager. These are *connection*, *observation* and *supervision*, and we can throw in *freedom* for good measure.

First, a close connection and understanding between yourself and your child provides a basis for the entire relationship. If your connection is consistent, positive, warm, open and stable, your child is more likely to take this into their outside world. Their social interactions and decisions will reflect this. They are more likely to respond to others positively and with compassion and understanding and have a healthy self-esteem and attract others to them with this attribute.

In addition to developing a close connection between yourself and your adolescent, it is important to observe when they may require supervision. Research indicates that teenagers really enjoy when their parents take a keen interest in their activities, even though at times they may not show it. Teens whose parents know who their friends are and what they do in their free time are less likely to get into trouble. In the context of a warm, kind relationship, this observation and supervision of your child's activities comes across as caring rather than being nosy and intrusive.

Your teenager will love it when you encourage them to experience some degree of their freedom. This should be nurtured in children. Encouraging independent thinking and expression of one's beliefs and unconditional love will promote a greater sense of autonomy in your child. The lesson here is not to control our children or try to make them into clones of ourselves.

If you wish to enrich your connection with your teenager, find activities you both enjoy doing together. Not only are you spending quality and fun time together, but you are also teaching honesty, trust, sportsmanship, and respect for each other, which are crucial attributes for effective disciplining. When necessary, it will be required that you enforce consequences if rules and limits are broken. By staying on top of it and following through, you will most definitely save yourself the heartache later on.

We need to remember that the motivating force of *all* teenagers is the necessity to challenge their freedom. They will not let you know they feel more secure and in control when they know you are setting firm boundaries for them. The limits you set, believe it or not, actually provide a sense of stability in teens while they are struggling to understand relationships and the roles they play in their community.

One of the major challenges we as parents have is the disciplining of our teenagers. If you were to include your child in establishing rules about appropriate behavior/limits and their consequences, much of the tension and disagreements would probably end. Once this has been accomplished, the responsibility belongs to them. Your role becomes one of calmly enforcing the pre-arranged consequence. This then becomes an opportunity for them to evaluate what decisions they have made, and make any necessary adjustments. Helping to set the rules may not stop your teenager from breaking them, but it will help you to avoid power struggles with them.

A very common trap we fall into is attempting to control our kids, believing that if we control what they think, this will translate into our wishful behavior for them. So quite often, we will shut them out, withdraw attention, and invalidate their beliefs or use guilt and shame. This actually creates a greater separation between our parent/child relationships. In addition, without knowing it, we are teaching them how to duplicate these behaviors in their everyday social activities. This will in turn show up in their other interactions and in their parenting style later on in life

Summary

In your relationship with your teenager it is important to:
- Pay attention when they talk.
- Watch as well as listen. Learn to know when they need you and when they don't.
- Do not take things personally when you are getting 'attitude' from them. We often see this as a lack of respect.
- Try not to interrupt when it is their turn to speak.
- Re-phrase his/her words, to be sure you understand them and that they understand you.
- If you don't have time to listen at the moment, set a time when it is convenient for both.
- It is okay to disagree, but disagree with respect for one another.
- Respect your child's feelings. Do not dismiss them. You may not always be able to help but they will know that you are there with your support and love.
- Yes, of course you will get angry, but do it rationally and in a calm way. Do it in a way that you are teaching them about their decisions. Stay away from character assassinations that become very disempowering.
- Channel your discussions towards solving problems. Be willing to negotiate and compromise. These are everyday life lessons taught in a healthy and open way.
- When rules are broken, *go ahead* and follow through. Don't be afraid to be unpopular for a day or two. Believe it or not, all children see the setting of healthy limits as a form of caring.
- Let your child be the teenager they want to be, not the one you wish them to be.
- Don't be afraid to share with them that you have made a mistake and apologize when necessary.

The common theme to all of the above is to communicate with your teen. Communication comes in all different forms, by talking, by listening, by watching and sometimes by just knowing not to say anything at all.

Game Plan

1. Create your own behavior plan using something that is currently happening.

_____
_____
_____
_____
_____
_____
_____
_____
_____
_____
_____
_____
_____
_____
_____
_____
_____
_____
_____
_____
_____
_____
_____
_____
_____
_____
_____
_____
_____
_____
_____
_____
_____
_____

2. If you have a teenager putting together all of the wisdom found in Chapters 3 and 4, create a plan of how you would adjust your way with them and then journal the observable results. Remember that you could always make adjustments. You can also check in with your kids to see how they are doing with it all. At first they will not trust, so you must persevere.

_____
_____
_____
_____
_____
_____
_____
_____
_____
_____
_____
_____
_____
_____
_____
_____
_____
_____
_____
_____
_____
_____
_____
_____
_____
_____
_____
_____
_____
_____
_____
_____
_____
_____
_____

Chapter 5

Tools for Communication

Body Language

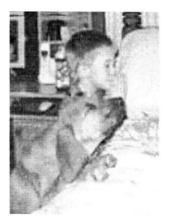

Did you know...?
More than 80 per cent of children aged 13 and under would rather talk about their feelings to their cat than to parents or friends.
(Source: Tenth International Conference of Human-Animal Interactions, Glasgow, October 2004.)

"Body Language" – Communicating as the Observer

"Warm, loving communication between you and your child enables them to build a sense of identity"

More than words:

Communication is a complicated process, with your child receiving a lot of 'information' from you. These include:

- the words you speak
- your tone of voice - loud, soft, harsh or whispered
- gestures
- how you stand
- Your facial expressions.

Your child has to watch, listen and react to an enormous amount of information and, in order to have a conversation with you, also judge when and how to take their turn.

Body language

The words you speak often carry less weight than the non-verbal parts of your communication. It's worth considering the impression you give through your facial expressions and body language.

Try these experiments

a)   Take a moment to look at your face in a mirror. How do you appear? Are you frowning, smiling, strained?
    Make a written or mental note of the following:

- Look at yourself in the morning as you wake up.

_____ .
_____
_____

- Look at yourself when you are happy, feel great, just did something that you are really proud of.

_____
_____
_____

- Look at yourself when you are angry, just heard bad news, your spouse has just reprimanded you for something, or you have just yelled at your child for doing something that displeased you.

_____

_____

- Look at yourself when someone has just told you how much they like you.

_____

_____

- Look at yourself when you are really exhausted.

_____

_____

- Look at yourself after you have just made love.

_____

_____

b) When you approach your child with a soft, smiling face do you think they'll be more receptive to your message?

c) Think about your posture. Do you stand over your child or get down to their level when you speak together?

d) Find a willing friend or partner and hold a brief conversation while they stand and you kneel on the floor. You may be uncomfortable listening and speaking to someone who's towering over you. This is how your child feels, so get down to their height to make the most of your communication.

Did you know?

The verbal impact of communication only accounts for 7% of your overall message? The bulk of our communication comes across in our appearance and body language, comprising 55%. Tone, speed and inflection of our voice make up the remaining 38%.

Thinking of Having Kids?

Lesson 8

1. Get ready to go out.
2. Wait outside the bathroom for half an hour.
3. Go out the front door.
4. Come in again. Go out.
5. Come back in.
6. Go out again.
7. Walk down the front path.
8. Walk back up it.
9. Walk down it again.
10. Walk very slowly down the road for five minutes.
11. Stop, inspect minutely, and ask at least 6 questions about every cigarette butt, piece of used chewing gum, dirty tissue, and dead insect along the way.
12. Retrace your steps.
13. Scream that you have had as much as you can stand until the neighbours come out and stare at you.
14. Give up and go back into the house.

You are now just about ready to try taking a small child for a walk

Did you know?

That during the first 7 years of a child's life that they have no filters on their brain. That means that they are like human sponges keenly aware of everything within their environment. At this stage they are the perfect student and are learning whatever they see, hear, touch, taste and smell, whether we are conscious of it or NOT!

Paying attention

Your child may know you care about them through your loving attention, but it takes extra effort to keep giving that message once they're away from you all day at school. The sort of attention you give will change in subtle ways as your child matures and their needs change.

At age five your child will still be keen on cuddles, tickles and hugs. They'll probably light up with pleasure if you wink, pat them on the shoulder, ruffle their hair or give them a thumbs-up sign. The rituals of saying goodbye at school can be important - a wave as they go in or through the classroom window shows you have them in mind.

Your child will tell you when they want your attention with the ubiquitous cry "Daddy, Mummy look at me!" or with more subtle approaches to show you their artwork or books.

This isn't showing off. Your child has asked because they need your approval and their self-esteem is often reflected in the attention you pay to them. Take these opportunities to stop what you're doing and show your interest.

How to get your message across

- **Get up close.** This means stopping what you're doing and going to within arm's length. If you call out from a distance or from another room, they may not hear your whole message above the chatter and noise around them. They'll also miss out on other information, such as the look on your face that shows whether you're serious or joking, and the gestures you use.

- **Use your child's name first.** This will get their attention - people are tuned to hear their own name above most other words - so they know the message is for them. If their name comes last they won't be sure who you're talking to and may miss the message. "Joe, come for your bath please," will work rather better than "Come for your bath please, Joe".

- **Keep your instructions positive.** For example, your child will respond better if you tell them what you want them to do, rather than what you want them to stop doing. Try "Emma, please hang up your coat," rather than "Emma, don't drop your coat".

- **Give your child a chance to respond.** Young brains take a few seconds to process what you've said and turn it into an action.

- **Keep it simple.** Your child can remember only about three subjects in any one sentence. For example, "Tom, please take off your coat, hang it up and then come here," will usually get a good response. "Tom, take off your coat, get your home-work, find the pens, then come here," will probably be too much.

- **Be clear.** It's good to give choices – this will build your child's independence. For example, "Sam, would you like beans or spaghetti for dinner?" But don't ask a question if you're really giving an instruction. Asking "Could you to go to bed now?" invites your child to say no!

Think ahead

Imagine traveling about 15 years into the future. If you asked your "now" adult child what messages they remember you giving them when they were little, what would they say? Would they remember the message, "I love you," or, "You're special"? What would you like them to answer?

Does Your Body Language Send the Right Signals?

Believe it or not, we speak to the world without saying a word through non-verbal communication. Almost every facet of our personality is revealed through our appearance, body language, gestures, facials expressions, demeanor, posture and movements.

In our professional and personal lives, we'd like to think we could make friends and influence people if we verbally articulate our message with optimism, enthusiasm, charisma, poise and charm.

Since non-verbal communication encompasses 93% of our overall message, let's take a closer look at what that entails.

- It can include your attire, tone of voice, clearing your throat, rubbing your eyes, crossing your arms, tapping your toes, scratching your nose.
- Eye contact, or lack thereof, gestures, crossed legs, open arms, and the scent we transmit are all forms of non-verbal communication.
- Through your choice of clothing, hairstyle, glasses, accessories, and makeup if applicable, your appearance also communicates a strong message. The way you dress plays a vital part in how listeners receive you and how others respond to you. (According to John T. Molloy, author of Dress for Success, clothes are used as a tool to control how others react to you and treat you.)

In an interview situation or during a business meeting, it is very important that you send out the right signals. Always look attentive and interested in the opportunity or conversation - do not slouch in your chair. If you fib, your body language, tone of voice or choice of words will probably give you away. Classic body language giveaways include looking everywhere other than the person you are speaking to and concealing your mouth behind your hands while speaking.

Not only is it important for us to be aware of our own body language, but it is as important to understand what body language means so we can effectively assess and react to others. For example, we may pass negative judgment on someone because they slouch, fidget, or pout. If we are aware of why we made the judgment, we can filter out our biases and understand what their body language means and what it is telling us about that individual.

Did you know?

The most significant fact you should remember is that non-verbal signals have five times the impact of verbal signals. When the verbal and the non-verbal parts of the message are congruent, the listener believes your message. If they are incongruent, usually your words are saying yes, but your body language is saying no.

Body Language and Parenting / Teaching

Being a parent is not an easy job at the best of times. While we all want to do the best for our children, we sometimes inadvertently allow the pressures and frustrations of everyday life to show themselves when we talk with our children.

Children are incredibly **perceptive to our moods and behavior. Why?** Because they have to be, we teach them almost everything they know in the first few years of life so they pick up on these things without really having to try very hard at all.

If we're lucky, we get to spend a lot of time with our offspring in those early formative years and how we talk, move and gesture to them signals our inner feelings, unless you're already very good and practiced in making that instant change from work mode to parent mode.

How often have you been talking with your spouse, partner or another adult about your really hard day at the office, factory, shop, etc? All of a sudden in burst the kids with their Barbie dolls, Action Man or some other toy, babbling on about what they've just done with it. You, still in work mode, wag the finger at them saying something along the lines of "Can't you see I'm talking, don't **interrupt**" sound **familiar?**

Of course it does, the words might not be exactly what you'd say but I can bet that at sometime in your life you've reacted something like this to your child. You don't have to be shouting at your child to give them the indication with your body language alone, that you are not in the best of moods or that this is not the best time to get the full attention of their parent and it would be best if they went away till you are in the right frame of mind to talk and play with them.

Why? Because they pick up on the **non-verbal** cues we all give off. It sounds very obvious and it is but how many times do we do things like this when interacting with our little loved ones. The answer for most parents unfortunately is a lot more than we should because we've not been able to immediately switch from one state of mind to another.

As children grow up with us as their mentors, they learn about the subconscious body language way before they learn the spoken language. They also learn about emotions we are expressing towards them through the tone of voice we use when speaking to them.

Can you imagine trying to **ok** a baby with an angry **voice?** How do you think the child would react to these gruff and loud noises coming out of your **mouth?** It just wouldn't work would it?

Because from the moment a **newborn** baby enters this world, the **influential** adults, especially the parents, talk in soft quiet tones along with gentle, soft movements. So the child learns almost immediately these people are nice, comforting and **non-threatening**.

Did you know?

Children are born with only two fears; the fear of falling and loud noises, everything else we or others teach them. This includes how to express themselves both positively and negatively.

If you don't **believe** this, watch your children and see just how many of your gestures, expressions and movements they **mimic** without even trying, you'll be surprised. How many times have you **said,** "You're just like your father/mother?

So when you are talking with your child try not to tower over them and talk down at them with the wagging finger or with your arms crossed in front of your chest. Try instead to sit side by side or with your child on your lap or crouch down to their level.

Talk where possible in softer tones with your palms facing upwards and outwards. This is an open, honest and non threatening hand gesture we all use when we're being open and honest with people, you can't stop yourself in everyday conversation without sitting on your hands or putting them in your pockets or under your armpits, even then the desire has to be **suppressed**.

Show them you are on concentrating solely on them by looking them in the eye, not at the TV, newspaper etc. Because although you may well be able to multi task different jobs, your child will perceive it as non interest and you won't get your point across in the most effective way.

We as adults spend our lives living with both the negative and positive affects of our parents, siblings and the other significant people in our lives. So make sure you pass on as many positive things to your children as you can and just taking a second or two to reflect on how best to handle your children in everyday situations.

There is nothing on this earth as precious as a child, they are each one is totally **unique** and their well being is in our hands.

Watch your body language. Verbal communication is the language of information. Body language is the language of relationships. Appear open, friendly and eager to join in and make friends. Stand up straight and look people in the eye. Respect other people's space by not standing too close.

Exercise: The Body Language Game

Do you remember playing Charades, how much fun it is by trying to guess what others are thinking or saying purely through body language?

Begin a tradition once per week of doing this with the whole family. I think you will see that everyone will begin to love this special time.

An Awareness

Children love to play. This is how they interact with their world. Play is an excellent means of facilitating child expression. We see therapists use play all the time to get children to communicate emotions they may be feeling.

Young children are straightforward and honest. They are extremely perceptive and pick up many nuances going on in the family we don't realize. They are generally willing to discuss these perceptions openly. Our position is to respect their sophistication, be aware of their world and meet them on their level.

Children are typically more concrete in their communication. It is necessary to gear your vocabulary to your child's level of understanding. The use of concrete examples will be helpful for your child to grasp the meaning.

Early school years are challenging for them, as they are required for the first time to conform to group rules. This conforming often requires postponing immediate gratification. Sometimes pressure to conform also leads to conflict with authority figures.

Early school years also represent their first social experiences within a larger peer group. We know that while the peer group influence factor is an important one, and in most cases a positive influence, it can also create some negative behaviors. It will be helpful for you to know how your child reacts within his/her peer groups.

How to Communicate More Effectively With Your Child

This may sound harsh but, if we were to look at it, we would see that children seldom get the undivided positive attention of a concerned and compassionate adult. However, they do get our undivided attention when they have broken some rule. Consistent positive attention places us in a position of teaching the child more acceptable behaviors.

As a parent, we can enhance our effectiveness by being *active listeners*. How frequently do we respond to our child's remarks before we truly understand what it is they are saying to us? Our quick responses often reflect our own judgments more than they do the views our child is attempting to express.

When children perceive they are not being understood, first, they may try to express their point again. Second, if it happens often enough, they will become discouraged and angry, and stop attempting to communicate in an open way. They will try to find other ways to express these now frustrating and angry emotions. When this happens, a door between you and your child has closed. All in all, what these hasty responses create for your child is a feeling of non-acceptance and lack of respect.

An Active Listener:

- Is a person who listens and attends to the child with all of their senses tuned in to the moment?
- Hears what their child is saying and tries to determine what is going on in the moment.
- Will focus on the child and only interrupts for clarity when it is appropriate.
- Will focus primarily on the feelings of the child.
- Reflects to the child what they have heard in your own words. Then the child can verify your understanding of what they have said and the way in which you interpreted it.

Examples of Active Listening at Work

Alice: "All the kids tease me. Some of them even pull my hair."

Mom: "You feel like the other kids are giving you a pretty hard time."

Carl: "I don't like my teacher; she is after me all of the time."

Dad: "Wow, it sure looks like she is not one of your favorite people."

Janet: "I don't want to do that today."

Dad: "Ahhh, I see you're not very excited about doing your homework today, right."

In each of these cases, the parent is validating their child's feelings and has left the door open for the child to continue the discussion. These open statements place the burden of responding on the child. Have you heard any of these door openers?

- "Tell me about it."
- "I see."
- "No fooling."
- "Hmm, tell me more."
- "Oh, this seems like something important to you."

Very often we get caught up in the 'I' and 'YOU' messages, such as:

I-message - "I feel really upset now."

You-message - "You've really messed up."

It is through honest 'I' messages that we can share feelings with our child. We may have to be patient with our child at the beginning (i.e., listening to our "I" messages) because a child's major concern is himself. The child's world is one of necessity and discovery; gradually, with maturation and patience, a child begins to realize that others have feelings, too. As a parent, you are showing them how to care and understand who they are. They will then be able to give it back to you. Gradually, a child learns that when you share with them, it means that he/she is important and worthy of your confidence and respect. Sharing with your child can be seen as one of the highest forms of acceptance.

Thinking of Having Kids?

Lesson 9
Repeat everything at least, if not more than, five times

Ways to Facilitate Communication

These can be called attending behaviors and can prove effective with all of our social contacts:

- **Have eye contact.** Be in a position to make eye contact. If it is not happening, gently bring their chin up to your face and teach them how to do it back to you when they feel you are slipping. Praise them when your eyes meet each other. There is a tremendous and very powerful exchange that takes place when you look at each other. You can tell a lot about a person through their eyes.
- **Physical posture.** Place yourself on the same level as your child. This may mean sitting in a small chair, perhaps on the floor or any way that puts you on equal levels. This indicates respect and a desire to communicate.
- It is important to express your desires and feelings through your tone of voice. A lot can be discerned through how you say things. Through this, your child learns and

feels compassion, love, limits, anger, frustration, judgments, etc. It is up to us to decide how we wish to express ourselves and what we want to teach to our child.

Probably the most important thing of all is to remember that our children are our teachers. They will teach us what their needs are through their interactions with us. Follow their lead, allow for them to teach us about who they are and what their needs might be. Let them teach us about who we are by how they see us interacting with them. It is our responsibility to create a more communicative atmosphere between our child and ourselves.

Just by being good observers and listeners, our job becomes an easier one.

Facilitating Better Interaction with Our Child

Qualities of love, communication, emotions and the desire for knowledge in our little ones can be nurtured by:

- Teaching them self-acceptance through acknowledgment for the things they do well. Always accentuate the positive aspects of their behavior. This allows for your child to identify with positive traits and characteristics about themselves.
- Being a mirror to your child's feelings, (e.g., "You seem especially happy today, Lisa."). This helps them identify and discuss what's going on in their life.
- Teaching independence and self-control by allowing your child to experiment and take risks in situations where you know that no harm will come to them. This reinforces new discoveries within their world.
- Allowing them to set their own goals and, once they have achieved them, let them know that you know they did a good job.
- Allowing them to make decisions for themselves and take responsibility for those decisions. This enables them to see consequences, both good and bad, which allows for them to make decisions to change the direction they are going in. Through your guidance, rather than control, you allow for them to develop their own paths.
- Learning to respond effectively. For example, you may say, "Sometimes I feel good just thinking about my friend." The expectation is that as your relationship strengthens, the child will behave more as you behave.

As a parent, it is important to have patience and understanding during the process. Remember, development happens in stages, sometimes moving slowly, sometimes more rapidly. Each child is unique and travels their journey at their own pace. We must be careful of high expectations and allow for them to come to their own realizations.

Communication and Your Teenager

For many parents it's one of the most baffling mysteries of parenthood: what turns a chatty ten-year-old into a tongue-tied teenager in the space of three short years? We may just have the answer, as well as tips on keeping the conversation going.

The need for privacy

There are two important reasons why an unnerving lapse in communication can occur in the early teenage years.

Firstly, your teen has a growing need for privacy. She may find her thoughts and feelings confusing, and she may feel uncertain, possibly even ashamed, of what's happening to her body and emotions. It's hardly surprising she wants to keep things to herself.

Secondly, your teenager begins to become sensitive to her lack of skills. She may feel that adults are good at talking. Adults seem to be able to find the right words, while she might feel unable to do this. So when it seems your child is a sullen teenager, it may be that she lacks confidence to express things in the right way.

Why do we need communication?

Communication is the key to good family relationships. Without being able to talk easily, your teenager can't let you know what she needs, you can't offer support and care, and neither of you can negotiate boundaries and acceptable **behavior**.

Different types of communication

Communication goes on all the time - even if no words are exchanged. It occurs through gestures, eye contact (or the lack of it), touch and even the way you stand when you look at someone. As a parent, you're communicating with your teenager all the time, even though she may not speak to you very much.

What you should do?

There are many ways you can encourage and help your teenager to speak with you.
- Make time to listen - many **teenagers'** say their parents don't listen to them. Communication is a two-way street: if you want her to listen, you have to make sure you're willing to do the same.
- Show respect for your teenager's point of view - take a deep breath and be willing to acknowledge that she may have something worthwhile to say.
- Try to act as a role model for your teenager - find ways of **modeling** good communication in your home, with your partner or with younger children.
- Be flexible - be willing to talk at times or in places that suit your teen, rather than you.

What shouldn't you do?

- Score points - like all of us, teenagers don't like being put down or feeling that adults are playing power games.
- Push your ideas down your teen's throat - if you try to impose them on her, she'll inevitably reject what you have to offer.
- Make snap judgments - listen to your teen before you jump to conclusions. There's nothing worse for a teenager than to find you have a closed mind and aren't willing to listen to her views.

Tips for Talking to Teens

- Take the cue from your teenager. There's absolutely no point barging your way in, saying you want to talk, when she's rushing to get ready for a night out. Try to catch her at a time when she's relaxed.
- Try to spend time alone with your teenager, without other children being around. Go out for a coffee or visit the cinema, if there aren't any opportunities at home.
- Share information about what's going on in your life, but only for as long as your teen seems interested. Teenagers are often much less fascinated by their parents than they were as younger children!
- Use open questions that don't just need a yes/no response. That is, "How did the music lesson go?" rather than "Did you have a good day?"
- Guard against using a chat as an excuse to nag or tell off.
- Never put a young person down for their views or ideas. Don't say: "That's so stupid. How can you possibly think that?" They need your approval, even though they'd never admit to it.
- Treat your teen with respect - much as you would another adult.
- When you both have different points of view and a disagreement is inevitable, it's better to negotiate a solution than enforce your demands, which will lead to resentment. This means compromise. So don't say "I want your room cleaned up tonight," but "I'm getting really upset at the state of your room. When do you think you can tidy it up?"
- Listen and reflect back what you hear. For example: "So, there's just too much coursework to manage?" Active listening such as this is also about looking beyond the words for what's really being felt and said.
- No matter how well intentioned your advice, your teen is probably not going to be keen to take it. What's important is paying careful attention to the young person, keeping quiet to give them a chance to talk and not rushing in with your opinion.
- Use all the informal opportunities you can to communicate - for example, driving them somewhere often leads to great conversations.
- Show you're genuinely interested when your teen tells things, by using body language and eye contact. Stop what you're doing to listen, if possible.

- Don't overreact or fly off the handle if you don't like what you hear. Comments such as: "Are you telling me they were smoking?" are the surest way to close down communication.

If there are really difficult issues you feel you have to talk about - such as bad grades or worries about risky **behavior** - it's even more important to find a time when there are no external pressures and you're feeling calm. Using "I" statements always helps. Say "I'm worried about the way your school work is slipping," not "You're doing really badly in school."

Explain your concerns calmly and listen carefully to her side of the story. It's fine to stress what you believe in and what your values are - and to be clear if there are any aspects of her **behavior** you want her to change.

****

A wise person once told me that with children, we share our feelings, not our burdens. Not to unburden ourselves, but to give of ourselves. Honesty, simplicity and brevity and a lot of discernment will make your 'I' messages very effective

Game Plan

Use this part of your game plan to monitor the shifts of the way you communicate. This is a good time to test out your skills of observation, reflection and resistance. Remember resistance is an impediment and will cause you to self-sabotage the way you relate to your child, your teen, your spouse, your boss etc.

Using the mirroring technique, note the changes in your relationships.

_____
_____
_____
_____
_____
_____
_____
_____
_____
_____
_____
_____
_____
_____
_____
_____
_____
_____
_____
_____
_____
_____
_____
_____
_____
_____
_____
_____
_____

Chapter 6

Balancing Work and Family - A Conundrum

Achieving a Balance between Work and Personal Life

Professionals have long assumed that the balancing act between work and personal life only results in problems such as time pressures, family/work conflicts, guilt, etc. However, new research is demonstrating that the balance (when done successfully) can produce benefits, too. People who perform multiple roles (worker, spouse, parent, caregiver, etc.) report that they experience greater overall physical health, relationship satisfaction and well-being. For example, Rosalind Chait Barnett, PhD, of Brandeis University found that among dual-career couples, positive involvement with family protected them from distress when their jobs became problematic.

Work/Life Balance from the Corporate View

Have you heard people say this before? "I like my job, I have wonderful kids and a supportive spouse, but I feel I am stretched to the limit. I never seem to have enough hours in the day to get my work done and still have time for family let alone friends or the things I really want to do."

They are not alone. Several studies have found high levels of stress are often associated with conflicting demands of work and home. One survey showed that even though job satisfaction may be high, a majority of workers rate balancing work and family as more important that any other employment factors. Job demands include "time pressures and deadlines, long hours, unclear or conflicting duties, having too much responsibility, or work that is too tiring or boring."

Work/life balance initiatives can help to bridge the gap between work and home responsibilities.

Work/Life Balance Initiatives

Work/life balance initiatives are any benefits, policies, or programs that help create a better balance between the demands of the job and the healthy management (and enjoyment) of life outside work. Work/life initiatives can potentially deal with a wide range of issues including:

- On-site childcare
- Seasonal childcare programs (such as March break or Christmas)
- Flexible working arrangements
- Family leave policies
- Other leaves of absence policies such as educational leave, community service leaves, self-funded leave or sabbaticals,
- On-site seminars and workshops (on such topics as stress, nutrition, smoking, communication, etc.)
- Internal and/or external educational or training opportunities
- Fitness facilities, or fitness membership assistance (financial).

Why should a workplace consider these programs? The need for balance is essential.

When we are 'out of balance,' we experience more stress and fatigue and tend to be absent from work more often and also unable to spend quality time with family. We become less focused while at work because we are worried about issues at home. The end result is that neither situation is healthy or productive; in short, it's a lose/lose situation for employees, their families and their employer.

Studies on work/life balance programs have reported such benefits as:
- Helps to retain staff
- Builds diversity in skills and personnel
- Improves morale
- Reduces sickness and absenteeism
- Enhances working relationships between colleagues
- Encourages employees to show more initiative and teamwork
- Increases levels of production and satisfaction
- Decreases stress and burn-out.

How does a workplace implement work/life balance initiatives?

Work/life balance initiatives can be part of a complete health and safety and/or a health promotion program in the workplace. The initiatives can be written as part of existing health and safety policy, or particular guidelines can be referenced in the overall company human resources policy or the collective agreement (if applicable).

Meeting both the employees' and overall business needs requires a significant commitment from senior management. Each workplace should tailor its work/life policies to suit their own particular needs and corporate culture. This 'best fit' should be done with frequent consultation with employees. As with other health and safety programs, for work/life initiatives to be successful and sustainable, both employers and employees must take responsibility for making the program work effectively. An evaluation or feedback systems should also be part of that process.

It is very important to remember that, for many workers, balancing work/life demands is just one of the many challenges they face on a regular basis. While most people would agree that these issues should be addressed, they may not know where they can be resolved. A program dealing with work/life issues could, for example, be part of a complete health and safety program. However, it should not take away resources or distract attention from addressing other health and safety concerns or hazards that may be present in the workplace.

Thinking of Having Kids?

Lesson 10
Go to the local grocery store. Take with you the closest thing you can find to a pre-school child. (A full-grown goat is excellent). If you intend to have more than one child, take more than one goat.

Buy your weeks groceries without letting the goats out of your sight. Pay for everything the goat eats or destroys.

Until you can easily accomplish this, do not even contemplate having children.

Creating balance by adjusting our view and attitude

The key here is alignment with our principles. We can control our actions, but the consequences that flow from those actions are controlled by our view. The body, the mind, marriage, family, all relationships – every natural system is governed by principles, by natural laws and the conditioned views that have resulted from our experiences.. This is particularly true as we consider how to find a sense of balance between work and family.

Now intellectually, this may not be hard to understand, but emotionally it's a tough idea because the social value system of most people is determined by some quick fix, some way of short-cutting this natural process. There is none.

We will always reap as we sow. I challenge anybody to find one exception anywhere of any person or relationship or enduring family that is not based upon principles. I do not think you can find an exception anywhere of a truly effective or balanced person or family that does not have at least a pretty good handle on the following principles.

Balance and Life Centers

Work-centered

I put my work at the center of my life. Everything is oriented around my work – all relationships, all pleasures – everything has to do with my work. How do I see my relatives? (As contacts, customers, referral sources.) How would you perceive your little children if you're work-centered? (Obstacles? "Oh, I have to deal with that, what an interference. Go through the motions, you know, try to do my family thing so that I can get back to work.")

Work-centered people may become 'workaholics,' driving themselves to produce and sacrifice health, family and other important areas of their lives. Their fundamental identity comes from their work. Taking care of one's family is a noble reason for making money. But to focus on money-making as a center will bring about its own undoing. (Money-centered people often put aside family or other priorities, assuming everyone will understand that economic demands come first.)

Possession-centered

Another common center for many people is possessions – 'things,' 'stuff' – not only tangible, material possessions such as fashionable clothes, homes, cars, boats and jewelry, but also the intangible possessions of fame, glory or social prominence. Most of us are aware, through our own experience, how totally flawed such a center is, simply because it can evaporate so rapidly.

Self-centered

Perhaps the most common center today is the self. The most obvious form is selfishness and greed, which violates the values of most people. But if we look closely at many of the popular approaches to growth and self-fulfillment and even approaches to work and family issues, we often find self-centeredness at their core.

Family-centered

Finally, what if we put family at our center? This, too, may seem to be natural and proper. Now I want to make a distinction here: I'm not talking about 'prioritizing' your family; rather I'm talking about putting your family at your center. As a center in and of itself, it ironically destroys the very elements necessary to family success and work-family balance. We could go through an analysis of every alternative center, or even a combination of them and I'll guarantee at the conclusion of it all, it will cause tremendous imbalance and your life will be unfulfilled.

Principle-centered

Only when we put principles at the center of our lives will we be able to bring a sense of proper pacing and a sense of proportion, perspective and appropriate balance to our family and work and other important roles in our life.

Principles would look like this:

- *My principles focus on children and are family centered.*
- I will act with integrity and compassion at all times.
- My focus is to keep an open mind and work as hard as I can to achieve my personal and family goals.

This sense of balance includes consideration of any number of relevant principles and not the elevation of a single principle to the exclusion of other principles. It allows us to be adaptable, flexible and sensitive, yet still effective, in a wide variety of changing circumstances and roles – while still being true to our deepest priorities in life. It allows us to deal with whatever changes may come along and gives us a constant frame of reference to make all decisions by.

Take time with your family and loved ones to make explicit what principles are. Principles ultimately govern.

Every individual struggles to gain and maintain alignment with core values, ethics and principles. Whatever our professed personal beliefs, we all face restraining forces, opposition and challenges, and these sometimes cause us to do things that are contrary to our stated missions, intentions and resolutions.

We may think we can change deeply imbedded habits and patterns simply by making new resolutions or goals, only to find that old habits die hard and that in spite of good intentions and social promises, familiar patterns carry over from year to year.

We often make two mistakes with regard to resolutions:

- *We don't have a clear knowledge of who we are.* Hence, our habits become our identity, and to resolve to change a habit is to threaten our security. We fail to see that we are not our habits. We can make and break our habits. We need not be a victim of conditions or conditioning. We can write our own script, choose our course, and control our own destiny.

- *We don't have a clear picture of where we want to go*; therefore, our resolves are easily uprooted, and we then get discouraged and give up.

Replacing a deeply imbedded bad habit with a good one involves much more than being temporarily 'psyched up' over some simplistic success formula, such as 'think positively' or 'try harder.' It takes deep understanding of self and of the principles and processes of growth and change. These include *assessment, commitment, feedback, follow-through.*

We will soon break our resolutions if we don't regularly report our progress to somebody and get objective feedback on our performance. Accountability breeds response-ability. Commitment and involvement produce change.

Breaking deeply imbedded habits such as procrastinating, criticizing, and overeating or oversleeping involves more than a little wishing and will power. Often our own resolve is not enough. We need reinforcing relationships, people, and programs that hold us accountable and responsible.

Remember: *response-ability is the ability to choose our response to any circumstance or condition.* When we are response-able, our commitment becomes more powerful than our moods or circumstances, and we keep the promises and resolutions we make.

We can overcome these restraining forces by making and keeping the following three principles

Principle #1: Exercise self-discipline and self-denial

To overcome the restraining forces of appetites and passions, **resolve to exercise self-discipline and self-denial**. Whenever we overindulge physical appetites and passions, we impair our mental processes and judgments as well as our social relationships. Our bodies are ecosystems, and if our economic or physical side is off-balance, all other systems are affected.

The principles of temperance, consistency and self-discipline become foundational to a person's whole life. Trust comes from trustworthiness and that comes from competence and character. Intemperance adversely affects our judgment and wisdom.

I realize that some people are intemperate and still show greatness, even genius. But over time, it catches up with them. Many among the 'rich and famous' have lost fortunes and faith, success and effectiveness because of intemperance. Either we control our appetites and passions, or they control us.

For example, many of us succumb to the longing for extra sleep, rest and leisure. How many times do you set the alarm or your mind to get up early, knowing all of the things you have to do in the morning, anxious to get the day organized right, to have a calm and orderly breakfast, to have an unhurried and peaceful preparation before leaving for work? But when the alarm goes off, your good resolves dissolve. It's a battle of mind versus mattress! Often the mattress wins. You find yourself getting up late, then beginning a frantic rush to get dressed, organized, fed and be off. In the rush, you grow impatient and insensitive to others. Nerves get frayed, tempers short. And all because of sleeping in.

A chain of unhappy events and sorry consequences follows not keeping the first resolution of the day to get up at a certain time. That day may begin and end in defeat. The extra sleep is hardly ever worth it. In fact, considering the above, such sleep is terribly tiring and exhausting.

What a difference if you organize and arrange your affairs the night before to get to bed at a reasonable time. I find that the last hour before retiring is the best time to plan and prepare for the next day. Then when the alarm goes off, you get up and prepare properly for the day. Such an early-morning private victory gives you a sense of conquering, overcoming mastering and this sense propels you to conquer more public challenges during the day. Success begets success. Starting a day with an early victory over self leads to more victories.

Principle #2: Lead your life and manage your relationships around principles

To overcome the restraining forces of pride and pretension, ***resolve to work on character and competence***. Socrates said, "The greatest way to live with honor in this world is to be what we pretend to be." This means to be, in reality, what we want others to think we are.

Much of the world is image-conscious, and the social mirror is powerful in creating our sense of who we are. The pressure to appear powerful, successful and fashionable causes some people to become manipulative. When you are living in harmony with your core values and principles, you can be straight-forward, honest and up-front. And nothing is more disturbing to a person who is full of trickery and duplicity than straight-forward honesty. It's the one thing they can't deal with.

Whenever we indulge appetites and passions, we are rather easily seduced by pride and pretension. We then start making appearances, playing roles and mastering manipulative techniques. If our definition or concept of ourselves comes from what others think of us from the social mirror, we will gear our lives to their wants and their expectations; and the more we live to meet the expectations of others, the more weak, shallow and insecure we become.

When we examine anger, hatred, envy, jealousy, pride and prejudice or any other negative emotion or passion, we often discover that at their root lies the desire to be accepted, approved and esteemed by others. We then seek a shortcut to the top. But the bottom line is that there is no shortcut to lasting success. The law of the harvest still applies, in spite of all the talk of 'how to beat the system.'

If people play roles and pretend long enough, giving in to their vanity and pride, they will gradually deceive themselves. They will be buffeted by conditions, threatened by circumstances and other people. They will then fight to maintain their false front. But if they come to accept the truth about themselves, following the laws and principles of the harvest, they will gradually develop a more accurate concept of themselves.

The effort to be fashionable puts one on a treadmill that seems to go faster and faster, almost like chasing a shadow. Appearances alone will never satisfy; therefore, to build our security on fashions, possessions or status symbols may prove to be our undoing. Edwin Hubbell Chapin said: "Fashion is the science of appearances, and it inspires one with the desire to seem rather than to be."

Certainly, we should be interested in the opinions and perceptions of others so that we might be more effective with them, but we should refuse to accept their opinion as a fact and then act or react accordingly.

Principle #3: Be of service to others

If people are 'looking out for number one' and 'what's in it for me,' they will have no sense of stewardship, no sense of being an agent for worthy principles, purposes and causes. They become a law unto themselves.

They may talk the language of stewardship, but they will always figure out a way to promote their own agenda. They may be dedicated and hard-working, but they are not focused on stewardship – the idea that you don't own anything, that you give your life to higher principles, causes, and purposes. Rather, they are focused on power, wealth, fame, position, dominion, and possessions.

The ethical person looks at every economic transaction as a test of his or her moral stewardship. That's why humility is the mother of all other virtues because it promotes stewardship. Then everything else that is good will work through you. But if you get into pride into "my will, my agenda, my wants," then you must rely totally upon your own strengths. You're not in touch with what Jung calls "the collective unconscious" – the power of the larger ethos which unleashes energy through your work.

Aspiring people seek their own glory and are deeply concerned with their own agenda. They may even regard their own spouse or children as possessions and try to wrest from them the kind of behavior that will win them more popularity and esteem in the eyes of others. Such possessive love is destructive. Instead of being an agent or steward, they interpret everything in life in terms of "what it will do for me." Everybody then becomes either a competitor or conspirator. Their relationships, even intimate ones, tend to be competitive rather than cooperative. They use various methods of manipulation such as threat, fear, bribery, pressure, deceit, and charm to achieve their ends.

Until people have the spirit of service, they might say they love a companion, company or cause, but they often despise the demands these make on their lives. Double-mindedness, having two conflicting motives or interests, inevitably sets a person at war within himself or herself and an internal civil war often breaks out into war with others. The opposite of double-mindedness is self-unity or integrity. We achieve integrity through the dedication of ourselves to selfless service of others.

Implications for Personal Growth

Unless we have control of our appetites, we will not be in control of our passions and emotions. We will, instead, become victims of our passions, seeking or aspiring our own wealth, dominion, prestige and power.

I once tried to counsel a junior executive to be more committed to higher principles. It appeared futile. Then I began to realize that I was asking him to conquer the third temptation before he had conquered the first. It was like expecting a child to walk before crawl. So I changed the approach and encouraged him to first discipline his body. We then got great results.

If we conquer some basic appetites first, we will have the power to make good on higher level resolutions later. For example, many people would experience a major transformation if they would maintain normal weight through a healthy diet and exercise program. They would not only look better, but they would also feel better, treat others better, and increase their capacity to do the important but not necessarily urgent things they long to do.

The key to growth is to learn to make promises and to keep them

The following are some additional principles on how to create balance. It is important to note that the skills you are developing as you build your self-mastery practice will help you in carrying out these tips. We all know too well that information is great; however it is the willingness to put the information into practice that is the real key to your success.

Several strategies can help you maintain a good balance between work and personal life, including:

1. *Learn how to set limits - and stick to them!* (Career and Personal) Setting limits (for how you will respond to demands from both your work and your personal life) will prevent you from over-committing yourself. But limits are only effective if you stick to them, so make sure you follow through on the decisions you have made about what to cut back on. As you are setting limits for yourself, it may be helpful to imagine situations in which you would be tempted to disregard your limits - and decide how you will handle these situations. That way, you won't be caught unaware in situations in which you might over-commit yourself.

2. *Take advantage of your workplace's family-friendly policies and supports.* (Career) If your workplace offers discretion over the methods, timing, or location of your work, use this flexibility to improve your situation.

3. *Prioritize your multiple roles.* (Career and Personal) When you become clearer about your priorities and values, it becomes easier to make decisions and set limits between the demands of work and personal life.

4. *Reduce the psychological conflicts you experience between work and personal life.* (Personal and career) Surprisingly, time is not necessarily the main conflict we experience between work and personal life. Instead, the psychological conflicts (guilt, difficulty 'turning off' work behaviors at home, pressure, anxiety, etc.) create the most problems. Clarifying your values, setting priorities, and actively reducing the psychological importance of one or more of your roles may be required to reduce the conflicts, and the negative emotions that arise from them.

5. *Protect each role from interference by the others.* (Personal, Relationship, Family) When you are at home, turn off your cell phone, laptop, beeper, or email, so that you can be fully 'present' during this time. Similarly, when you are at work, try to limit personal life intrusions. This will help you be more efficient and effective during your workday.

6. *Develop stress-management skills.* (Relaxation, Interests, Friends and Family) The ability to take care of yourself by doing things you enjoy – reading, exercising, or indulging in a favorite hobby – is essential to maintaining the proper work / personal life balance. Caring for yourself in these ways will allow you to reduce your stress and reward yourself for a job well done!

The following represent some common questions and suggestions that may help when constructing your Balancing Plan.

How can I make mornings go more smoothly?

1. Follow the same consistent routine each day so your children know what to expect.
2. Get up before your kids do to exercise or have a quiet cup of coffee.
3. Get showered and dressed before your kids wake up.
4. Set out your kids' clothes the night before so there's no arguing about what to wear.
5. Pack your children's lunches and backpacks the night before.
6. Let children do as much as they can by themselves – get dressed, brush their hair or pour themselves cereal. This can help them feel independent while also freeing you up to do other things.
7. Keep breakfast simple and portable.

Keep It Moving – An excerpt

We have a routine, and it works. I'm up by 6:30 and showered and dressed (mostly) before the kids are awake. At seven, I wake up my two sons and my daughter. Clothes are laid out the night before – that way there is no arguing about what to wear. The boys share a room and have a TV in their room (I know, I know), and they use the TV as their timer: They know they must be ready to leave before their favorite program is over. During that time, all I have to do is worry about getting myself ready, keeping the boys on track and getting my daughter dressed.

Breakfast is simple and something portable – usually granola bars or waffles. The kids eat in their room while finishing getting dressed. Backpacks and lunches are packed the night before. Once they grab those, we're out the door. I have to make three drop-offs before I head to work, so keeping everyone moving and happy is critical. It all comes down to the kids knowing the routine and expectations and not varying it

How can I stay involved in choosing child care?

1   Go on school field trips or volunteer in the classroom if you can take time off from work.
2   Volunteer to help after work hours – plan parties, prepare crafts, and make phone calls.
3   Stay in touch with your child's teacher or caregiver by phone and email.
4   Donate snacks and supplies for parties or projects.
5   Channel some of your work talents into volunteerism. Help build a web site for your child's daycare center, for example.
6   Ask your caregiver to keep a journal of your child's activities and milestones.

How can I build a positive relationship with my caregiver?

1.   Look at the relationship as a partnership.
2.   Work together to solve behavior problems both at childcare and at home.
3.   Drop by as often as you can to say "hello" – share your ideas, express your interests and volunteer to help.
4.   Recognize your caregiver's good work. Send a thank-you card or a small gift.
5.   Bring surprise treats to day care like snacks, crafts or toys for the kids.
6.   Keep your caregiver informed of any changes in your child's schedule.

Stay Apprised of Your Child's Development – An excerpt

My daughter's babysitter keeps me up to date on meals, naps, play dates and other activities by writing it down in a daily journal. We also talk twice a day – once in the morning and once in the afternoon so that she can share any stories with me.

What can I do when my child is sick and I need to work?

* Decide in advance how you and your husband will share this responsibility.

My husband and I take turns staying home with sick kids when necessary. I am also lucky enough to have my parents and my in-laws in the area. My mother-in-law is wonderful about taking a sick child at the last minute. Often I can drop off my son at her house and go into work for an hour or so and then come home to get him. It is important to think about what you will do in this situation *before* it arises and line up people to be your backup. Talk to neighbors who are stay-at-home moms or family members. You may be pleasantly surprised how many people are willing to help out in a pinch!

* Split the day with your husband.

When my kids are sick, they stay home and we find a way to work around it. Usually my husband and I split the day. I go to work in the morning, from 7:30 until 12:30, come home, and then he goes in and works from 2:00 until 8:00. If the split shift doesn't work for that day, then one of us will take the day off altogether. Another word of advice: Never apologize to your boss for being a mom. It only feeds prejudices. Don't *ask* to take time off when your kid is sick; *tell* your boss you will be taking time off. But meet her halfway by working at home if you can, and get your spouse to take time off to care for the kids too.

* Work at home if you can – Save Your Sick Days

My husband is able to work at home more effectively than I am, so he typically stays home with our kids more often. Otherwise, I am happy I have a job that is not customer-centered or requires travel, so that I don't have a problem staying home when I need to. I try to save my sick days so that I don't have to take unpaid days. My company is pretty flexible, and everyone here has kids so they understand. -

* Line up someone locally who can care for your child on short notice.

How can I make the most of evenings at home?

Tips for Making the Most of Your Evenings at Home

1.   Serve Kid-Friendly Meals

I leave my office at 4:30, pick up the kids at 5:15 and get home about 5:30. It really helps to have dinner already made. The kids want to eat about 6:15. I use my Crock-pot a lot and serve lots of kid-friendly meals. My kids love frozen vegetables, especially broccoli, so it's easy to slip some nutrition into the mix. I also serve them hot dogs, chicken nuggets, chicken breast pieces, and sometimes we have breakfast for dinner – eggs, bacon and cereal. About once a week, we go out for fast food. Often my husband and I eat later, since it's too much to try and get everyone to the table at the same time. But we do have dinner together as a family on the weekends.

2.   Discuss Your Day During Dinner

I work 7:30am to 4pm, so I can have the children picked up and dinner started by 5:30. That gives us a little breathing room in the evenings. The kids get to play or watch a little TV before dinner, but TV is definitely off during dinner. Aside from eating, we discuss our days and other issues during dinner. After dinner, there might be some more play time, but usually it's PJs, teeth brushing, story time, then bed. After the kids are in bed, I clean the kitchen (if it isn't already done), prepare lunches for the next day, and perhaps start dinner for the next day. I also set up the coffee on a timer for the a.m. Then I hopefully get an hour of TV before bed.

3.   Plan Ahead

I am trying to plan more dinners ahead, so that chicken, steak or salmon is marinated overnight. Then I can leave instructions and dry ingredients and sauce packets out on the counter and my husband can cook it while I work out. My girls are two and five, and after dinner the goals are: two-year-old goes to bed by 8:30, five-year-old by 9:30. I alternate fun 'rewards' with required 'work.' Bath is fun, pajamas are required, snack is fun, brushing teeth is required, stories are fun, bed is required. I also threaten that if we don't move it along, we won't have time for stories. Also they get to pick shower or bath, and we wash hair and bodies, and then get out the toys. They play in the water for 15 to 20 minutes while I clean up after dinner.

4.   Find Time to Relax—and Have Fun

There are three huge timesavers I use for after school and work. First, I go into work early, before 8, so that I can leave work by 4:30 and get home before 5. My kids don't usually want to eat dinner until after 6 so I can actually relax, read the mail, and sit for a few minutes before starting dinner. Second, I make sure dinner preparation is easy, no more than 15 minutes. I use the 'make ahead' method. That is, I usually have a few things in the freezer that I can simply defrost and cook like casseroles, marinated chicken, burgers, etc. Either that or I put something into the Crock-pot before work and it's cooked when I come home. Third, my son's school provides after-school care. During that time, he gets most of his homework done, so when he comes home, there's more downtime for him to enjoy and less whining. Before dinner, my kids usually do their own thing – TV, games, outdoor play if it's warm and light out. After dinner, we usually hang out together in the family room, either with the TV on or without. Bath time starts at 7:30 and we try to get the kids in bed (if not actually asleep) by 8:15.

5. Treat yourself to dinners out on occasion.

6. Stick to a routine so your kids know what to expect.

7. Factor in fun and time to snuggle.

Between working all-day and dealing with the kids at night, how can I maintain a healthy relationship with my spouse? How do I stay connected with my spouse?

1. **Make Time to Talk:** After the kids are asleep on the weekends, my husband and I often just sit in the living room with the lights off and talk quietly and unwind.

2. **Create Couple Time:** Go to bed early sometimes. Turn off the phone. Decline some social invitations to make just couple time. Have at least one night a week be 'couple time.' Email and talk during the workday. Put the kids to bed early.

3. **Make Lunch or Dinner Dates:** My spouse and I go out for lunch about once a week. We email each other quite a lot during the day. We send jokes and links to web sites. We have even worked out some bigger issues via email, because then you have to think over your reply and not fire back some off-the-cuff response that you can never take back. We also try and plan nights out alone together.

4. **Make Love!:** I would say that, hands down, the years when children are young are the most difficult for a marriage. The most important thing to remember is that times will change and little ones won't be so dependent as time goes on. Although most of us struggle with this, the single most important thing one can do to maintain a healthy relationship is make sure you have a healthy sexual relationship. Lock doors, sneak into other rooms after the kids are in bed, whatever you have to do.

5. **Share Chores:** My spouse and I generally talk, read or watch TV together after the kids have gone to bed. We'll also wash/dry/fold laundry and sometimes do other chores during the commercials. Each of us has some nights where our own activities are scheduled. He has church folk group practice on Wednesday nights. I go to school fundraiser meetings or the occasional "girls night out." And, of course, there are times where what we do to entertain ourselves after the kids are asleep is not fit for discussion.

    If the reason is based on how *you* feel about yourself (if you feel you don't see your family enough or that you're too involved with work), then by all means seek a change. Shorten your hours, cut down on travel, split shifts with your spouse, or be bold and change careers. Do whatever it takes to make you feel good about yourself. Just be sure that you're doing it for you, your spouse and your kids and not for someone else.

How can I let go of my feelings of guilt about working?

1. **Get to the Root of It:** Ask yourself why you feel guilty. If the reason is based on how another person feels (your mom, your mother-in-law, the stay-at-home mom down the street), forget about it. They don't have your life so they have no right to make you feel guilty any more than you have a right to make them feel guilty about their life choices.

2. **Change Your Way of Thinking::** Guilt is a useless emotion. It can make you unproductive, resentful and depressed. In our supportive corner of the Web, we all understand how hard it is to leave your child in day-care and go out into the workforce. It is so easy to identify ourselves as having only one role in life – mother – and leaving it at that. However it is important for us to maintain separate identities, for our children's well-being and our own. I am one of the few who actually enjoys working, and that makes it so much easier for me. While I'm at work, I give 100 percent of myself to the task at hand and take great pride in doing a good job. The same is true when I'm at home with my children.

You only get one chance to live this precious life. You have to make the most of it while you are here. I don't identify myself by what I do any more than I identify myself by my children. I am a person in my own right and I (usually) am fairly happy with who I am. Mother, wife, employee, and student – these are just labels. I don't feel guilty about working any more than I feel guilty about taking classes. I am happy with the choices I've made regarding child care. My boys know who their mommy is and they are well adjusted little guys who are happy to go to school and learn new things.

How can I work to be a better partner with my school?

- **Volunteer at Night An - Excerpt**

Not only am I a working spouse, but I am a fourth grade teacher, too, so I see this issue from both sides. I stay involved in my son's preschool by signing up for parties and bringing treats. Field trips are a good way to get involved, too. There is generally more than a week's notice for any school trip so that a working parent can arrange their schedule to help out the teacher. There are also opportunities to volunteer outside of working hours. Call your child's teacher and ask if there are any calls she needs made to other parents or any parties she needs help planning. Primary grade teachers often need help with cutting patterns or tracing things, which can easily be done at night if the teacher sends it home with your child. The PTO/PTA in your school will have lots of committees to volunteer for that meet in the evenings. Just be proactive and make the call to your child's teacher. As a teacher, I love to hear from parents who want to help. The feeling of support and community is great!

- **Do Something You're Good At**

Here's a good rule for school involvement: Volunteer to do one or two things very well rather than a bunch of things not so well, and make it something that you enjoy doing. Also, pick something you can do in the time you have. If you work locally, volunteer to be a lunch or playground monitor. Or channel some of your work talents into volunteerism. This has two benefits: It allows the school to get some free professional-level consulting, and it gives you some experience as a private consultant, which may prove useful someday if the layoff fairy visits. I've focused my school involvement this year on helping to build our school's Website into a better communication tool for parents and students.

- **Stay in Touch with the Teacher**

I generally cannot be at my child's school during the day, but I've found other ways to stay involved. For example, my children's teachers will at times send me homework to do, which can be anything from cutting a million triangles to recording a book on audiotape. I also send in supplies, snacks and donate whenever I can for projects. I also take time off from work to go on field trips, and always attend any plays, parties or other special events going on in the classroom. There are so many ways to get involved. Parents must simply ask the teacher, "How can I help?" Now that email is so prevalent, communication is much easier. Use it! Teachers are responsible for too much today.

Creating Your Family Plan

When creating your family plan, it is suggested that you use the following 2 models:

1. The Balance Wheel:

a. Fill in the balance wheel with the 6 aspects:

- Career/work
- Relationship
- Interests
- Family
- Friends
- Relaxation

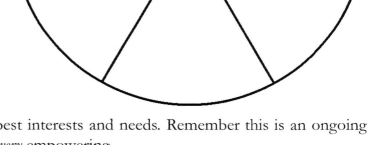

b. Put in the approximate percentages of time during the course of your day, week and month that you spend on each one of those aspects.

c. This will give you a snapshot of your life and you can make adjustments at any time that meets with your best interests and needs. Remember this is an ongoing process and is in itself *very, very* empowering.

2.   A Weekly/Monthly/Yearly Calendar

- Weekly Calendar
- Monthly Calendar
- Yearly Calendar

Game Plan: Work / Life and Balance Proposal

Schedule proposed (*Provide details of the schedule proposed. This diary approach may help*)

	Hours/times	On-site	Home
Sunday			
Monday			
Tuesday			
Wednesday			
Thursday			
Friday			
Saturday			
Total /weekly hours			

How will the proposal contribute to creating balance in your life?

_____

_____

_____

_____

_____

_____

_____

_____

_____

_____

_____

_____

_____

Who will be affected? How?

_____

_____

_____

_____

_____

_____

_____

_____

_____

_____

_____

_____

_____

What are your suggestions regarding this?

_____
_____
_____
_____
_____
_____
_____
_____
_____
_____
_____
_____
_____
_____
_____
_____

What expenses might/will this incur?

_____
_____
_____
_____
_____
_____
_____
_____
_____
_____
_____
_____
_____
_____
_____
_____
_____
_____

What review criteria would you suggest for you and your principal/manager to assess how your performance is meeting expectations?

_____
_____
_____
_____
_____
_____
_____
_____
_____
_____
_____
_____
_____
_____
_____
_____
_____
_____
_____

What changes will you practice to achieve set goals?

_____
_____
_____
_____
_____
_____
_____
_____
_____
_____
_____
_____
_____
_____
_____
_____
_____
_____

How will you monitor these changes?

_____
_____
_____
_____
_____
_____
_____
_____
_____
_____
_____
_____
_____
_____
_____
_____
_____
_____
_____
_____
_____

As part of your Family Plan, you have the option to do all 3 calendars incorporating the 6 Life Aspects, which have been previously mentioned. You now have 2 very visual pictures of what your life looks like. We talk about how difficult it is to keep pace with our life and how busy we are, how little time we have for ourselves, for our relationship and for our family. This will give you an excellent picture of where you can make modifications.

We think you will see that, in analyzing your thoughts and your actions, how much energy is spent on your negative thoughts. We also believe you will be able to modify your time so that it is spent more constructively. This is also an excellent management skill to teach to your kids.

What you are doing here is based on now being more aware of your daily, weekly, monthly practices that you can create a new practice, which is empowering to all. This you will see can change your life, your family's life to one of more peace and harmony.

Remember, by this point you are already practicing the skills you will need to achieve your goals. Yes you already have the tools necessary to take yourself to a different level. Empower your family by first empowering yourself.

Congratulations!

Chapter 7

We Are Each Other's Teachers

Each child comes into this world as a unique individual. They are born as pure, unconditional loving, honest; trusting beings, open to the world and what it has to offer. Their uniqueness is further established through their interactions within the family and outside socially.

There are however, some common elements in their humanness, which they share with others. Among the most important of these is the characteristic of being a social animal with a strong desire to have acceptance, to find their place in life, and to have a relationship with others that gives them a sense of identity and security.

Children's needs are very basic. They need to:

- Have a sense of physical and economic security.
- Love others and to be loved.
- Have a sense of personal worth.
- Experience life through their own mind, body and spirit.

Probably the most important thing of all is to remember that our children are our teachers. They will teach us what their needs are through their interactions with us. Follow their lead, allow for them to teach us about who they are and what their needs might be. Let them teach us about who we are by how they see us interacting with them. It is our responsibility to create a more communicative atmosphere between our child and ourselves.

Just by being good observers and listeners our job becomes an easier one.

This chapter is made up of several interviews which have allowed children of all ages (6 – 18) to express themselves freely about how they view their home, their school and themselves.

It also allows you, the parent, an opportunity to express how you see yourself as an individual, as a parent and as a family.

The goal here is to allow both of you to see each other through your worlds, learn from each other, respect one another and use this as a very important opportunity to experiment with change which will ultimately transform relationships within the family.

Please note that our interviews have NOT been edited. The way you read it, was the way it was spoken.

Thinking of Having Kids?

Lesson 11
1.   Hollow out a melon.
2.   Make a small hole in the side.
3.   Suspend it from the ceiling and swing it from side to side.
4.   Now get a bowl of soggy Cheerios and attempt to spoon them into the swaying melon by pretending to be an airplane.
5.   Continue until half the Cheerios are gone.
6.   Tip half into your lap. The other half, just throw up in the air.
You are now ready to feed a nine-month old baby.

The Child Interviews

We do all have a purpose!

The following questions can be given to and answered by children themselves, or can be used in an interview. Questions you and the child may want to think about before moving on:

- What does it mean to be gifted?
- What does it mean to be handicapped or have a disability?
- What does it mean to be normal?
- *What Am I?*

There are many questions that will follow, some you may be able to answer easily, and some will be more difficult. Answer those you feel comfortable with. You do not have to answer each and every question. What is important is that YOU tell your story!

You guys are playing a very important part as to how we want others to see us, to take care of us, to teach us, to talk to us, to know us. Your answers will help us caretakers shift, so that a new way of parenting, teaching and communicating will be created. A way that will allow for you to be our teachers and us yours with a sense of balance and ease.

1. Questions that have to do with school

1. What are my academic strengths?
2. Do I know how I learn best?
3. How do I learn, visually, hearing, touching?
4. What do I like about my classroom?
5. How could my teacher make learning easier for my classmates?
6. How does my teacher help a classmate who is having difficulty?
7. What could a teacher do to make them a better teacher?
8. Do teachers like their jobs?
9. Are teachers a little like my mom or dad? Should they be?
10. What does a teacher do that gets me upset or happy?
11. What type of teacher would I work best with, what are they like?
12. What could make learning more fun?
13. How could school make learning feel better, safer, or how could my teacher get me to be more motivated.
14. What kind of rules do I think are important to have in school?
15. What can I do to motivate myself?
16. How would I like my teacher to talk to me?
17. How can my teacher bring out the best in me?
18. What can the principal do to make the school a better place?
19. Why do I have homework?
20. What could my teachers do to help me with stress?
21. How does stress affect my performance?

2. Questions that have to do with home

1. What do I think of my mom ... my dad?
2. What can my mom do to make life better for me?
3. What can my dad do to make life better for me?
4. Are parents teachers?
5. What do mine teach me?
6. Do I teach my parents? If so, what?
7. Are parents here to guide me, to counsel me? To help me do homework? To speak up for me?
8. How do I feel about living with my parents?
9. Do I get a chance to speak up? Do I feel like I am respected?
10. What could I do to make things better with my parents?
11. What kinds of things do I like to do at home?
12. What are my favorite activities?
13. Are there things I could change about myself so that I would be happier?

14. Are there things my parents could change about themselves that would make them happier... more harmony in the family?
15. What would they be?
16. Do I like my house, and where I live?

3. Questions that have to do with me

1. What do I know about me that I do not share with my parents?
2. Am I happy with me?
3. Have I ever thought about what I would like to do ... in school, in life?
4. Do I have the freedom to do what I really want to do?
5. Do my parents understand me?
6. Do my teachers understand me?
7. Do my friends understand me?
8. What could my parents do to help me with school?
9. How could they help me to achieve my goals?
10. Am I frustrated, angry, happy, sad, and/or afraid?
11. Do I know what these feelings are?
12. What does it feel like to be successful?
13. What does it feel like to be a failure?
14. Am I a success or a failure or in the middle?
15. What can my parents do to help me feel more successful?
16. What can I do to help myself feel more successful?
17. Is my mom, happy, sad, angry, afraid?
18. Is my dad, happy, sad, angry, and afraid?
19. How does one change their feelings?
20. What kinds of activities do I like to do in my free time?
21. Do my parents know if I am stressed, unhappy, angry, joyful, whatever?
22. What can my parents do to relieve the stress?
23. Am I a good communicator?
24. Are my parents good listeners?
25. Do they listen to me?

Time for the kids!

Elissa's answers *(age 13)*

Questions that have to do with school.

What are my academic strengths? - English and History

Do I know how I learn best? - Visual and Oral

How do I learn, visually, hearing, touching? - All

What do I like about my classroom? - That the windows and doors are always open, letting in fresh air and sunlight.

How would I change it so that learning would be easier? - Provide more visual and hands-on experience.

How could my teacher make learning easier for my classmates? - In my pervious year, my teacher brought in a laptop, projector, and many new Microsoft programs. This allowed us to visually see pictures, movies, and formats for whatever task we were trying to complete. He also followed up with a lecture, and sometimes an experiment. This made class very enjoyable for everyone.

How does my teacher help a classmate who is having difficulty? -My teacher will re-discuss the lesson, simplifying it, while those who understand begin to work.

What could a teacher do to make them a better teacher? - Talk to their students. I like to know who my teacher is. I like to know a little about them so that I trust them more easily, knowing that they're real people too. Some of the teachers never told the class anything about themselves, which makes me think that they were probably robots with no lives.

Do teachers like their jobs? - It just depends on the teacher. I find that younger teachers prefer their jobs, as opposed to older teachers. I believe this is so because older teachers tend to teach with old methods such as, talking the whole period then assigning endless amounts of homework, never relating to your situations, always believing they're right, etc. The younger teachers seem to relate better, as they still seem to remember what school was like. They find fun ways of presenting things and students react better to them.

Are teachers a little like my mom or dad? -Teachers aren't like mom or dad at all.

Should they be? - No, they shouldn't be. It's a nice change to get away from your parents, that way you don't feel they are invading your space. If kids feel invaded in their space they will turn to other places, such as a bad crowd, skipping classes, and other places. It's nice to have a change of scenery, that way when you get home, you are glad to see your parents.

What does a teacher do that gets me upset or happy? - Teachers get me upset when they think they know it all. This happens all the time. My math teacher in previous grades used to say, "Your mark is your mark, it doesn't matter if it was wrong on a question, I was more then generous on other things. If you bring it up to me, with something wrong you might risk me finding places where I was generous and I'll take those marks away. So you'd better be sure that's what you want." Teachers make me happy when they give praise when deserved, and don't single out people.

What type of teacher would I work best with, what are they like. - A fun, free spirited teacher that tries his/her best at making things fun and enjoyable to learn. My grade eight teacher was a great example of this.

What type of teaching techniques would work best for me? - For me to work on my own, hands on, talking etc. I like to work on a little bit of everything.

What is my school like? Do I like learning? Why? -My high school is huge, and has a lot of students. The teachers I have seen so far have been nice. I like learning because it keeps my mind quick, and helps me understand why things work the way they do.

What could make learning more fun? -More trips and hands-on experiments.

What is school for and do I have a picture of what I would want my school to look like? - To me, school is a place for learning about the world, meeting new people, and having fun.

How could school make learning feel better, safer, or how could my teacher get me to be more motivated? - I would feel better and more motivated if the school budget was spent better. In my previous years I did an experiment. I made a list of all the things the school budget and fundraisers should have been spent on; such as curtains in the girls change room, new paint on the exterior of the school, new lockers, newer computers, etc. None of these issues we dealt with. Instead a newer camera was bought to replace the other camera purchased the year before.

Why follow rules? What are they for? -Some rules are good, some are just useless. Some good ones are for protection, safety, and professionalism. The useless ones are like; no talking in class, use black or blue pen only, go to the bathroom in two minutes, having to put up your hand, having to wear a uniform, etc.

What kind of rules do I think are important to have in school? - Respect, non-violence, and power balance rules are good.

What can I do for myself to be motivated? - Take part in activities, so that when I'm in class I'm ready to learn.

How would I like my teacher to talk to me? - With equal respect.

What are teachers for? Are they people too? - Teachers are to aid and to teach us different things. The majority of teachers are real people, but others I'm not too sure of.

How can my teacher bring out the best in me? - By being happy, human, and easy to talk to.

What can the principal do to make the school a better place? - Be cheery, non-threatening, and down to earth.

Why do I have homework? - I have no idea.

Am I stressed? - It depends on how much I have going on in my life, and how much the teachers expect.

What could my teachers do to help me with stress? - Give less homework.

How does stress affect my performance? - It becomes harder to real focus and concentrate on a new task.

Does my teacher know about my stress? Some understand, some don't seem to care.

How can they help me to cope with it better? By understanding, giving less homework, and not expecting so much.

Questions that have to do with home

What do I think of my mom? My dad? - My mom is really cool. She loves pretty much everything, especially helping people. My dad and I have a funny relationship. We don't really communicate how we feel, but I know he loves me through things that he does. He demonstrates his feelings through actions more than words.

Why do I need parents? What are they for? - To keep me in line, and tell me when I'm wrong.

What can my mom do to make life better for me? - Just continue loving me the way she does.

What can my dad do to make life better for me? - Stop thinking that I want things, and spend more time with me.

Are parent's teachers? - Parent's are teachers in everyday life.

What do mine teach me? - My mom teaches me how to love unconditionally, and my dad teaches me how to deal with group situations.

Do I teach my parents? If so, what? - I teach my parents different lessons. I teach my mom about as many little life lessons as she teaches me. I am teaching my dad a different outlook on life.

Are parents here to guide me, to counsel me? - I believe parents and kids are here to guide each other.

To help me do homework? - No, they don't remember half the stuff they learned.

To speak up for me? - Yes, my mom speaks up for me a lot. I hate confrontation, and making people angry. My mom is almost always there to help me, and teach me to speak up for myself.

To tell me things that they want me to do? - No, parents are much more then that.

How do I feel about living with my parents? - I love living with my mom. I'm very happy just being me.

Do I get a chance to speak up; do I feel like I am respected? - At my mom's house I can say whatever I like. At my dad's house it's a little bit different. I feel like I can never get a word in edgewise. Someone is always saying something.

What could I do to make things better with my parents? - I could talk to my dad more, and he could talk to me.

What kinds of things do I like to do at home? What are my favorite activities? - I like to play piano, play guitar, sing, write stories, and take nature walks.

Are there things that I could change about myself so that I would be happier? - I would probably loose some weight, and stop chewing my hangnails.

Are there things that my parents could change about themselves that would make them happier... more harmony in the family? - Mom-

Are there things that would make the family function better? What would they be? = Nothing.

Do I like my house, and where I live? - I love it!!!

Where would I like to live? - In a big house with a kitty

What things would I have in my house? - Wood furniture, beautiful colors, and pets.

Where would I like to live? Why? - I would like to live closer to my high school.

Questions that have to do with me

What do I know about me that I do not share with my parents? - I don't share everything with my dad. I don't tell him how I feel most of the time.

Do I ever tell them? - I tell my mom almost everything.

Am I happy with me? - Definitely

Have I ever thought about who I really am? - Yep, many times.

Have I ever thought about what I would like to do... in school, in life - I would like to be a teacher, an author, and a musician.

Do I have the freedom to do what I really want to do? Do my parents understand me? - My mom understands me, but my dad doesn't really; even though he thinks he does.

Do my teachers understand me? - Some of them do, but others don't.

Do my friends understand me? - My friends all understand me.

What could I do to help others understand me better? - I could tell them how I really feel.

How could they help me to achieve my goals? - By encouraging me.

Am I frustrated, angry, happy, sad, and/or afraid? - All of the above at different times.

Do I know what these feelings are? - Most definitely.

What does it feel like to be successful? - It feels amazing. It's like a big breath full of fresh air.

What does it feel like to be a failure? - It feels like a slap in the face. It hurts and stings but you learn next time to duck.

Am I a success or a failure or in the middle? - I am a success.

How can I feel like I am a success? - By doing the things I love.

How can I be made to feel better about myself? - By playing my piano or singing a song.

What can I do to help myself feel more successful? - Keep a positive outlook.

Do I know what self-esteem is… what is it? - Self-esteem is how you judge yourself.

Do my parents know what these feelings are? - My mom does.

How does one change their feelings? - By finding something good in life.

How can my mom or dad change the way they feel? - By doing something they enjoy.

How can they help me to change the way I feel? - By talking to me.

What kinds of activities do I like to do in my free time? - Music related things, writing, and singing.

What could I do to relieve the stress? - Play my piano.

Do my parents know I am stressed, unhappy, angry, joyful whatever? - My mom does, my dad gets it sometimes.

What can my parents do to relieve the stress? - Relax and take a break.

Am I a good communicator? - Pretty good.

Are my parents good listeners? Most of the time.

Do they listen to me? - My mom definitely, my dad, I know he hears it but whether he does anything with it is beyond me.

Lucia's Answers (age 18)

(Lucia is from Argentina, her native language is Spanish and she wrote out her own answers in English and did a great job)

Questions that have to do with school

1. My academic strengths consist principally in my great sense of responsibility, in the way in which I commit myself with every activity.

2. Yes, with the years I could learn the way that I help me to make easier the learning process, it consists of visualising the information, of summarising, of making charts.

3. The way that results me more efficient is visualising the information that I need to understand or to memorise

4. Sincerely I do not like very much my classroom, I believe that a more agreeable environment would optimise the learning process

5. I think that plants, mirrors and an interesting colour in the wall would do that you feel more comfortable in the classroom, and it would generate more desire of remaining in it.

6. I believe that when a professor is interested in what he had to teach and feels passion for teaching he can transmit to the pupils how interesting and necessary is to learn. Apart from of this, he would have to study at least a bit of psychology,

pedagogy, because there are lots of teachers that know too much on the contents, but very little of how they must teach.

7. I think that the most important thing to help the pupils who have difficulties in learning is not to humiliate them and make them feel that they are not different when they do not understand something. To give them the space to ask, or give them extras exercises.

8. I understand for my experience as pupil that the teachers from whom I learn more are with those who feel passion for what they have to teach and love to be between pupils dictating classes.

9. Sincerely, I believe that at the beginning of their careers the majority of the professors feel very much pleasure on teaching but with the years they are few ones who can fight against the routine and preserve the passion for teaching.

10. When you are small you shares great part of the day with teachers, learning to behave in society, learning to learn, then I do not still have doubts that the teachers have the same function that parents have.

11. Certainly that must be like mom and dad, must give love and attention and teach things that would impact for the rest of life.

12. It irritates me when the teachers don't assist to the classes or are unpunctual, when they do not correct the duties that asked me to make. I believe that it is a lack of respect to pupils who deposit in the school activities a great effort.

13. The teachers with those who I work better are those who have a great sense of humour, are dynamical and update day after day their exercises and their classes

14. The techniques of learning that are more effective are those in which I have to participate constantly, to think, to elaborate and not those in which only I must limit to listening and memorising.

15. My school is excellent , I like the environment, I love that the teachers get enthusiastic so much with the classes, that they enjoy sharing their time with the pupils, I am fascinated by the exercises that I must realise, I feel comfortable between my companions

16. It fascinates me to study and to learn.

17. Because I believe that all the human beings must grow and to know the history of every thing is necessary to understand the present.

18. I think that learning might be more entertaining if we can break with the routine if there would be more freedom, and to incorporate more technology into the classes with we great.

19. The college is the place where children begins to socialise, to learn how to give and receive, to share the time with people, learns to respect the authority, learns the pleasure of learning.

20. I believe that what a pupil needs is attention, to feel the recognition for expiring with the predetermined aims, feeling that it is progressing.

21. The social rules are indispensable to achieve a good living together. It is true the phrase that says " the right of one ends when begins the rights of the other " or the

one that says " do not do to other one what you would not like that they do you to you ", they are the bases of the rules, one must learn to respect the others for obtain the respect of others, also it is important to be tolerant and to learn to forgive the others when they break the rules and not to punish the bad behaviours but to explain the reasons for which one must follow the rules.

22. I like that my teachers talk to me with respect, do not raise the tone of voice ever and for any reason, I think that this is not a caprice, but the way for which they teach me to speak with respect to the others.

23. Obviously that the teachers are persons also, but they should be professionals and not take to the classroom their personal conflicts, to have good humour constantly in spite of the problems that could have out of the classroom.

24. My teachers can obtain the best of me when they motivate me, when they can catch my attention, when they recognise my effort, when they speak to me with respect, when they are responsible with their work and when they don't lose of sight the aim that consists basically of the fact that I learn what they teach me.

25. The director would have to take charge joining all the persons who are members of the school, proposing collective activities, which involve both teachers and pupils, in order that each one could feel that belongs to that college, to feel that it is not the same going to any other one.

26. I believe that the homework is useful when it is an activity that if was done in the classroom would be a loss of time, for example, to read a book or to watch a movie, or activities that need more concentration of the pupil, but if not I believe that they are not good, because it is necessary that pupils have free time in order to do another kind of activities, to practise sports, to learn to play some musical instrument, to learn another language or simply to spend time with their friends or their family.

27. Often I feel stress; in several occasions I feel that I do not have the time to do everything that I must do, and it generates me sadness and anxiety. I believe that the reason is the disorganisation, if I could learn to organise better I would have the necessary time to do everything that I have to do.

28. To teach myself to organise, to teach me the most productive way to do the exercises and to teach me to see my aptitude to solve any problem that could happened.

29. The stress affects me in a negative way because if I feel pressure I am less efficient and my creativity is limited. I believe that when one is in harmony has more aptitude to solve problems, to understand, to memorise, and to create. On the other hand if one is a bit worried stress cannot concentrate at the maximum and start thinking what you did not do and what you still have to do.

30. I believe that the teachers don't understand the stress of the pupils they cannot even perceive it.

Questions that have to do with home

1. I believe that my parents are very good persons, who worry for the well-being about the others that they try to make me happy and that they want the best for my, but I believe that though they try to do the best and I could recognise their effort and their good intentions in many occasions they cannot understand me, though I believe that the reason is that I do not express with clarity.

2. I need parents in order to learn to give and receive love and to feel protected.

3. They are to give me love and protection, to help myself in everything, to share my time with them, to help me to be happy and to be with me in all the projects that I propose, to help myself to achieve my aims.

4. I believe that my parents should understand that in spite of that they have given me lots of things, my life is mine and from nobody else. I need the independence necessary to be able to grow and to be able to find my own way in life.

5. My parents had teach me everything that I learned in life, everything.

6. My parents taught me that the important thing in the life is to be happy, and one is happy if it is in peace and if gives and receives love, if it shares his time with friends, with family.

7. Teach different ways of seeing the things , teach them to be more tolerant and to extend their capacity of comprehension

8. My parents must guide me, but I believe that maintaining a prudent distance, giving me the place I need, I could solve my matters without depending on them, it is the only way in which I can develop my capacities.

9. They must not help me with the homework because they are mine, and I must do them by myself.

10. They must not speak for me; I must learn to defend alone, and to solve the conflicts for my own ways.

11. They have the right to give me their opinion, but only in an informative way, they have a lot of experience and are probable that they are right in their advice, but I must acquire my own experience and must take decisions alone.

12. I feel comfortable living with them, in spite that in many occasions we discuss, I feel happy sharing my daily life with them.

13. Always they gave me the place to give them my opinion and the always listened to me and can apologise and give me the reason when they believe that I have it.

14. I believe that modifying some conducts will make the living together more pleasant.

15. In house I like to read, to cook, to watch TV and movies, to paint, to listen music, to write, to have dinner with my parents, to take mate with my friends, to sunbathe.

16. Obviously that there are many things that I can change to be happier, the point is that they are too much and to change is not an easy work, needs time and effort, I changed many things and I am happier that before, I believe that with the years I will be able to change everything but must be patience.

17. My parents should learn to speak with more respect and without raising the tone of voice, I believe that they shout very much and that they do not realise that the shouts breaks the climate of harmony that it should reign in our home

Questions that have to do with me

1. To speak itself more respectfully, to be more tolerant, to understand that not always everything is like one wants.
2. I love the place where I live, and I feel comfortable in my house, though I believe that it is too untidy
3. In my house there is going to be a garden full of plants, mirrors, pictures, books, and a big and great kitchen.
4. I believe that I would like to live always in Adrogué because it is my place, I belong here. But I believe that the contact with the nature would make me much happier that to live surrounded by cement.
5. Be many things of me that I do not share with my parents, and seem to me that it is ok, because they are not my friends, they do not have my age, and there are many things that they cannot understand. I must preserve my intimacy.
6. If I feel I the need to tell them something I do it.
7. Not always I am satisfied with what I am, I know that I have many virtues and know that I have many faults and in spite of that I make a great effort to be the best that I can be. I often do things that not make me feel well, but I have the hope that in some moment I am going to be the happiest I can be with what I am.
8. I always think who I am really and it make me laugh when I realize that in spite of having lived with me I cannot know with absolute security who I am really.
9. I always think what I would like to be, for moments I know it but it I changed with too many speed my plans for the future, I also believe that with the years I will know it, I think that not everything depends on me, but on the circumstances that they present and on how I take advantage of them.
10. Certainly that I do not have all the freedom to do what I want, my freedom is determined by my familiar and the social context and by my faults.
11. They not always understand me and it is logical, not only because they are my parents, but for the generational difference.
12. My teachers not always understand me; also it is because the generational difference and because we are too many pupils.
13. My friends understands me.
14. I should express with more clarity and express more my feelings and thoughts in order that they all could understand me, but sincerely there does not matter much that they understand, in many occasions I know what I want and why so does not seem to me that I need the comprehension of the others.
15. To help myself in the college they do not have to do anything.
16. They must be to my side when I needs them to help me to achieving my goals.

17. My state of mind depends on the context though I try to be always in peace with myself.
18. I understand what these feelings mean because I have felt them.
19. To feel that one has triumphed is a very pleasant sensation, increases the self-confidence.
20. Failing is not a nice feeling, but it is when I learn more.
21. I feel that in many things I am successful and in others I fail.
22. I am successful when I propose something to myself and obtain it.
23. Changing what I cannot stand of my, it can do that I feel happier with myself.
24. They can make me feel that I triumph when they recognise my achievements.
25. Admitting that I do the best that I can, though often I could not achieve my aims and paying more attention in the effort I made and not in the results.
26. My parents are happy and have many desires of living, always they have future plans, projects, desire of continuing progressing.
27. I feel that when I do things that they do not like they get irritated, but this is a problem of them that must resolve for themselves.
28. Only with the example they help me to changes the way I feel, especially when I am sad.
29. In my free time I like to be with my family and my friends.
30. For not being stress I must realise that nothing is so important, must not be dramatic and not exaggerate the situations, must understand that everything has a solution.
31. My parents always knows how do I feel, it is not always necessary for me to says them, they can realise when I change my routine.
32. I am not good at communicating my feelings.
33. My parents are not good listeners they not pay attention when I try to share with them some problem.

Nick's answers

Questions that have to do with school

I learn best through variety, meaning that I enjoy a combination of visual, auditory and touch activities. I find that using the same learning method can be too repetitive, but when teachers change things once in a while, it keeps things unpredictable. I like that atmosphere in my classroom because it is very open. We often have free discussions and everyone can share their opinions. When some students have difficulties understanding things, there are several things my teacher could do. If it is only a couple of students, he/she should ask them to come in after school so as not to waste class time. If there are many students who are confused, the teacher should organize an activity or somehow clarify the problem. Some of my teachers seem to enjoy their jobs, where as others seem to be bored by it. Whether or not they liked their jobs, it is important to prevent that from being shown in the classroom.

The teachers that I like best are the ones that see their students for what they really are: we are no longer young children, we are teenagers. I like teachers that are not offended by swearing, that do not act surprised when we talk about mature and serious things, teachers that treat us more as their equals, not as inferiors. They are still the ones in authority, but they should give some independence here and there. Kids get angry when they feel like they are restricted by tons of rules, so it is good to consider whether certain rules (like swearing once in a while, as long as it isn't at other people) should be abandoned as students get older. It is important to have rules to instill morals into students, especially when they are younger, and to make sure that there is an organized atmosphere at the school. Personally, I get all the motivation I need from within myself, and my teacher is there to teach me new information that I can apply to my assignments and hopefully to something later in my life. Homework is important for practice, but sometimes should not be necessary, especially for older students. This would be preparation for university. If you know the stuff and you don't feel like you need to do the work, you shouldn't be forced to do it. Pacing oneself is important to avoid stress, and if under stress, teachers should be able to help their students organize themselves and avoid being overwhelmed when it is time for exams.

Questions that have to do with home

My parents have given me everything, and I appreciated that now. They pushed me to try out different sports, to get involved at school, to make sure I did not forget my first language, and although I sometimes hated them for it in the past, I am extremely grateful now. They gave me the opportunity to find what I love to do (gymnastics), and they exposed me to lots of different things as a child. Sometimes I teach my parents, for instance when it comes to letting them know what goes on in the "teenage world" or when it comes to letting them know something about myself, for they are largely responsible for the person I have grown to become. My parents have always helped me and continue to offer my help. When I was younger, they helped with homework. Now, they help me with other decisions in my life, such as those regarding university and my future. There are things that I could change in myself to make me happier, but they are things built into my character, and although I acknowledge them as my weaknesses, I cannot change them. They are a part of who I am, and I have learned to live with them. If I could, I would make myself more easygoing in that I would not be so stressed out about little things, and would take criticism easier. My parents have always made the atmosphere at home very pleasant, and I have a great relationship with both of them. Sometimes they worry about me too much and this causes them to get angry, but it is understandable. Sometimes they criticize me and I think they are wrong, and we end of getting angry at each other. I am working on dealing with criticism, however. Lately, I have been very busy. I would like for us to have more time to spend together. That is very important for a family, especially when the children are young. I LOVE my house!

Questions that have to do with me.

There are very few things I don't tell my parents: things regarding my personal life and things that would worry them that they do not need to know because I know that they are not a big deal. (Sometimes my parents blow things out of proportion). I believe that I have the freedom to do as I wish. I have a great family and friends and I am happy that they understand me. My teachers understand me as well as they can, considering they do not really know me the way my parents and my friends do. I am very happy with who I am and consider myself to be a happy person. Obviously there are times when I am angry and upset, but this is natural. I think my life so far has been a success: I have hobbies outside of school that I love, I have wonderful friends and family and I am doing well in school. My parents are lenient and let me do almost anything that I want, as long as they know where I am at all times. Sometimes they bother me about my plans for my future and I get angry and say things I don't mean, but I know and they know that this hot-temperedness is in my nature. Just as any family, we fight once in a while, but we always work things out. My parents always know how I'm feeling because they know me and they can just tell, and they do everything they can to help me. Sometimes when I'm upset I would like for them to just give me my space, but they care too much and are unable to step aside. When I want to be, I am a good communicator, and they are generally good at listening. Sometimes, however, they jump to conclusions and assume things that aren't true, and this makes me very frustrated. If they listened to me completely open-mindedly and the made conclusions, it would be far more effective than already having their minds made up before I say anything.

Allan's Answers *(age 16)*

Questions that have to do with school

When it comes to school everything is like a blur. I am good at gym. I love athletics and I seem to be pretty good at everything that I try. I like football, hockey and track. I am very quick and a good sprinter. My favorite day at school is track and field day. Boy, I could really show off my good skills.

As far as being a student, I seem to be afraid all of the time and because of this I don't do very well. I get really nervous on Sunday nights knowing that school is the next day. I believe that I learn best through touching and seeing. I learn best through experience.

I really think that I have pretty good teachers. They are very caring, they work hard, they are nice, and they go out of their way to help us and seem to like their job.

I see my teachers as people that need to be listened to and I do everything that I could to be nice to them. I respect all of the rules. I work best for those teachers who take an interest in me personally.

I guess that teachers would be really great if they can make subjects really interesting and fun. What a great quality for all of them to work towards having.

When a teacher gets angry and punishes others, I get really nervous and want to run away. I make a promise to myself that I will not break any school rules. Boy it really looks like I am a goody-two-shoes.

I feel that school could be better if the classes were not so big and I could have more personal attention. Not enough teachers seem to be really paying attention that much to the kids. In this way maybe they could be more like a mom or dad, that is ask us how we feel about things and help to teach us how to solve our own problems and also help us to feel better when we are unhappy. It would be great if I could have some private time.

AS to the question of stress, I think that if they did this then they could help me when I feel stressed.

Oh this question of motivation, that is a difficult one, I think that if teachers listened to me more, found a way for me to be do well, tell me that I am doing good and if I am not doing well help to show me how to do better. If they were able to do this well I would want to do better and also try harder.

The principal… mmmm.. That is an interesting question. I am not so sure what he is supposed to be doing. I know that my parents go and talk to him and I know that he talks to kids when they break really big rules. He also talks a lot to teachers and he is an important person in the school. What else. Well, I am not so sure.

Questions that have to do with home

What do I think of my mom and dad? For me that is a difficult question, there are good and bad things. My father is very, very strict, he gets angry a lot and I am afraid of him. There are times that I think that he cares for me, but since he is angry so much I am not really sure. My mom is really busy; she stays at home and takes care of us four boys. I guess she tries to keep things organized. She is a good cook and does her best. Because she is so busy doing all of the little things, I think that she does not have the time to really play with me, ask me how I am feeling. I kinda get the feeling that she does not really understand me too well. Because of this I do not share too much with her or my dad.

Parents are there to take care of us and keep us safe, also to teach us the right and wrong things to do. I wish my parents would be there more for me and really show me that they are here to support me.

I get really upset when my father gets angry with me and it seems like he is always angry, I feel like I want to run away and hide. I know that I would do better if they were nicer to me. I am afraid to talk to them, to tell them how I am feeling and what is going on in my life. When I have done that either they have not listened or they have yelled at me and told me what I have done wrong. Whenever I come home with a bad report card, my father always tells me that I am going to be "a ditch digger." This makes me feel really bad. When he does this, my mother just listens and does not say anything.

I guess I would like more support.

Parents are here to do many things. They are here to teach us, to listen, to help with homework, to have lots of patience, to be understanding, to communicate, to help me when they can and to speak up for me when they need to.

In my house, I am afraid to speak up, and there are many times where I wish that I were living somewhere else with nicer parents. A place that was calmer, more together, more caring. One of the problems is that I am confused, I don't know how to make things better, how to change things. just run away. I wish things were different.

Questions that have to do with me

I do not share hardly anything with my parents, most of the time when I do they find a reason to find something bad to say. I am happy when I am outside playing with my friends and those are the times that I feel free.

Do my parents understand me? NO!

Do my teachers understand me? NO!

Am I happy? NO

I am not sure exactly what I am feeling other than being afraid to say things, I am afraid I am going to make mistakes all of the time.

As you ask me this question, I guess I am sad.

Beau's answers (age 13)

We are all gifted—It's true I have a lot of friends who have their own unique gifts, some are smart in school, some are smart while playing an instrument, even kids that have a disability are especially smart in one area.

What does it mean to be gifted? A special talent that most other people don't have that is unique to that person.

What does it mean to be normal? To fit into a special stereotype.

Questions about school

I find that I am good at presentations and writing stories, I am not so good at math. I am good at science. I learn best through hands on learning I remember it best that way. I do well in science because it is hands on.

I like when the classroom is set up in a circle rather than rows. It is not so traditional that way and that the teacher is in the middle rather than up front.

My teachers get best results from us kids when they present the class in a fun way. All teachers are different though, so, it depends. We learn best when she thoroughly completes a unit knowing that everybody understands before moving on.

I like teachers that enjoy teaching, not just because they get summers off. I had one teacher who I wanted to talk to and he told me to shut-up and go away. I then wrote a letter to the principal. Some teachers are stressed out with their own lives and they show it.

A good teacher is someone who has patience and the ability to understand what it is like to be a kid and teach to us kids.

Teachers are like moms and dads because they need to care about us and when they do; kids will begin to care more about learning they also teach us about life about rules just like our parents.

The biggest issue with teachers is not seeing things as being fair or not, so the need to understand each other and communicate.

I like learning but sometimes school is the harder way to learn, an easier way is like the discovery channel, computers, hands on learning.

Teachers can get me better motivated through encouragement, building my confidence level, being positive and interested in my learning.

It is important that teachers teach in the area that they are comfortable with. I now have a science teacher that has never taught science before and the class is unhappy including herself, we are not learning and so many of us are not doing well. We know that she doesn't know what she is talking about it. I also know that she is stressed out as well.

A good teacher is one who can create an understanding of their content and be able to reach all or most of their students. Then with the understanding, learning becomes a lot more fun.

How can a teacher help those kids that are having difficulty learning? The teacher needs to be aware of this as well as the students.

Stress, yes I know it, when it comes to doing homework. The stress comes form both peers and doing the work. The teachers need to be aware that stress exists with us and be compassionate and caring.

Questions that have to do with home

I couldn't imagine having any other mom, anybody that is as caring and present as she is. She teaches me things that I cannot learn in school, special things. My mom teaches me about discipline and to be balanced in my emotions. She helps me when it comes to judging others. She tempers any anger that I have and helps me put it into perspective. Through her compassion I have learned to have compassion for others. On the other hand my dad does not seem to care.

Basically my mom is a free counselor in my life.

I teach my mom songs that I write, I teach her board games. I teach her special facts that I learn in school like how far is the earth from the sun.

My mom is really eager to help me with my homework and is always there to help me with personal problems. If I do need to seek others for guidance, I usually will talk about issues with close friends.

My mom always asks me what she can do to be a better parent. I feel that I am respected in this family. My mom treats me in the same way that she would expect to be treated herself. With compassion, understanding, and cooperation.

If I had to change something about myself, it would be to limit my sarcasm with others. That would make me happier.

For my mom if she was more organized, for my dad if he could get through some of his defensiveness.

If I had a sound proof room in my house that would be great so that I can play my guitar.

I think it would be magic if I could build my own house with secret places, a big mall right next to it and a place called Kids World where I can go to play.

Things that have to do with me

I feel happy, I know that I have problems but I also know that I have the ability to solve my own problems. For example I wish that things were different with my dad and when I get down about it, I will play my guitar or watch my favorite TV show.

I have thought about going to a school for the arts. I like the thought of being an actor. Also I would enjoy working in marketing and advertising, I also really like photography. Also my mother is supportive when it comes to all of this.

I feel that my mom understands me, my dad doesn't understand me, it's as if he does not respect my ideas and my likes and dislikes. He does not take the time and listen to what I have to say.

To feel successful means that you have accomplished something that you have done a good job. There is a big difference between success and failure, success means to achieve a goal failures get me depressed.

I feel great when I make up my own music to play on my guitar I feel really proud when I let them know that I did it.

When it comes to success and teachers, I feel that it is their job to help me get good grades and if they can do this then I will feel successful. I also will feel that this means that they were successful as well.

Self-esteem is about feeling good about myself, which I do. My mom is taking a course and is working on feeling better about herself.

I would like my dad to change within him the fact that he does not understand that I have a mind of my own and that I have good judgment.

We change through experience, sometimes we have life altering experiences like bad accidents, sometimes we change when we just get angry about something that causes us to be unhappy about something.

My mom is a good listener, my dad is different he cuts me off and wants me to do what he wants. I think that it is really important to listen. I feel respected when people listen to what I have to say. We can learn from each other only when we give ourselves the chance to listen to one another.

JJ (age 6), Cameron (age 8), Lissanne (age 7) and Vanessa (age 8)

Do I have any secrets that I do not share with my mom or dad?

JJ: I always have secrets that I tell my dad.

Cameron: I don't have any secrets.

Lissanne: I really don't have any secrets because I am close with my mom and dad.

Vanessa: I don't have any secrets cause I tell my mom everything.

Do you have the freedom the things that you really want to do at home?

Vanessa: It depends on what I want to do. If I want to make my own clothes and do the cutting No because she spends lots of money on them, but when it comes to playing, she usually lets me.

Cameron: Most of the time.

JJ: I don't have the freedom, my mom or dad tells me what to do and I like it.

Lissanne: No comment.

Do my parents understand who I am?

JJ: My parents understand that I am a kid.

Lissanne: My mom understands who I am because anytime I need to I can just go and talk to her.

Vanessa: My parents know how I feel and they are there to help me in school and with my friends.

Am I happy?

Vanessa: I am happy; I get to spend time with all my friends and my family.

Lissanne: Sometimes I am unhappy with myself because I do things that I shouldn't do, right now I am not so happy because I don't like my haircut.

Cameron: I am happy with myself, I don't know why I just am.

JJ: I am happy because I have a horse which I love to ride.

Do my teachers understand me?

Vanessa: Yes they do but when I am mixed up they don't.

Lissanne: Sometimes they do not understand but there is one who does and she is my favorite teacher.

Cameron: Most of my teachers they do not understand me, because I am usually pretty crazy and they cannot figure me out.

JJ: When I do not listen to them, they do not understand me.

Have I thought about what I want to be in life?

Vanessa: I want to be a teacher, because usually I get A's on my report card.

Lissanne: I want to be a daycare teacher because I like little kids; they are fun to play with.

Cameron: When I grow up, I want to be a video game tester.

JJ: When I grow up I want to be a dancer.

What does it feel like to be successful?

Vanessa: It is just like taking a test, when I think that I am going to get it wrong, I get it right.

Lissanne: When I accomplish something, it feels great. When I feel I cannot do something I end up doing it great.

JJ: Pass

Cameron: Pass.

How does it to feel not to be successful?

Lissanne: When I am not successful and it ends up that I cannot do something, I feel bad. When I see that other people got it and I haven't it feels weird.

Cameron: I feel sad and that I will probably get into trouble.

JJ: I feel really small when I make a mistake.

Vanessa: I feel like I am not smart.

What can my parents do to help me become more successful?

Vanessa: They can buy me a whole collection of "Baby Brats."

Lissanne: They can help me by giving me money.

Cameron: Pass

JJ: Whenever I break a toy my dad fixes it.

Do I tell my parents what is on my mind?

JJ: My dad is always around when I need to tell him stuff.

Lissanne: I keep things to myself.

Vanessa: Sometimes, I don't talk to them when I need to and keep things to myself.

Cameron: Pass

Are my parents good listeners?

Vanessa: They are good listeners and how I know that is because when they visit my school they come and talk to me about how I can improve.

JJ: My parents are sometimes too busy, to listen.

Lissanne: My parents are there to listen to me when I am not so happy.

Cameron: My parents, listen to me when I tell them that I want a new video game.

Are my parents happy?

Vanessa: My dad is usually happy, because he loves to play with me.

JJ: Pass

Lissanne: I guess so, because they laugh a lot.

Cameron: Pass

Do my parents know when I am feeling stressed?

Vanessa: They do know when I am stressed because I usually talk to them when things are bothering me at home or at school.

JJ: I tell my mom or dad when I am not feeling good and then they go buy me more toys.

Lissanne: They do know because they see it in my face.

What do I like to do in my free time?

Vanessa: I like to play tag with my friends Maggie and Nicholas.

JJ: I like to play basketball; I am really good at it.

Lissanne: I usually read or I will go play with my friends.

Do I like my house?

Vanessa: I like to do many things in my house. I love my Nintendo.

JJ: I like to play a lot in my house.

Lissanne: I like my house, I would not like to move because I would miss them. If I had to move I would not like to live in the mountains because I would be afraid of getting lost.

Cameron: I love my house, I feel really good there

Do I think my parents are my teachers?

Vanessa: Yes I do, my parents help me with my homework.

JJ: My parents teach me about what to do when my brother is not being good.

Lissanne: My parents help me to remember things.

What do I teach my parents?

Vanessa: I talk to them about the things that I need.

JJ: I don't teach them anything.

Lissanne: I let them know sometimes about how I am feeling.

The Parents' Speak

What follows is a list of questions that were used for the interviews.

You can also check in by asking yourself these questions. Please remember that you can interview yourself or your kids as often as you wish and as part of your journal note your changes, your kids' changes, the family's changes.

Parenting – Adult Questions

1. How did parenthood affect your marriage?
2. Did you make any major life changes in regards to the birth of your child?
3. Upon being a new parent, did you receive help and support? And by whom?
4. Where did you learn how to be a parent?
5. Did you and your partner suffer form post-partum depression?
6. What guidelines do you use?
7. How did parenthood affect your family?
8. How did parenthood affect your personal life, your other adult relationships?
9. Your self image?
10. Did you feel inadequate?
11. Did you feel angry, deprived, fulfilled, confused, happy, at peace?

12. How do you cope with these feelings?

13. With whom do you share them?

14. How has your idea of parenting changed with experience?

15. How do you see yourself now as a parent?

16. How does your child see you as a parent?

17. Do you have a family plan?

18. What would be in your family plan?

19. Do you belong to support groups?

20. How does the everyday stress of life affect you in your parenting ways?

21. Do you understand how you interact with my child?

22. What is your parenting style?

23. What is your spouse's style?

24. Do your spouse and you see yourselves as one? Are you consistent in your disciplinary techniques?

25. How do you see yourself communicating with your child?

26. Give examples of situations of communication (any recent experiences).

27. What do you perceive to be balance in your life before kids and what is it now?

28. How important is it to have balance in one's life? Without it?

29. How has having a family affected you as an individual?

30. What has your child taught you about yourself?

Melanie (Beau's mother)

As a parent I want for them to feel that they can use all of the skills which they have. I want them to feel good about themselves and happy and empowered.

I try to let them be themselves, to allow for them to explore their own interests. I teach them the values about commitment and that they take their responsibilities to completion.

Parenting a teenager

One of the challenges of having a teenager is that I wanted to be cool. I thought that if I could be their friend, like one of them that this was the door to having a good relationship. Boy was I in for a shock. I realized that being the authoritative parent, the guiding parent, the parent who was there to advocate, that there was no room for friendship. In remembering myself as a teenager, I realized that the reason I got into trouble was that I wasn't thinking so that my role here is to think for them, to protect them because they are not thinking. I was afraid for them. I know that their desire is to be on their own but it is difficult to hold back and allow them to experience life. It is hard to know when to draw the line, when to step in. When to say, "I really don't care that you want to do this." "You have to do it my way." This is the conundrum. What is scary is when to know when to step in or when to stay out of it.

For parents who have teenagers, I would suggest that you keep a watchful eye on them. Try to find a way to get them talking. Find ways that you can do things with them. Trust them, respect them, and listen to them.

Parenting Style

The problem with my spouse and myself that we had drastically different parenting styles and we could not meet some place. Because of this the kids got mixed messages and this confused them and us as well.

How do you see the role of a teacher?

They have a huge role. Most teachers go there for the right reasons. They are dedicated to teaching children. A good teacher is one who can teach to the kid's level and style of learning. A good teacher is one who is flexible enough to understand their kids. A good teacher is one who can listen and respect their students.

How do you motivate your kids?

I am there as their supporter and show them this any way that I can. That I am there to show them where they have come, how they have grown. What they have accomplished or not.

To motivate means to be consistent. What ever you say you must follow through and it must be relevant.

Kids need to know that you are going to be there for them. Forgiveness is really important. There is no paycheck for this job; it is the hardest job in the workplace. I think that you need to appreciate the small things, the small accomplishments. Those special times where you see your kids are growing and in a subtle way benefiting by the teachings that you as a parent are offering to them

An Interview with Colleen, Kelly, Inca, Patrick, Allan and Marianne

How did having a child affect your relationship?

Colleen: My gut feeling, my intuition helped me to understand what to do when I had my first son. I guess I am just blessed to be in a really great relationship. My husband and I communicate really well. He has always been there for me and I for him. Actually he has always kind of worshipped the ground I walk on. This made it really easy to deal with the ups and downs of having children.

Kelly: Having kids really changed the relationship with my husband. I saw things in him that I never new existed. Things that made me feel really uncomfortable we had very different styles and he withdrew from the relationship. After a few years we ended up going our separate ways.

Inca: Having children for me was the most natural thing I have ever done. I guess that explains why I have five children. I feel perfectly natural with them. I feel that my life never skipped a beat.

Patrick: I was not totally aware, but having a child was really fabulous, but I felt that I didn't have the skills to deal with what my role was. At the time I was out in the workforce and my wife was at home. Because she was overwhelmed with Patrick Jr. we ended up reversing roles. That didn't work well, we ended up both being overwhelmed and after a few months we made the decision to separate.

Allan: We did not have kids for a few years after we were married, but for me, it was the most natural progression. I always loved the thought of having children. I felt that I would just know what to do as a parent. I would have been more than happy to be a stay-at-home dad. When I finally did have kids, my thoughts proved correct. It was just great.

How do you create balance with your spouse?

Colleen:

Kelly:

Inca: We find that we have to organize our day. Our weeks so that we honor ourselves as individuals. One day a month we do something special together. This is special time for my husband and myself.

Marianne: I reflect. In the morning I light my candle, reflect, and visualize on how I want my day to look like. One of the intentions I make is that I will not yell at my kids. Instead that we will discuss issues work them out. They understand that they are playing an important role in the family,

Patrick: We need to take care of ourselves to honor ourselves.

Kelly: I find that you can really beat yourself up, that it is important to take things as they come. If not chaos seems to reign all of the time. I try to follow the old adage "Don't sweat the small stuff." To have a family is hard work that each and everyone have to do their part for it to work. That we need to work at creating balance within us as individual family members.

How do we see discipline in our family? What is the difference between discipline and punishment?

Marianne: Punishment is a negative way for teaching boundaries. I must admit that at times I fall into this negative trap, sometimes it seems easier to be negative. It also can be very draining. I try to remain conscious that I must approach discipline from a more positive way.

Patrick: There is one time that I was working with a client and there was a woman who came to my home she brought her son who began to play with some toys which were there. When it came to leave her son wanted to take a toy, she explained to him why he could not setting the proper boundaries. I see this as teaching discipline.

Colleen: I think punishment is power and control. As a parent we have to be conscious of what we are and whether or not if this is the way we want to, look at discipline. As for me, I opt to teach my kids about choices and decision making as my way of modeling discipline.

Kelly: Discipline is a way to instill in your child what is good and not good to adopt.

Marianne: My children have choices; I view teaching discipline about giving choices.

Jessica (Marianne's daughter): I see my mom more as a friend. I talk to her as a friend, which is a good quality. In my family I see discipline as a loving caring thing, I know that my mom is not doing it to be mean, but that she is teaching me about that if I do something wrong that I have to deal with the consequences.

As far as being about a teenager, it is not easy. There are a lot of things that you cannot talk to your parents about because you feel that they may not understand.

What do you think about our tendency of labeling our children and the prevalence of medication as a teaching tool?

Colleen: Parents have the final choice when it comes to testing. There are other options like naturopaths; homeopaths always go with your gut feeling.

Kelly: They don't need medication they need meditation.

Marianne: I am a teacher so I know that if a child is having difficulty with attention but as a parent I would agree with Colleen that before a parent decides on medication that all the options should be examined

Patrick: Celtic sea salt some form of seaweed or algae, flaxseeds, hemp, olive oil. That this phenomenon that we are seeing in our schools and homes has to do with malnourishment. That our children are calling out for more attention, for a greater understanding of who they are and how they learn.

General overview of what it is like to be a parent?

Colleen: I think that it is about being the best parent that we can be. That there is no right or wrong. There are no mistakes that can be made. Ours is to be able to be good observers and learn from what we do and make the necessary adjustments. We must keep in perspective here that there is another human being on the other end of the line here. Someone who is totally independent of our world. We must never forget that and always respect that and them and ourselves as well. It is good to ask ourselves questions because it shows an awareness. It shows that we are looking to grow.

Inca: I think that when we share our lives with our kids. We share our happiness and sadness our goodness and badness. They learn so much about life, They learn about communication how to solve problems and all along we are learning about the same things as well. Yes it is all about balance You have to be in balance with yourself, take care of yourself. That you are happy, then you are more ready to be happy with your kids and spouse. You have to evaluate all of the time what is good for you and what is not.

Patrick: If we are assessing ourselves about how we are doing. I we are always saying yes to our children and then we hear that it is good to be firm with our kids. We get confused. It is about asking ourselves questions and checking in with ourselves whether or not this is safe or not. If it is not safe then we have learned this from someplace.

The above questions were designed to help you in getting to know your kids as they grow and develop. By using them you may also become a better interviewer. This may help in your overall relationship building.

I would love for you to send me your results of your interviews.

Thinking of Having Kids?

<u>Lesson 12</u>
   Learn the names of every character from Sesame Street, Barney, Disney, the Teletubbies, and Pokemon.
   Watch nothing else on TV for at least five years.

Your Interview

If you wish you can use the questions to interview yourself, your spouse and of course your children. You may be very surprised at what you can learn. Another technique is to interview someone else's kids as they may feel more comfortable. You can switch on and off. This may be a lot of fun.

_____
_____
_____
_____
_____
_____
_____
_____
_____
_____
_____
_____
_____
_____
_____
_____
_____
_____
_____
_____
_____
_____
_____
_____
_____
_____
_____
_____
_____
_____
_____

Chapter 8

The Impact of Media on Our Children

In today's society, electronic media are thoroughly integrated into the fabric of life, with television, movies, videos, music, video games, and computers central to both work and play. Recent studies indicate that even the youngest children in the United States are using a wide variety of screen media, many at higher levels than recommended by child development professionals.

Pediatricians, educators, researchers, and policymakers have raised particular concerns about electronic media use among very young children. Developmental science suggests that children may be the most vulnerable between birth and school age to certain negative effects of media use such as obesity, aggression, fear, and sleep disturbances. Paralleling this vulnerability is a unique responsiveness to educational programming that has been linked to both immediate and long range educational benefits.

Neuro-developmental research indicates that, unlike other organ systems, the human brain is embryonic at birth – it completes the majority of its development over the first 18 – 24 months of life. The experiences that optimize brain development during this time include interaction with parents and other humans, manipulation of environmental elements like blocks or sand, and creative, problem-solving activities.

Because screen media do not perform any of these functions, the American Academy of Pediatrics (AAP) officially state that the risks of infants using media outweigh the benefits and thus recommend against screen media use for children zero to two years of age.

What is of concern is that research has provided us a link between the exposure that we have to television and computer games and the onset of obesity, diabetes and the substantial increase in violent behavior.

In addition to this, I will pose a very scary question to you. "Is there a link between the amount of time that our kids are watching TV (6 – 7 hours per day), the vulnerability of their brain (for the first 6 years of life, there are no filters), the speed at which they are learning via our media (warp speed), and the speed that we are teaching them at school (turtle speed) and the huge increase of our ADHD population?

To clarify, the main symptoms of Attention Deficit and Hyperactive Disorder are lack of focus and an inability to pay attention. That is to say, "Can we hypothesize that our kids are not being challenged enough in school, that they are bored and are losing interest?"

To support this, data from the National Longitudinal Survey of Youth indicated that TV viewing at age one and three was associated with parental reports of attention disorder symptoms at age seven. Attention disorder symptoms were indicated by parent response to the five-item hyperactivity subscale of the Behavioral Problems Index (BPI), which assess concentration, impulsivity, and restlessness. For every additional 2.9 hours of TV viewed per week at age one, a child was 28% more likely to exhibit attention disorder symptoms at age seven (Christakis, Zimmerman, DiGiuseppe, & McCarty, 2004).

These results need to be taken very seriously as we may be affecting the educational, emotional and social development of an entire generation of youth.

Despite the attention the AAP has given to the potential harmful effects that media is having on our children, recent studies examining media use by very young children have indicated that the vast majority of parents have never heard of the recommendations and continue to allow and even encourage their very young children to use screen media.

This chapter is designed to create a greater degree of awareness. After all isn't that what this book is all about? That is creating awareness's and then working to develop a better plan that gives us the opportunity to develop a healthier environment for ourselves and our kids?

The Modernization of TV Watching

For those who grew up in the 1950s, 1960s and 1970s, television was fairly uncomplicated and modest in its content. There were only a few major networks and, of course, no cable networks with its hundreds of channels to surf through.

In the 1960s, kids spent an average of 30 hours a week with their parents. Today, kids spend only about 17 hours. In the average household, the TV is on between six to nine hours per day. Some latest alarming statistics are telling us that preschoolers are spending about 60 hours per week in front of the TV and by the time children reach the age of 18, they have spent more time watching TV than at school.

So what do we do in order to protect the best interests of our children when it comes to media exposure? Do we pull the plug and throw out the TV or maybe the computer? There are those who would tell us that that is exactly what we should do. But in reality, that probably isn't going to happen.

The truth of the matter is that the technology isn't going to just go away. The key may be to find the best way to live with it and use the various media technologies to serve us in beneficial ways, while not allowing them to take over our lives and adversely influence the well being of our children.

In order to establish a sound foundation on which to base our decisions as parents, we need to examine as many aspects of the question at hand as possible.

One of the most serious and far-reaching considerations of how television may negatively affect our children is the question of whether television can change our children's brains.

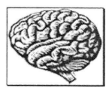

How the TV and Computer May Affect Your Child's Brain Development

Many experts, both in the field of neurology and psycho-neurology, agree that your child's brain development can, and is affected particularly by watching too much television, especially with young children.

The blank look on your child's face when watching a show like *WWF Smackdown* might reflect what's going on in his brain – and be a warning sign of things to come.

Indeed, for several years child psychologists have been warning parents about the dangers of repeated exposure to violent video games. Now, there may be medical evidence to back their claims.

Researchers in Indiana have measured the effects on a brain scan. The study's principal investigator, Dr. Vincent Mathews, said prolonged exposure to violence actually affects brain function and behavior. "The parts of the brain we looked at are the frontal lobe — the area of the brain involved in emotional control, inhibition of behavior and impulse control."

The frontal lobe also works somewhat like a filter or screening device and organizer of incoming information, helping the child to make sense of, process and incorporate information.

The idea is that those parts of the brain don't work as well (after prolonged exposure to all of these video games our children are becoming addicted to), and because of that, they don't control their behavior as well."

Given a child's natural hormonal mood swings, adding a steady diet of these video games is like pouring gasoline on a fire, according to Dr. David Walsh, of the National Institute on Media and the Family.

"There are two things going on," Walsh said. "One is the anger is getting amplified by the repetitious acts of violence in the game; then at the same time the buffer to that is less active." He said the content of most popular games today has no positive value and might shock most parents. "What good could possibly come from having your child spend hours and hours and hours decapitating people and organizing drug rings and murdering prostitutes?"

It is suspected that prolonged participation affects the child's ability to hold and form healthy images in the mind, which is an essential function in the development of their imagination, self-esteem and self-reflection.

"TV rots the senses in the head!

It kills the imagination dead!

It clogs and clutters up the mind!

It makes a child so dull and blind.

He can no longer understand a fantasy,

A fairyland!

His brain becomes as soft as cheese!

His powers of thinking rust and freeze!

— Ronald Dahl from *Charlie and the Chocolate Factory*

Television – The Stressbuster Myth

I know, you come home from a hard days work, and you have had a really stressful day and you can't wait until dinner is finished, the kids have done their homework and are and either sleeping or off doing their own thing. Yes it is time to do the couch potato thing and just relax, and veg out. Another scenario is for you to catch some time for yourself by getting the kids to watch their favorite TV shows or video games. They love it, they are occupied and you are home free for a little while.

What we do not realize is the unseen physical responses both yourself and your kids are having while watching.

Television is designed to evoke a response from you. It may be fear, anger, love, sex and so on. It has to be that way because it is a product that is being sold. If it didn't elicit an emotional response from either yourself or your children, then you would just turn it off.

Physiologically, a hormone called Cortisol is released from your body. Cortisol basically is responsible for sending a message to the body that its muscles need extra energy to interact with a specific experience. In this case, it may be experiencing the action being portrayed on the screen. If you think about it, television is very manipulative and we just give ourselves up to whatever we happen to be watching.

Once released into the bloodstream, Cortisol can stay circulating in the body for up to 24 hours. Research shows that a sustained high level of Cortisol can contribute to a long list of health-related problems. Among these is an increase in appetite and cravings for certain foods, particularly the junk foods we see advertised on television so much. Our mind automatically begins to produce Cortisol once it begins to witness the content of the show you are watching, which automatically stimulates you to go to the fridge to eat or order your favorite pizza, wings or Chinese food.

It is not surprising then to hear that obesity and diabetes are becoming an ever-growing problem within our current generation of children. Ask yourself could this be one of the contributing factors as to why adults in their 30s and 40s are now requiring gastric bypass surgery.

Research also indicates that our Asian neighbors and most other cultures living away from North America are not exhibiting these most disturbing emotional and health related trends.

Among some of the other less known things that can result from stress and Cortisol production are:

- Impaired digestive functioning
- Memory and learning impairment
- Increased anxiety and depression

As Marie Winn writes in her book, *The Plug-In Drug*: "Television producers and, particularly advertisers, know that in order to capture the attention of a casual viewer and hold the attention of a serious viewer, they must produce a steady flow of startle flickers. These are quick changes in camera angle, rapid changes in sound, punctuation in color and movement—all of these produce very small startle responses in the brain, preparing the body to react and riveting attention to the television just as surely as it would be riveted to a cobra or tiger. The effect of this is a continuous stream of low-level Cortisol entering the bloodstream."

How Do TV and Other Electronic Gadgetry Affect Your Child's Learning ?

Learning to pay attention is one of the most essential learning skills and one of the things most threatened by over-stimulation, whether it be by television, computers, video games and the like.

Another problem with paying attention and plays into ADHD is something that is called being *stimulus bound*. This means that every time something changes, the child's focus will shift and they will react to it. Although it is quite natural for young children's attention to jump from one thing to another, it is felt that forms of electronic media may contribute to prolonging this behavior. The child's brain function can often end up being trained or altered in such a way that it is difficult for the child to hold attention on any one thing for any length of time.

This is quite serious because if this is what our media is doing to train our brains then we must consider the effects this is having on our child's learning capabilities in an educational system which is not teaching its students at the same pace.

Actually to me this is quite scary since we are drugging those kids who are having difficulty paying attention.

Bottom line: Children under seven years of age will learn more from their own experience in the real world, interacting with other people. Electronic machines introduced at this time are of little or no use and perhaps have harmful consequences.

After the age of seven, most experts agree that the developmental stages of the brain are now complete enough to start introducing some electronics such as computers. In fact, they suggest that constructive computer use combined with other activities and perhaps within some kind of social context, may actually be of benefit to the child. The child is now better equipped to begin to understand and deal with technologies

Urie Bronfenbrenner, a prominent sociologist, describes what he considers the effect of television viewing on our children:

"Like the sorcerer of old, the television set casts its magic spell, freezing speech and action, turning the living into silent statues for as long as the enchantment lasts. The primary danger of the television screen lies not so much in the behavior it produces –although there is danger there – as in the behavior it prevents: the talks, the games, the family festivities and arguments through which much of the child's learning takes place and through which his/her character is formed. Turning on the television set can turn off the process that transforms children into people."

Teaching Your Child to Be a Critical TV Viewer

To help our children become media smart, we as their teachers need to do only three basic things: watch, listen and talk.

1. Watch

Watch television with and for your child. This allows you to make yourself familiar with what your child is watching, make decisions about the appropriateness of the program and its messages, and discuss these with your child.

An added benefit of watching with your child is that you might actually enjoy some of the programs yourself and get some relaxation in, too, while sharing this time with your child. Young children will usually appreciate have mom or dad's company and older children will appreciate your interest.

2. Listen

Listening without judging. It's about guiding and working through any possible disputes with your children and helping them to become conscious, selective and critical TV viewers.

3. Talk

This allows your child to share. At the same time they are developing their own abilities to discriminate. Be a mirror for their thoughts, this helps you become a better active listener. They will love this and this can only enhance your relationship with them

This would be a good time to set your expectations around what you would like to accomplish in respect to TV watching and your family. For example:

- Do you want your children to watch less TV? How much less?
- Do you want your children to be less influenced by TV messages?
- Do you want your children to watch only educational/quality programs?

Part 2 - Action Plan

The Family TV Use Chart

The TV Use Chart is a good tool to begin assessing your family's TV watching patterns and ways in which family members use TV. It might be a good idea to post it on the refrigerator door, or near the TV, or in some other place where it is in plain sight and will act as a reminder to fill it out.

For the most part, a family's TV viewing patterns are fairly consistent over the course of each week, so filling out the chart for one or two days will pretty much give a good idea of the family's patterns and where problems may lay.

The TV Chart

- Everyone in the household should be included and should fill out a chart.
- Indicate on the chart every time the TV is on, whether or not anyone is watching it.
- Be aware of the 'conscious choice' aspect of your family's TV use as indicated on the chart. If someone is interested in or likes a particular program and watches it, that's still a conscious choice.

Some TV Guidelines:

- No TV during meals.
- No TV before or during homework.
- No TV before chores are finished.

Choosing Programs – Developing a Family TV Plan

How do you go about making selections?

- First, if you involve your children in the decision-making, your kids are much more likely to abide by the choices that are made.
- Next, find a good source of TV program listings. Using a guide, your family can sit down together and plan out a schedule.
- Selecting programs that are age appropriate is important. Watching the program beforehand is a good way to determine this.

COMPUTERS, VIDEOS AND VIDEO GAMES

Do we no longer have a choice?

Computers, video games, and the Internet have become entrenched features of our daily lives. Computer use has reached beyond work and is now a major source of fun and entertainment for many people. For most people, computer use and video game play is integrated into their lives in a balanced healthy manner. For others, time spent on the computer or video game is out of balance, and has displaced work, school, friends, and even family.

What is computer and video game addiction?

When time spent on the computer, playing video games or cruising the Internet reaches a point that it harms a child's or adult's family and social relationships, or disrupts school or work life, that person may be caught in a cycle of addiction. Like other addictions, the computer or video game has replaced friends and family as the source of a person's emotional life. Increasingly, to feel good, the addicted person spends more time playing video games or searching the Internet. Time away from the computer or game causes moodiness or withdrawal.

When a person spends up to ten hours a day or more rearranging or sending files, playing games, surfing the net, visiting chat rooms, instant messaging, and reading emails, that easily can reach up to seventy to eighty hours a week on-line with the computer. Major social, school or work disruptions will result.

Symptoms of computer or video game addiction:

For children:

- Most of non-school hours are spent on the computer or playing video games.
- Falling asleep in school.
- Not keeping up with assignments.
- Worsening grades.
- Lying about computer or video game use.
- Choosing to use the computer or play video games, rather than see friends.
- Dropping out of other social groups (clubs or sports).
- Irritable when not playing a video game or on the computer.

For adults:

- Computer or video game use is characterized by intense feelings of pleasure and guilt.
- Obsessing and pre-occupied about being on the computer, even when not connected.
- Hours playing video games or on the computer increasing, seriously disrupting family, social or even work life.
- Lying about computer or video game use.
- Experience feelings of withdrawal, anger, or depression when not on the computer or involved with their video game.
- May incur large phone or credit bills for on-line services.
- Can't control computer or video game use.
- Fantasy life on-line replaces emotional life with partner.

There are even physical symptoms that may point to addiction:

- Carpal tunnel syndrome.
- Sleep disturbances
- Back, neck aches
- Headaches
- Vision problems
- Obesity
- Dry eyes
- Failure to eat regularly or neglect personal hygiene

For the computer or video game addicted person, a fantasy world on-line or in a game has replaced his or her real world. The virtual reality of the computer or game is more inviting than the every day world of family, school or work.

Can a Computer Play a Positive Role?

Computers can:

- Provide access to an almost limitless amount of information.
- Allow us to organize information.
- Allow us to learn about the world from many perspectives.
- Allow us to perform tasks in science, medicine and mathematics that would be otherwise very difficult.
- Help us control and run machines that help us in our daily lives.
- With creative planning, add positively to shared family time (when the children are the appropriate age), and can promote some good conversations.

The reality seems to be that most families will choose to have a personal computer in their home. As with the television, most parents understand that inappropriate or excessive use can become a serious issue. With that in mind, setting some rules and guidelines about the use of the computer in your home is a good idea.

Guidelines for Computer Use in your Home:

- Just like the television set, locate the computer(s) in a location where it is easy for you to watch and monitor computer activities.
- Negotiate appropriate time limits on the use of the computer for family members.
- Make computers off limits after school until chores and homework are completed, unless it's being used for doing homework.
- Set some strict rules around Internet use and make sure you check in often with your kids to ensure that the rules are being followed. Talk to them about the dangers that can occur when using the Internet.
- Remember, starting children too early on computers isn't a good idea.
- Especially for younger children (preschoolers), other specific guidelines may be necessary.
- Choose interactive, problem-solving types of software programs that facilitate your child's need for flexibility and their need to discover and explore answers to things for themselves.
- Help your kids to see that working on a computer can also be a fun and helpful social experience you can share with friends, peers and your family. Encourage this type of interaction over solitary use.

- If your child starts to show signs of addiction, cut down on their screen time or pull the plug. The key here is to always have lots of interesting alternatives to keep them keen on doing other things.

Tips for Safeguarding Your Children:

- Use a detachable keyboard if necessary, and keep little bodies 30 to 36 inches from the computer screen (even more for TV) and at least four feet from the sides and back.
- When purchasing a computer, check them out and get one that emits as low and electromagnetic field (EMF) as possible. Ask the retailer questions and for information from the manufacturer on what safeguards they have in place on their equipment.
- Ask about any other devices that might help cut back on any EMF emissions.
- In school (or home), don't line computers up back-to-back. Remember, most of the harmful stuff comes out from the sides and back. And also that these fields can travel through walls. Keep this in mind when locating computers either in the home or school.
- Do your homework and look for ways to cut down on all electromagnetic emissions around your home. Turn things off, especially the TV and computer, when they are not being used. It is even better to pull out the plug if possible. It is especially important that a child's bedroom be 'clean' of electromagnetic pollution. Most of the body's repair work is done while at sleep. So perhaps it would be wise to remove all electrical gear from their bedroom or at least unplug everything before saying goodnight.

Vision

Eye problems rank at the top of the list of problems being reported by doctors and parents. Many eye specialists are naming children's computer use as the main culprit. There are several problems with the way in which the technology is set up and how it is used that creates visual problems.

Firstly, the screen is flat and usually close to being on a horizontal plane with the eyes of the user. Because of this, the eyes do not move around to observe something as the visual system is set up to do. The systems are set up to view things at varying distances at different heights.

The consequences of this may result in nearsightedness. Also, kids tend to blink less and stare more (static stare) when they are working on a computer screen. This leads to eyestrain and eventual visual deterioration.

Also computers screens (video display terminals) are what are termed 'illuminated.' This illumination maintains itself by refreshing its phosphorous coating approximately sixty times per second, creating what is called 'flicker.' Although we are not aware of this perceptively, this process is very stressful on the brain and the visual system.

Because heads are usually looking straight ahead when working on a computer (and not looking more downward as we would if we were reading a book), the user's eyes can be exposed to other light sources in the room, especially from overhead ceiling lights, all of which add extra strain on the eyes.

Tips for Safeguarding Your Children's Eyes

- Check for and eliminate any sources of light that may be directed from either outside or from within the room into your children's eyes when working on the computer. Also eliminate any glare or any type of reflection on the screen. Close blinds or curtains if need be or set the screen up in such a way so that glare and reflection is not a problem. Use antiglare screens in cases where glare may be an issue. Use desk lamps instead of ceiling lights if possible, especially if the overhead lights are fluorescent.
- Make sure the screen is always kept clean.
- Experiment with different type fonts and screen colors if necessary to make reading easier.
- When setting up the computer and screen for your child to use, drop the screen down so that they have to look slightly down to see what is on the screen (ten to twenty degrees approximately).
- Remind your child to give their eyes a rest when working for longer periods on the computer. A good rule of thumb is a total of fifteen minutes for every hour spent. Have them get up, walk around, look out the window, go outside for a minutes or two to get some fresh air, get a drink of water, etc. Take a few seconds to look away at something every ten minutes or so. And also remind them to remember to blink!
- If you have a heavy user, make sure they get an annual eye examination.

Obesity

Obesity among American children today has grown to epidemic portions. How can things like sitting in front of a computer or television contribute?

First, if the child is sitting and watching, and not participating in something that is more active. Secondly, especially passive television viewing usually leads to active munching … and it's not usually carrot sticks if the child has a choice. But worse than that, according to some research done on kids watching TV, it was discovered that their metabolic rate actually drops to a level between sleeping and resting. Apparently they have the ability to burn more calories just sitting there daydreaming than they do watching TV. So as strange as it might seem, the very act of watching TV can contribute to your child becoming overweight.

Eating Disorders

The media has a huge impact on our children's self-esteem and self-image. Eating disorders such as bulimia or anorexia can often come as a result of a child, especially young girls, being 'taught' through ads and programs portraying "thin is beautiful" images and themes, that if they want to be popular and acceptable to their peers and the world, then they must look the same way. The real damage occurs when a young person watches and accepts what they see in the media, before they have the opportunity to develop their own individual identity, self-image and self-esteem in the real world.

Diabetes has also become an epidemic among our young people today and being severely overweight is one of the chief contributing causes.

A decline in overall fitness levels of our children is also of deep concern. Physical activity, especially out-of-doors, is essential to good health. This helps kids to wear off that extra energy, to sleep better, and to better deal with anxiety, stress and depression. Regular exercise also increases blood supply to the brain, helping to improve children's abilities for learning and memory functions.

So let kids get outside and just let them play! If you feel they need to be watched over, perhaps you can join them and get some exercise, too! Preplanned, competitive sports with all that goes along with them will not benefit your child as much as plain, spontaneous play.

That is how nature designed things.

The picture painted about the effects of media is quite catastrophic. To me the process looks like this: While we are watching TV, our bodies are being conditioned to produce Cortisol, thus we are eating more while watching. At the same time through advertising, we are being offered foods that are saturated with sugars and unhealthy fats. The result of this is an increase in obesity, diabetes, clogged arteries, poor focusing, etc, etc. On the other hand, and again through advertising, we are being conditioned to think that in order to be acceptable to others, we must be thin looking. Is this not giving us a mixed message which is filled with a recipe for disaster!

The Ways Television Can Affect Our Children

- TV watching becomes addictive.
- TV time takes away the opportunity for children to be engaged in other activities.
- TV can block the healthy development of a child's brain.
- TV often interferes with the parent-child bond.
- TV can interfere with the development of focusing and attention skills of the child.
- TV can lead to hyperactivity and increased distractibility of the child.
- TV acts as a potential deterrent for families to spend quality time together.
- TV may impede the development of a child's imagination.

- TV may contribute to health related concerns such as diabetes and obesity.
- TV may contribute to a lack of school performance.
- TV increases the eating of junk foods.

Summary

Within the past 2 years Senator Joseph Lieberman, Sam Brownback and Hilary Rodham Clinton have lobbied for funding to the tune of $100 million research dollars to investigate the effects that media is having on our children.

Below are there anecdotes. My question is, should we not follow their leads and make it our responsibility to examine the potential effects that TV and computers are having on the social, emotional and academic development of our children

"America is a media-rich society, but despite the flood of information, we still lack perhaps the most important piece of information — what effect are media having on our children?" Lieberman said. "As policymakers — and as parents — we have a responsibility to examine the positive and negative effects of media on our children, a responsibility this legislation can better enable us to fulfill. No one is looking out, in a systematic way, for what media our children are using. The questions about the effects of media on our children's health, education and development are too important to go unasked and unanswered."

"The development of our nation's children is vital, and understanding the way in which media impacts their ability to grow and develop is imperative," Brownback said. "Providing parents and guardians with the most accurate information and current research regarding the impact media has on their children is essential. To do anything less would be a terrible injustice to our children."

"One of our challenges as parents and policymakers is that technology keeps advancing. The definition of media in our children's lives is a moving target," said Senator Clinton. "We need better, more current research to study the impact of the new interactive, digital and wireless media dominating our kids' lives, and that's what the CAMRA Act will give us."

Remember, that you, your child's parent, will always know your child better than anyone else. Parenting is as many people have said, the toughest, most important job you will ever have. It is you your child will model after.

Perhaps, it's time to slow down, reorder our priorities, decide what we truly value, and then take the necessary action. Turning off the TV or the computer entirely or just for a while might be a good place to begin.

This chapter is all about media literacy. Each and every day we are afforded the opportunity to learn just a little bit more about our relationship with ourselves and others. What follows is a quiz related to media literacy. I believe that you will find the results intriguing.

Enjoy this part of the process

PBS Media Literacy Quiz

1. What percentage of American 8-18 year-olds have television sets in their bedrooms?

- ☐ a. 14%
- ☐ b. 25%
- ☐ c. 42%
- ☐ d. 68%

2. The average American seventh grader:

- ☐ a. watches three hours of TV per day
- ☐ b. listens to three hours of music per day
- ☐ c. surfs the internet and communicates via e-mail three hours per day
- ☐ d. plays video games three hours per day

3. Excessive TV viewing has been linked to:

- ☐ a. nearsighted vision
- ☐ b. obesity
- ☐ c. attention deficit disorder
- ☐ d. fine motor skill impairment

4. What percentage of young people say they either talk on the phone, instant message, watch TV, listen to music or surf the Web for fun "most of the time" while they're doing homework?

- ☐ a. 30%
- ☐ b. 75%
- ☐ c. 89%
- ☐ d. 93%

5. What percentage of children willingly share personal information about themselves over the Internet in exchange for goods and services?

- ☐ a. 12%
- ☐ b. 28%
- ☐ c. 47%
- ☐ d. 75%

6. Researchers estimate that children view an average of how many TV ads per year?

- ☐ a. 3,000
- ☐ b. 15,000
- ☐ c. 40,000
- ☐ d. 90,000

7. Among the top 20 most watched shows by teens, what percentage include sexual content?

- ☐ a. 10%
- ☐ b. 50%
- ☐ c. 70%
- ☐ d. 100%

8. The TV rating code "TVY7, FV" indicates that:

- ☐ a. program is appropriate for kids over age 7, although it contains animated and/or live action violence.
- ☐ b. program is appropriate for kids under age 7, with parental supervision
- ☐ c. program is normally appropriate only for kids over age 7, but this is a family version
- ☐ d. program has been screened so it doesn't contain ads that are inappropriate for children under age 7.

9. An online journal or Web log is commonly referred to as a:

- ☐ a. DVR
- ☐ b. mp3 file
- ☐ c. blog
- ☐ d. pod

10. Approximately how much money was spent on presidential election advertising during the 2004 election?

- ☐ a. $10 million
- ☐ b. $50 million
- ☐ c. $100 million
- ☐ d. $530 million

11. According to a 2006 survey, what percentage of teens own at least one video game platform?

- ☐ a. 99%
- ☐ b. 81%
- ☐ c. 56%
- ☐ d. 34%

12. Minimum wage and allowance adds up! How much money did teens, ages 12-19, spend in 2005?

   ☐ a. $250 million

   ☐ b. $900 million

   ☐ c. $3 billion

   ☐ d. $159 billion

13. According to a 2005 survey, 9% of people in their 60's list the Internet as a main source of news. What do you think the percentage is for people under the age of 30?

   ☐ a. 10%

   ☐ b. 36%

   ☐ c. 67%

   ☐ d. 92%

14. 63% of American families "usually:"

   ☐ a. allow kids under 18 to see R-rated movies

   ☐ b. keep the TV on while eating dinner

   ☐ c. have the radio on while traveling in the car

   ☐ d. allow kids to surf the Web unsupervised

15. What percentage of Americans under the age of 30 read a newspaper on a typical day?

   ☐ a. 12%

   ☐ b. 23%

   ☐ c. 62%

   ☐ d. 87%

Quiz Answers and Sources

1. What percentage of American 8-18 year-olds have television sets in their bedrooms?
Answer: D. Children's bedrooms have increasingly become multi-media centers, raising important issues about supervision and exposure to unlimited content. Children who have TV's in their bedrooms watch an average of 1 ½ hours more TV in a typical day than children who do not have TV's in their bedroom.
(source: Kaiser Family Foundation Study: Generation M: Media in the Lives of 8-18 Year-olds, 2005.)

2. The average American seventh grader:

Answer: A. In addition, seventh – 12th graders spend an average of 2:16 hanging out with friends, 0:53 talking on the phone, 0:50 doing homework and 0:32 doing chores.
(source: Kaiser Family Foundation Study: Generation M: Media in the Lives of 8-18 Year-olds, 2005.)

3. Excessive TV viewing has been linked to:

Answer: B. No studies have conclusively demonstrated a link between TV viewing and attention deficit disorder, although research in this area continues. Excessive TV viewing has been linked to obesity, and may lead to decreased school achievement, poor body image, increased aggression and increased risk of substance abuse.
(source: Kaiser Family Foundation Issue Brief: The Effects of Electronic Media on Children Ages Zero to Six: A History of Research, 2005.)

4. What percentage of young people say they either talk on the phone, instant message, watch TV, listen to music or surf the Web for fun "most of the time" while they're doing homework?

Answer: A. Children and teens manage to pack increasing amounts of media content into the same amount of time each day because of the amount of time they spend using more than one medium at a time.
(source: Kaiser Family Foundation Study: Generation M: Media in the Lives of 8-18 Year-olds, 2005.)

5. What percentage of children willingly share personal information about themselves over the Internet in exchange for goods and services?

Answer: D. To help protect children and teens, experts recommended that adults understand and discuss the dangers of the Internet with young people, as well as use filtering and blocking software.
(source: Cyberangels Statistics.)

6. Researchers estimate that children view an average of how many TV ads per year?

Answer: C. While older children and adults may grasp the inherent bias in advertising, child development research shows that children under the age of eight are unable to critically comprehend televised advertising messages and are prone to accept advertiser messages as truthful, accurate and unbiased.
(source: American Psychological Association Task Force Report: Television Advertising Leads to Unhealthy Habits in Children.)

7. Among the top 20 most watched shows by teens, what percentage include sexual content?

Answer: C. When these popular teen programs contain sexual content, only 10% provide a reference to sexual risks and responsibilities at some point in the episode. In addition, one in every nine shows across the TV landscape (excluding newscasts, sports events and children's programming) includes scenes in which sexual intercourse is either depicted or strongly implied.
(source: Kaiser Family Foundation: Sex on TV 4, 2005.)

8. The TV rating code "TVY7, FV" indicates that:

Answer: A. "FV" stands for "Fantasy Violence," and "Y7" lets parents know a program probably isn't appropriate for kids under age 7.
(source: TV Ratings Guide for Parents.)

9. **An online journal or Web log is commonly referred to as a:**

Answer: C. The term blog comes from the word Weblog. Blogs are Web sites that are frequently updated with reverse chronological posts. They gained popularity due to cheap, easy tools that allow anyone to start one. To keep up to date on such terms and how media is changing society and culture, visit PBS's MediaShift Web site.
(source: MediaShift Glossary.)

10. **Approximately how much money was spent on presidential election advertising during the 2004 election?**

Answer: D. This figure is more than double the $200 million spent during the 2000 presidential campaign.
(source: Online NewsHour Ad Watch.)

11. **According to a 2006 survey, what percentage of teens own at least one video game platform?**

Answer: B. Interestingly, in this same survey, almost 80 percent of teens indicated that they intend to spend less time playing video games in 2006 and nearly 70 percent indicated that their interest in playing video games is decreasing.
(source: Taking Stock With Teens' National Study of Teen Shopping Behavior and Brand Preferences, 2006.)

12. **Minimum wage and allowance adds up! How much money did teens, ages 12-19, spend in 2005?**

Answer: D. This figure is actually down 6% from 2004; however, teen spending is expected to increase in 2006.
(source: TRU Projects Teen Spending Total for 2005 at $159 Billion.)

13. **According to a 2005 survey, 9% of people in their 60's list the Internet as a main source of news. What do you think the percentage is for people under the age of 30?**

Answer: B. While online news consumption is highest among young people (those under age 30), it is not an activity that is limited to the very young. Three-in-ten Americans ages 30-49 cite the Internet as a main source of news.
(source: Pew Research Center Report: Public More Critical of the Press, But Goodwill Persists, 2005.)

14. **63% of American families "usually:"**

Answer: B. In many young people's homes, the TV is a constant companion. In addition to families keeping the TV on during dinner, 51% of children and teens say they live in homes where the TV is left on "most" or "all" of the time, whether anyone is watching it or not.
(source: Kaiser Family Foundation Study: Generation M: Media in the Lives of 8-18 Year-olds, 2005.)

15. **What percentage of Americans under the age of 30 read a newspaper on a typical day?**

Answer: B. That statistic is sharply lower than for older populations — six in ten Americans age 65 and older read a newspaper on a typical day. According to the Pew Research Center for the People and the Press, the age gap in newspaper readership continues to widen.
(source: Pew Research Center Report: Where Americans Go for News, 2004.)

Scoring:

12-15: Congratulations! It's clear you're nobody's fool when it comes to media matters. You're probably already integrating media studies into your classroom curriculum—interested in seeing what PBS might add to the mixture? Check out our list of media-related PBS Online sites and television programs.

7-11: Good for you! Your knowledge of media literacy has a good foundation, but could benefit from further study. Learn more about the media through our list of related sites and studies. We suspect you're already talking about media literacy with your students, but for some fresh alternatives, explore the activity ideas posted on this site.

6 or less: You're on the right track, but you're not ready to run the media literacy marathon just yet. Improving your media literacy skills will not only help you as an everyday media consumer, but will also help your students' critical thinking skills - no matter which discipline you teach. To learn how you can begin integrating media literacy into your curriculum, spend some time with our activity ideas.

Chapter 9

Cultivating Balance

Introduction

Cultivating balance paves the road to creating healthy relationships within ourselves and furthermore with our children. In creating balance, the body arrives at its natural state, the breath is calm and controlled, the mind is expansive and open, the intellect and memory is sharp and the ego is not a burden to the self. We experience this, some more than others and for some with heightened awareness. When we are in our natural state, there is harmony; it's naturally within us. It is not something that goes away; it's always there. By creating balance we create joy. Joy keeps company with discomfort/pain and dullness/tedium. They interact with another providing us with the beautiful tapestry of so much that life offers. The trick is to cultivate and nourish the joy that resides in each of us while acknowledging and embracing that two other aspects. This is balance.

Children of today challenge us because they are tapping into our higher consciousness. They are seemingly "more intelligent" and some authorities believe they "demand" that we live with a greater sense of awareness in order for them to be understood properly. With respect to that, adults need to unlearn beliefs from our current past and adapt new ways of thinking and doing about every aspect of life.

This chapter is about achieving balance and health and is focused around the principles of Ayurveda, the 5,000-year-old system of natural healing that comes from India. Ayurveda is known as the mother of healing: *ayu* means life, *veda* means knowledge/science. Within Ayurveda, we learn how to cultivate a life of fulfillment, in every facet of our body, mind and spirit. Knowledge of the subtleties of nature, healing protocols and treatments, lifestyle approach and diet and exercise are all contained in Ayurveda and its sister discipline, Yoga. Practical tools are presented here along with case studies to inspire you and enrich your life towards a path of balance, harmony and joy.

Balancing Act in the Body

We know balance and moderation are the keys to creating health. Creating balance within our lives can involve not allowing any particular daily consumption of the senses to overtake us. We experience life through our senses, for example, working too much, over-eating, getting caught up with our emotions, watching too much TV, or staying up late. We are hardwired to live in harmony and balance within our body, mind and spirit and within nature.

When the senses are over-stimulated, the body finds ways to rebalance itself. The body, innately, keeps us balanced. In physiology, this is called homeostasis. It seems we can go for quite a while without having to practice any kind of health maintenance within our body, mind and spirit. Symptoms such as muscle and joint pain, fatigue, decreased mental clarity can be early signs of more serious issues. Homeostasis will set in and the body will balance itself.

One significant example of homeostasis involves pH balance in the body. Consumption of mostly acid-forming foods will result in excess acid substances being deposited in the tissues and joints to maintain the blood's normal blood pH of 7.4. The "potential" of hydrogen (pH) is the amount of hydrogen in a solution, measured between 0.00 − 14.00. The more hydrogen ions, the more acidic the solution. Below 7.0 is acid and above 7.0 is alkaline. 7.0 is neutral. With a typical North American diet of high protein, high refined sugar, low complex-carbohydrate diet there is a trend toward acidity in the body.

Complex Carbohydrates	Simple Carbohydrates	Refined Carbohydrates Avoid completely
whole grains vegetables legumes	fruits fruit juice	white flour white/brown/raw sugar honey molasses corn syrup malto-dextrin glucose fructose sucrose

Source: Rowland, David, "Client Support Resource Program", pg. 2 Copyright 2004

Overall, the body cannot be too acidic or too alkaline. (There are specific areas in the body that need to be more acidic, like the stomach). Chronic inflammation is a sign of acidity in the body. Inflammation sets in the body as a signal that an area is combating an intruder/infection or some kind of irritation or pain. For example, when one feels muscle or joint pain or stomach cramping, inflammation is or already has taken place. Pain that keeps coming back (chronic pain) can mean chronic inflammation. Chronic inflammation can lead to overall increase of acidity in the body and in some cases can result in degenerative conditions such as osteoarthritis, osteoporosis, fibromyalgia, and chronic fatigue. Recent studies have shown that cancer patients have a low (acidic) pH level.

A response to chronic inflammation is utilizing minerals in the body to keep the pH level in check. If need be, the body will go to the muscle and nerve cells to get these minerals to buffer acidity in the body. In addition, depletion of minerals causes muscle stiffness, fatigue and other symptoms. As a massage therapist, I have taken saliva tests with pH paper to determine pH level of the blood before and after a treatment (saliva is an accurate measure of blood pH). I have found that about 40% of clients show an increase of 0.5 to 1 on the pH scale. This shows that activities of a nurturing nature can lead to increase alkalinity. We can conclude that nurturing, healing therapies and life affirming behavior have a physiological effect on our bodies.

Thinking of Having Kids?
Lesson 13
Move to the tropics. Find or make a compost pile. Dig down about halfway and stick your nose in it. Do this 3-5 times a day for at least two years.

The Qualities of Nature

When we pay attention to nature, our surroundings, observe our minds and our bodies, we can see the many activities that interact with one another. We begin to acknowledge the subtleties of nature and how these qualities affect us. In nature, there are three main qualities that reside in everything, and each quality is in constant interaction with the others. In Ayurveda, these qualities are known as *Gunas: Sattva, Rajas and Tamas.* These are subtle yet pervasive qualities, in which one out of the three will dominate, and the dominant of the three can be felt and observed in the qualities of people, animals, food, workplace, and shopping malls and in anywhere or in anyone. One can be said to be more sattvic, more rajasic or more tamasic. Have you ever observed a situation or been in a situation where there was a beehive of activity, for example a shopping mall on a weekend or the subway during rush hour? In terms of the Gunas, we say this is rajasic. A dull situation or a boring party, we say is tamasic. Eating a home-made cooked meal free from additives and preservatives is sattvic.

Today, the predominant quality of our air and water is tamasic. Modern North American food is both rajasic and tamasic. These foods are heavily seasoned, sometimes overly spiced, stored overnight, reheated or micro-waved, all of which are qualities of rajas and tamas. The condiment industry is a huge, multi-million industry producing items that are very rajasic in nature. The processed food industry produces food that is dull, dead and devoid of prana. Sattva is lacking in these foods. The qualities of purification, rejuvenation, prana, life-enhancing are lacking in many of our food choices these days. We must slowly return to a diet of simplification, life-affirmation, nurturing and balancing. Providing our bodies with more sattvic foods will bring increased energy, clarity of mind, calmness, a higher state of consciousness and all the qualities we must strive for to increase the quality of our relationships within ourselves and our children.

In Ayurveda, balance can be observed in the body through the Dosha System, known as *Vata, Pitta* and *Kapha.* These three operating systems in the body are governed under the principles that go beyond the European/North American scientific understanding of physiology, psychology, medicine and nutritional science. To fully appreciate the doshas, we must think outside the box and bring an open mind and heart to the knowledge of Ayurveda.

SATTVA	RAJAS	TAMAS
purifying	transformative	inertia
light	stimulating	heavy/dullness
life promoting	aggravating	stillness
meditation	shopping mall	oversleeping
yoga	running	couch potato/lack of exercise
peaceful, optimistic discussion	yelling, aggressive argument	suspicious, delusional conversation

ELEMENT	DOSHA	QUALITY	BODY PART	SENSE	5 ELEMENTS
Space & Air	Vata	Unresistant	Ears	Hearing	Space
		Dry, Rough	Skin	Touch	Air
Fire & Water	Pitta	Heat, Clarity	Eyes	Sight	Fire
		Soft, Cold	Tongue	Taste	Water
Water & Earth	Kapha	Solid, Stable	Nose	Smell	Earth

Fundamentally, we are all born out of the five elements of nature: Space, Air, Fire, Water and Earth. Because the Gunas are all around us, they interact with us and the doshas.

The qualities of the Gunas are present in us through the doshas as Vata, Pitta and Kapha. Being born out of the five elements as represented through Vata, Pitta and Kapha, the senses also correlate to the five elements as shown on the table.

Responsibility

We are now living in a time in which we are acknowledging what it takes to accomplish what needs to be done to create a better place for ourselves and for our children. The consciousness of every single person is being elevated whether we like it or not. We are being guided towards proper thoughts, actions and deeds through knowledge and experience.

A new standard of living is being created and with this, better relationships will be cultivated within us, with our children and with nature. It begins with getting back to the basics of living by cultivating the body, mind and spirit through proper nourishment, proper exercise, moderate sleep, moderate work and devotional practice. This may sound elementary and you know this, but that's the point. We know that simplicity works; natural solutions work. For example, we see a rise in natural healing therapies today. Natural and traditional approaches to health are growing, bringing about greater public awareness and greater demand. The World Health Organization recognizes the growth and demand for traditional medicine in the last decade leading to increased interest in both the government and academic population. In North America, more and more people are turning to "alternative" therapies to facilitate healing for common everyday ailments. (See Table 7: Use of Alternative Therapy for the 10 Most Frequently Reported Principal Medical Conditions.)

"In a study published in the Archives of Internal Medicine, employees with chiropractic insurance coverage had 41 percent fewer hospitalizations for back pain than employees without chiropractic coverage. They also had 32 percent fewer back surgeries and significantly lower utilization rates for CT/MRI scans and X-rays than employees without chiropractic insurance."

"Also, employers are interested because of growing employee demand for complementary health services. According to a recent Centers for Disease Control study, 36 percent of consumers use some sort of complementary or alternative therapy. And in a 2005 Consumer Reports survey of 34,000 readers, consumers preferred hands-on therapies such as chiropractic treatment over conventional therapies, including prescription drugs, for back and arthritis pain."

(© 2006 PRIMEZON, Internet www.chron.com/disp/story.mpl/conws/3730053.html)

Table 7: Use of Alternative Therapy for the 10 Most Frequently Reported Principal Medical Conditions					
Rank	Condition	Percent Reporting Condition	Percent using Alternative Therapy in Past 12 Months*	Percent Who Saw a Provider in Past 12 Months*	Percent Who Saw a Doctor in Past 12 Months*	Therapies most Commonly Used
1	Back or neck problems	30%	71%	32%	11%	Chiropractic, Spiritual healing
2	Allergies	29%	60%	21%	9%	Relaxation Techniques, Spiritual Healing
3	Arthritis or rheumatism	20%	60%	18%	8%	Spiritual Healing, Relaxation Techniques
4	Difficulty walking	17%	67%	22%	10%	Spiritual Healing, Relaxation Techniques
5	Frequent headaches	16%	65%	29%	8%	Spiritual Healing, Relaxation Techniques
6	Lung problems	12%	62%	20%	11%	Spiritual Healing, Relaxation Techniques
7	Digestive problems	12%	63%	25%	10%	Spiritual Healing, Massage Therapy
8	Gynecological problems	10%	70%	29%	9%	Relaxation Techniques, Spiritual Healing
9	Anxiety attacks	9%	69%	19%	10%	Spiritual Healing, Relaxation Techniques
10	Heart problems or chest pain	9%	59%	19%	6%	Spiritual Healing, Relaxation Techniques

*Percentages are of those who reported the condition. Provider denotes a provider of care who is not a medical doctor. Note: Double counting may occur because some patients may have seen both a medical doctor and an alternative provider.

From *http://oldfraser.lexi.net/publications/pps/21/table7.html*

Proper Nourishment

It is mentioned in the ancient Vedic text (Shaka Ayurved Tradition) that the combination of prana and the physical body constitutes life. Prana follows the individual soul and, as the soul descends into the embryo, prana follows and "enters the 'body' endowing it with life". Prana is a key element in life and we cannot overlook the valuable role it plays in maintaining life. Prana is in food, water and air. (Dr. Mishra: pg 4 *"Ayurveda and Beyond"*)

Food, water and breath provide nourishment to the body, but also thoughts, feelings and ideas are ingested and assimilated in our system. Foods that are non-supportive to the body should be eliminated, just as thoughts, feelings and ideas that are not supportive should be, as well. The subject of food – what is good and bad for us – leave most of us confused. We hear red wine and dark chocolate are loaded with anti-oxidants but others would say they are "bad" for you. Drink soy if you're allergic to milk, but now they say soy can cause breast cancer. Two things apply here, awareness and moderation. When you hear contradictions in the media about what is good and bad for you, be moderate in your use of that particular food and be aware of the role media plays in the promotion of products.

Educate yourself. Attend community workshops; visit a health and wellness clinic that promotes prevention and natural healing as alternatives to creating health. In the next ten years, the wellness industry is estimated to become a trillion dollar industry with the baby boomers leading the way.

LIFELESS FOOD	TROUBLESOME FOOD	INTELLIGENT FOOD
any leftovers some fast food	food served in any fast food industry	a home-cooked meal utilizing fresh ingredients
any boxed cereal with preservatives & colors	any boxed cereal	whole grain cereal prepared fresh
any microwavable frozen entrée with preservatives & colors	microwavable frozen entrée	freshly prepared meal
store bought apple pie with preservatives & colors	apple pie	fresh apple
all junk food (pop, chips, candy bars, juice with sugar, preservatives & colors)	store bought juice	fresh squeezed vegetable or fruit juice

Use common sense and as much as possible provide proper nourishment to your body devoid of unnatural substances, such as preservatives, stabilizers, colorings found in many processed foods these days. Fueling your body with denatured food only leads to dullness, lethargy, cloudiness of the mind and promotes inhibitions and fear. To experience lightness, clarity of mind, creativity and joy through food, the body must be fueled with high prana food. This is "intelligent" food – natural, wholesome, made with love, no preservatives, no stabilizers, no additives or coloring. A home cooked meal made with fresh ingredients is an example of intelligent food.

Looking at this table, the average person has had his/her fair share of all three categories. The strategy to creating health is to minimize or avoid completely the troublesome food and stay completely clear from the lifeless category. Why? Because, the intelligent foods contain more prana than "troublesome" foods or "lifeless" foods. Most people are familiar with energy, measured by the amount of calories a food has. Prana, chi, life energy or SOEF (Subtle Organizing Energy Fields) [Cousens, Gabriel, *Conscious Eating*, p. 275], whatever you want to call it, is the subtle energetic force that is found in food.

Most North Americans regularly consume foods found in the troublesome food category. We must avoid this category of foods if we are to be masters at creating health and cultivating healthier relationships with our children. When we choose intelligent food. the body reciprocates by giving us the intelligence to make better choices for ourselves. Better choices lead to openness, understanding, compassion and unconditional love. We are then equipped to nurture our children in the most honest, sincere way.

Intelligent food has a vibrant nurturing life force. It is packed with prana because it is in its most natural state, devoid of being denatured. There are varying degrees of intelligent food. Raw food / live-food eaters believe heating food higher than $102 - 104\,°$ C denatures food. Ayurveda, the traditional healing system of India, believes certain foods must be cooked and considers them intelligent and infused with prana when prepared appropriately.

Food prepared with love and made at home is intelligent food. Food prepared in a restaurant, even if the ingredients are fresh, may be for reasons beyond your control, such as the mood of the person who prepared it, which can greatly affect the quality of the food. How it's prepared plays a role in the quality of the food. Meals prepared with love and kindness are infused with prana and is life-supporting.

How a food is eaten and the mood of the person eating also has subtle effects on the body. Another subtle example is to be aware of how you are feeling while eating. If you are stressed, upset, preoccupied, all this will have an effect on the totality of your being. Eat your meal in a peaceful state of mind. Giving thanks before you eat will help set the tone of at meal time.

Another factor to consider is eating more alkaline foods versus acidic foods. To maintain good health, a 20:80 radio of acid to alkaline foods is recommended. One cannot tell if a food is acid-forming or alkaline-forming by taste. An example of this is lemon. Although it tastes acidic, it actually has a high concentration of alkaline minerals. (Calcium, magnesium, sodium, potassium and iron are alkalinizing minerals.)

For every bodily function, there are hormones, enzymes and neurotransmitters that participate in the beautiful orchestra of the body to keep it performing. We are all generally playing the same tune, in that the body requires protein, carbohydrates and fats but each with our own theme (the types of food we eat, the lifestyle we uphold) and variations of the theme (fluctuations in our feelings and emotions), but a body that is "in tune" with the harmonies of nature is cultivating health as opposed to one that is "out of tune". How do we become "out of tune"? By creating disharmony in the body with improper choices mostly through the food we eat, the thoughts we allow to manifest and the actions that follow. Scientists have begun studying the more subtle aspects of our being, coming closer

Selected Acid and Alkaline Forming Foods				
Very Acid Forming	Acid Forming	Neutral	Alkaline Forming	Very Alkaline Forming
unripe cranberries	unripe fruit		sweet/sour cherries	figs
watermelon seed	prunes		ripe fruit	ripe lemons
walnuts	plums		most vegetables	chaparral
peanuts +++	yeast		tomatoes	carrot/beet juice
raw apple cider	pasteurized/raw		millet buckwheat	vegetable juice
vinegar	yoghurt		kelp	miso
sauerkraut	pasteurized milk		raw cow's	vitamin K
fermented foods	cheese		milk ++	calcium ascor-
eggs +	pasteurized butter		raw goat's milk	bate (vitamin C)
flesh foods +	animal fat +		bean sprouts	wheatgrass
vitamin A	white sugar+		string beans	juice
ascorbic acid	most beans		azuki beans	
(vitamin C)	lentils		soy beans	
	kidney bean		lima beans	
	soy sauce		onions	
	soft drinks +		wheatgrass	
	medical drugs +		sprouted	
	alcohol +		almonds	
	most cooked grains: rice, oats etc		brazil nuts	
	soaked sprouted grains		alfalfa sprouts	
	soaked sprouted wheat		sunflower	
	most nuts: soaked sprouted nuts		sprouts	
	most seeds: Soaked sprouted seeds			
	soaked sprouted alfalfa seeds			
	soaked sprouted sunflower seeds			
	raw butter *			
	avocado *			
	vegetable oils *			
	honey**			

+ Included for completeness but not recommended.
++ There is disagreement whether raw milk products have an acid/alkaline effect on the body. For example, clinical research by Dr. Crowfoot on urine pH after ingestion of raw milk suggests that raw milk has an alkalinizing effect. On the other hand, Dr. Morter contends that the recent increases in protein in the diet of dairy cows has resulted in a higher protein in milk, and therefore a higher acid ash that creates a more acid effect in the body.
+++ Dangerous quantities of pesticide residue on non-organic peanuts make them the most pesticide-saturated food in the American diet. A mold called aflatoxin which is carcinogenic often grows even on organic peanuts. Sun-dried organic peanuts may prevent aflatoxin growth and are without high toxic residues. Arrowhead Mills has such a peanut product.
* Between neutral and acid.
* Between neutral and alkaline.

Source: Gabriel Cousens, *Conscious Eating*, pg 251-252, First Printing 2000

to the kernel, the seed of our existence and life. In a relatively new branch of science, Psychoneuroimmunology (PNI), researchers are discovering how the healing arts (visualization, positive affirmations, breathing, yoga, massage, etc.) have a positive effect on the immune system and recovery of patients with varying illnesses. In a recent health symposium sponsored by the Art of Living, doctors and researchers provided scientific proof on the positive effects of meditation and breathing exercises on the whole physiology.

The Path to Joyful Living

Below are tools that when practiced regularly will reconnect and realign our body, mind and spirit, cultivating peace and understanding and promoting joy. We are living in a crucial time in history where proper practices must be utilized by every individual to create a more peaceful, harmonious world for ourselves and our children. It starts by choosing activities that nurture our body, inspires our minds and enlightens our spirit. There is no waiting around, the time is now and we have the resources, tools, knowledge at our disposal.

Exercises & Tools to Cultivate Balance & Harmony

1. Self-empowerment
2. Mindfulness
3. Self Therapies
4. Yoga
5. Meditation
6. Music
7. Detoxification

1. Self-empowerment

Empower yourself with the right knowledge.

You have the power to make any choice you want; it's your given right bestowed upon you. When it comes to nutrition, there's plenty of knowledge out there in this age of information. Put simply, eat natural, organic foods as much as possible and stay away from as much toxins as possible. We are living in a toxic world and one must be pro-active in choosing the best for ones body to get proper nutrition. If you have to eat fast food, do so knowing the implications as was discussed above in the three qualities of food. We know that children learn by example, so create a great, healthy and informative environment around food. You can start at the grocery store.

On your next trip to the grocery, you and your child could read the labels of all packaged foods and household products. Or if your child cannot read yet, go through ingredients with them. Knowledge leads to empowerment. Note such ingredients as artificial flavors and colors, preservatives such as calcium chloride and magnesium sulphate, modified milk ingredients, polypropylene, tartrazine, dextrin, modified oils, aspartame, glucose, fructose and lactose. Artificial flavors and colors are very common in all cereals, so have your child be aware of these ingredients and offer an alternate choice. The key here is to raise awareness, and doing so on regular trips to the grocery store will do this. Offer alternatives to your child. Most grocery stores now offer healthier choices, devoid of most of these if not all of the ingredients listed above.

A special note about colors and additives found in many foods, frozen, packaged or boxed: There are approximately 200+ food colors, most of which are artificially made from petroleum byproducts. In Canada, the government approves even the harmful ones, such as tartrazine (FD & Yellow No.5). In 2003 the U.S. FDA issued a warning to hospitals when 12 people died in relation to Blue Dye No.1 which was used in enteral feeding. In Japan, Red Dye No. 2 induced DNA damage in the colon, glandular stomach and bladder.

You will notice in boxed cereals, for example, that the healthy choice contains less ingredients, eliminating the colors, extra sugars and additives. You will also find more grain choices. Wheat is still a very common grain used in many products. But with the rise of wheat allergies and intolerances, there is more variety commercially available now than 10 years ago. When choosing grains, go for variety even if you have no allergy or intolerance. Quinoa, amaranth, barley, kamut, millet, brown rice are becoming common these days. Minimize on the processed grains, for example, pastas. Instead, reach for the whole grain and prepare meals using these grains. If a recipe calls for pasta, substitute it once in while with quinoa, amaranth, barley, brown rice, kamut or millet.

2. Mindfulness

In any given moment, most people are either thinking of the past or the future, rarely being in the present moment. Mindfulness is being aware of the present moment, becoming an observer of yourself instead of generating thoughts about yourself. Observe your mind and how it is functioning and when you find yourself in the past or the future, shift gears and bring your mind to the present moment. Shifting gears to allow your mind to be in the present moment requires no thinking. Just as when you are driving a standard car and you have to shift gears, you just do it or else the car will stall. Just as the mind stalls in the past or future, shift gears to the present moment. It takes practice but in time the shift will happen naturally.

Practice mindfulness always: when you are washing dishes, loading up the dishes in the dishwasher, preparing a meal or when you are getting dressed. Even when you are having an upsetting moment, be with your feelings and allow them to express what needs to unfold and be done with it. The idea is to observe the beauty of every single moment and pay attention to the events that unfold. Be with life every single moment and you will experience the totality of being. You remain grounded and firm in the moment when you do not allow thoughts of the past or future expectations to interfere with the present moment. What can stop us from experiencing the present moment? The mind.

If the mind had a job, it would be to wander off on its own and that is exactly what it does. It does so cleverly, going through five different modes at any given moment. The mind can experience one or two modes simultaneously, sometimes getting stuck on one mode, but the mind will jump from one state to another, mostly subconsciously. The modes are:

1. The mind wanting proof.
2. Imposing your own values, feelings and ideas onto other people.
3. Getting caught up in wrong knowledge and hallucinating, for example, it's common for people to jump to conclusions by thinking they know what the other person is thinking about.
4. Sleep.
5. Delving into memories.

The key to heightened awareness and thus mindfulness is to transcend all five and allow the unfolding of life to happen without the emotions taking over you.

3. Creating Harmony through Self-Therapies

Paying to attention to our body is a gift we give to ourselves and enhances the delicate harmony and balance within our body, mind and spirit.

Baths are an excellent way to relax and unwind. Add some essential oils to promote deep relaxation such lavender, peppermint or chamomile. If the muscles are tight, consider adding Epsom Salt, which helps facilitate the release of lactic acid that builds up in the muscles as toxins. Gently use a dry brush before a bath to remove debris off the surface of the skin and open up the pores. Once in a while, add mineral salt to help replenish the body with minerals, important in many functions of the body.

Another simple therapy you can do at home is marma therapy. It is acupuncture without needles. Marma Therapy was introduced to me by Vaidya Rama Kant Mishra (Vaidya is an Ayurvedic doctor). I had never heard of marma before and a friend suggested I take a course that was happening out in Sarnia. At the time, I was looking for some other therapy to do in my massage practice but was hesitating on pursuing acupuncture. Marma was the answer! It is simple and effective and doesn't require needles! The principles work similarly to acupuncture In that specific points are stimulated through gentle touch. With acupuncture, needless are used, but with marma, your ring finger (an energetic channel linked to the heart) administers the stimulation accompanied with a mantra.

A mantra is a sacred text recited many times that invokes a specific meaning. Reciting a specific mantra evokes results based on the frequency it maintains through the sounds that emanate. This is vibrational healing and is most powerful in its healing capabilities.

Do the following exercise with this mantra:

Om

Aing

Hreeng

Kleeng

This is the seed mantra, the elements of prana. This mantra is repeated several times in multiples of 7 while doing the following steps.

1. Make small gentle circles with your ring finger in the middle of your palm. Repeat with the other hand.
2. Repeat Step 1 but with the feet, making small gentle circles at the middle of the foot adjacent to the arch.
3. Using your left ring finger, make the circles at the top of the head

These are preparation marmas. Doing this marma exercise has a most relaxing effect on the body. By stimulating these marmas, you are promoting the reception and flow of prana as it enters and leaves the body. Prana is what ultimately heals the body. Blocked prana in the nadis (energy channels) impedes healing. A marma practitioner should be consulted to pursue other areas in the body that requires specific attention.

4. Yoga

Yoga is a gentle exercise that can be done by every one of all ages, shapes and sizes. The beauty of yoga lies in its rich history that can be traced back to at least 5,000 years – a time when the ancient sages meditated and received knowledge and understanding of life, humanity and the universe. For some, Yoga today is another form of exercise. For others, it is a relaxing gateway to uniting with the body, mind and spirit. It is not a competition. It is about abiding in your limitations, exceeding them and coming away energized, full of life and with increased awareness. Be gentle and regular with your practice and you will reap the benefits. Even if you don't have a full hour for a proper session, at least do 5 – 10 minutes of some of the postures daily instead of none at all.

For beginners, go to a beginner's class or rent a Yoga video from your local library. I suggest Hatha Yoga for beginners. Explore other styles, such as Iyengar, Ashtanga, Flow, Vinyasa, Power, Bikram after you are comfortable doing the basic Hatha postures. A word of caution about Bikram: Because it is practiced in a heated room, it is important that your blood pressure is normal, not too high or low and that you have not experienced any dizziness, vertigo, nausea, ear aches or eye problems within the 24 – 72 hours prior to the start of class. Also, doing Bikram yoga can give rise to "false flexibility" due to the fact that heat will naturally lengthen muscles which can lead to overstretching. Heat is also pitta aggravating, therefore be aware of how it is affecting you, particularly those who are prone to pitta aggravation.

Children as young as five can do Yoga; however, they should not hold the postures for too long because their bones and joints need to move for them to grow. Have children count in their head to five when holding a posture. Counting in their heads will also help with concentration. The session can last anywhere from 5 to 20 minutes.

5. Meditation

Meditating brings peace to your life. When you are calm and centered, you are ready to tackle anything, even the most demanding children. Practice meditating on a daily basis, even if it's just for five minutes. Practice the *Om* meditation daily, morning, afternoon and evening. It is simple and effective and requires only five minutes out of your day.

Om Meditation:

Close your eyes. Recite *Om* and pay attention to your chakras (energy centers in the body) starting at your root chakra (located at the base of the spine) and up towards the navel, the heart, throat and finally the third eye (located at the brow). Meditate on *Om* while visualizing each chakra for about five seconds.

Om is the primordial sound and connects you the universal consciousness.

You can meditate with eyes open or closed, depending on the style and method you have learned. Meditating will allow the dissipation of stress, relaxing the mind and establishing a sense of harmony with all creation. If your mind wanders here and there, a good tool you can use to remain focused is a candle. Focus on the candle and do not allow your eyes to wander. Remain focused on the candle and allow your mind to relax.

6. Music

It is an uplifting experience to celebrate life with music. Celebrating life with music is missing these days in our daily lives. More often, we listen to music to unwind and relax. Children naturally love to sing and dance; it's an expression of life. Let us promote this life-affirming activity with ourselves and our children.

Satsang, in many cultures in India, is practiced in the evening with singing and dancing. Often, bhajans or devotional songs are sung to honor the Gods, creation and life. In North America, it is practiced in churches with hymns.

After dinner or before bed time, sing with your child his or her favorite tune. For young children, use classic tunes such as "Row Row Row Your Boat" or "London Bridge". Then get creative and give it a spin by making up your own lyrics using the same melody, with themes such as their favourite animal, your past childhood stories or something that happened to your child that day.

THREE PILLARS OF AYURVEDIC DETOXIFICATION		
(To achieve individual balance, *Prakrit Sthapana*)		
SHODHANA Gentle cleansing with correct preparation	**SHAMANA** Balancing Vata, Pitta and Kapha	**RASAYANA** Ayurvedic Rejuvenation Combination of herbs

Source: Mishra, R. K., *Ayurveda and Beyond*, pg. 2, copyright 2005

7. Detoxification

Detoxification is the elimination of toxins in the body. Many toxins pollute the body and some are excreted while others pollute the body. Toxins in the body include undigested material and emotional toxins (negative thoughts and feelings). A body overburdened with toxins disrupts metabolism, enzyme activity and nutritional assimilation, affecting immunity which can result in poor health and vitality.

It is safe to detoxify the body, but proper guidance is essential to monitor the individual to do a proper detox. In Ayurveda, there are 3 pillars for proper detoxification. Properly done, an Ayurvedic detox produces excellent results in the balancing of the body, mind, emotions and spirit.

Some other detoxification programs may include:

- Cleansing Diet
- Exercise
- Body Therapies
- Herbal Therapy
- Vitamin/Supplement Therapy
- Chelation Therapy
- Fasting
- Colonic Therapy
- Hydrotherapy
- Infrared Sauna Therapy

Consult an Ayurvedic Doctor or practitioner, natural health care practitioner, naturopath or nutritionist or a professional trained in a detoxification therapy to determine what best suits your needs.

Case Studies

Case Study #1

Name: N.S.

Occupation: Banker

Health Concerns: Stress, Muscle pain

Background: very considerate, conservative, spiritual, pleasant male in his mid 30s with stressful job at a bank, just got a promotion, loyal, hard-working, likes to please others, got married last year, bought a house and is now expecting their first child; under a lot of stress, has chronic back pain and occasional neck pain; client's goal is to help manage stress and help reduce back pain occurrence; already has background in Ayurveda and is looking for further recommendations to improve current status; practices mediation and Pranayama; husband and wife support each other and are persistent in nurturing their health

Natural Constitution: Vata/Pitta

Imbalance: <u>2 pitta imbalances</u> (liver & digestive fire); <u>1 vata imbalance</u> (downward movement involving elimination/constipation); <u>1 kapha imbalance</u> (clogging channels due to 2 factors: (1) client is naturally vata (dry) and since vata is aggravated, the body naturally compensates by over lubricating the body and (2) improper food choices leading to clogging of the channels); client shows undigested material/toxins in the blood and muscle tissue

Recommendations:

Diet:

Herbal Tea, Spice Mix, no processed foods or leftovers, no preservatives, no canned foods, no acidic food or vinegar or bottled dressing—lime okay, no large beans, smaller ones instead like lentils, dhal; Avoid bananas, potato, tomato, bell pepper, eggplant and winter squashes; whole grains only, for breakfast stewed apples or pears.

Client was given an herbal tea to drink daily from morning until 5 pm to prepare the body to eliminate toxins, support & strengthen the immune system, increase digestive fire and provide stamina. The spice mix was to help with elimination, detoxification, increase nutrient absorption, detoxify liver and support metabolism and mental acuity. By avoiding processed foods, leftovers, preservatives and canned foods, the client would be avoiding any additional toxins and undigested material being deposited in the blood and muscle tissue. Smaller beans help with digestion by decreasing the burden on the digestive system. Bananas and winter squash clog the channels. Potato, tomato, bell pepper and eggplant are avoided in traditional Ayurvedic diets and some people consider it poisonous because it belongs to the night shade family. Whole grains contain more nutrient value than processed/refined grains. Stewed apples/pears in the morning are easy to digest.

Lifestyle/Exercise:

Main concern is to manage stress. Herbs used for this is Ashwaganda, which can be applied transdermally along the cervical and sacral spine. Avoiding excess TV, computers and cell phone will help with the elimination EMF that can cumulatively affect vata. Arjuna is for emotional support.

Regular sleep before 10 pm is important to allow the body to recuperate from the day's stress and support the nervous system.

Yoga will tone the body and decrease the chances of muscle spasms and back pain, nourish the body, mind and spirit, create balance, increase energy and alertness. With regular practice of Yoga and meditation, stress can be managed effectively allowing for greater awareness, gratitude and joy.

Case Study #2

Name: A.W.

Occupation: Manager

Health Concerns: Stress, Headache, Muscle pain

Background: conservative, pleasant, introspective, 38-year-old female. Got married last year and now expecting first child; lives in the city, sensitive to environment, gets frequent headaches, under much stress and has chronic neck and back pain; open to natural remedies and generally lives a healthy lifestyle, practices meditation and Pranayama; husband and wife team supportive of each other and persistent in bettering their health.

Natural Constitution: Pitta/Vata

Imbalance: 3 vata imbalances (1. downward movement involving elimination/constipation 2. mental energy and creativity 3.distribution and circulation of prana to the whole subtle and physical body); 1 pitta imbalance (liver); 1 kapha imbalance (clogging of channels)

Recommendations:

Diet:

Herbal Tea, Spice Mix, do not skip meals and food should be well cooked. Client is quite acidic having a 6 pH level, therefore, no processed foods or leftovers, no preservatives, no canned foods, no acidic food or vinegar or bottled dressing—lime okay. These foods promote acidity. Client is recommended to supplement with coral calcium to buffer acidity, supply calcium and increase soma (counteract with pitta imbalance). No large beans, smaller ones instead like lentils, dhal; avoid bananas, potato, tomato, bell pepper, eggplant and winter squashes; whole grains only, for breakfast stewed apples or pears.

Client was given an herbal tea to drink daily from morning until 5 pm to prepare the body to eliminate toxins, provide emotional support and to moisten, cool to balance the pitta and vata. The spice mix is to help with digestion and elimination, detoxification, increase nutrient absorption, detoxify liver and support metabolism and mental acuity. By avoiding processed foods, leftovers, preservatives and canned foods, the client would be avoiding any additional toxins and undigested material being deposited in the blood and muscle tissue. Smaller beans help with digestion by decreasing the burden on the digestive system. Bananas and winter squash clog the channels. Potato, tomato, bell pepper and eggplant are avoided in traditional Ayurvedic diets and some people consider it poisonous because it belongs to the night shade family. Whole grains contain more nutrient value than processed/refined grains. Stewed apples/pears in the morning are easy to digest.

Lifestyle/Exercise:

Main concern is to manage mental emotional stress. Client was recommended Arjuna is for emotional support. Applied transdermally to the heart, lungs liver marma points will help with this.

Brahmi applied to the cervical spine to help with the vata imbalances and promote spiritual bliss.

Fennel is cooling and balances pitta aggravation and good for digestion. Daily self-massage is recommended as an adjunct to support and nourish the body and mind.

Avoiding excess TV, computers and cell phone will help with the elimination EMF that can cumulatively affect vata.

Regular sleep before 9:30 pm is important to allow the body to recuperate from the day's stress and support the nervous system. Transdermal cream with bacopa, gotu kola, poppy seed and lavender will promote sleep and can be applied on the cervical spine.

Yoga will tone the body and decrease the chances of muscle spasms and back pain, nourish the body, mind and spirit, create balance, increase energy and alertness. With regular practice of Yoga and meditation, stress can be managed effectively allowing for greater awareness, gratitude and joy.

As you may see that "Cultivating Balance" creates a formula for you to adopt and then teach your kids. This is based on knowledge that is thousands of years old and is proven to have dramatic results.

Thinking of Having Kids?

<u>Lesson 14</u>

Make a recording of Fran Drescher saying "mommy" repeatedly. (Important: no more than a four second delay between each "mommy"; occasional crescendo to the level of a supersonic jet is required). Play this tape in your car everywhere you go for the next four years.

You are now ready to take a long trip with a toddler.

Game plan

Your goal is to attain a Saatvic state of harmony. You are now on the road to achieving this goal.

As part of your game plan list some of the lifeless foods you are deleting from your diet and the foods you are replacing them with.

As you begin practicing the Marma exercises, take note of the new levels of relaxation you are attaining.

Yes relaxation, visualizations, meditations, jogging, reading, healthy eating etc, etc. are all Saatvic practices.

This is an opportunity for you to journal these new pieces of your life plan.

_____
_____
_____
_____
_____
_____
_____
_____
_____
_____
_____
_____
_____
_____
_____
_____
_____
_____
_____
_____
_____
_____

What does my Saatvic Plan look like?

Chapter 10

Rituals in the Family

Thinking of Having Kids?

Lesson 15
Start talking to an adult of your choice. Have someone else continually tug on your skirt hem, shirt- sleeve, or elbow while playing the "mommy" tape made from Lesson 14 above. You are now ready to have a conversation with an adult while there is a child in the room.
(Author Unknown, but they must have had kids...)
This is all very tongue in cheek, but as a mother of six, I can attest to the fact that there is a lot of truth in it. Share it with your friends, both those who do and dont have kids. I guarantee theyll get a chuckle out of it.
Remember, a sense of humor is one of the most important things youll need when you become a parent.

Most of us participate regularly in rituals without realizing it. You may not think that a daily trip to the playground or a family breakfast qualifies as a ritual, but it does. I call them *unconscious rituals*. Sadly, while we do these things often and may even look forward to them as part of our routine, we don't recognize their significance in our lives.

Many ancient cultures have used rituals to strengthen their family ties and to deepen their relationships. For example, in South America, it's common practice for a mother or grandmother to bless each person as he or she leaves the house in the morning, with the intention of strengthening the family bond as well as each family member's connection to

Spirit. In Mediterranean cultures, as in Italy and Spain, it's customary for everyone to come home for lunch. Dad leaves work, the children get a break from school, and everyone, even grandparents, takes part in a midday family meal.

Rituals can mark everyday moments or significant times; they can ease us through transitions and. especially in times of rapid change, bring structure and stability into family life. Family traditions and rites help establish a common spiritual ground on which bonds can be forged – bonds that transcend age, gender, and individual interests. Indeed, a strong spiritual life can help a family achieve harmony, even when there are unusual differences. As Annie, a mother who had adopted eight children from different countries told me, "Our family rituals bridge the gaps between cultures. They give us an even playing field."

We no longer have the option to look at life in the same way as our grandparents did. Change and transition are the only stable things left in our lives. As the world changes and the makeup of our family structure changes, we need to incorporate meaningful rituals that give substance and guidance to the way we will experience the world.

Children and Rituals

Rituals are particularly wonderful for families, because they bring adults and children together in a sacred space. If we take the time to stop and bless what we have – our loved ones, our food, our home – and to honor the seasons of change, both within the family and on the planet, we can learn to appreciate each moment and gain happiness from living in the fullness of the present.

By using rituals, we help ourselves and our children make better sense of the world. They begin to regard even the mundane – a bath or family dinner – as sacred moments of connection and togetherness.

We must educate our children and ourselves about other cultures and races. Our country is truly a global village and to ignore this fact leads to the disintegration of any real communication for the future. It will be more and more important as we move into globalization to make sure our individual identities do not get squashed and homogenized.

Think of it as weaving a tapestry. Each one of us brings our own unique flavor to the whole. This is the source of our creativity. Without this, our world will be a dull place to live.

Wisdom of the Elders

For thousands of years, the elders of a tribe contributed to the education of the children. They shared their wisdom, stories and expertise and were a valuable part of the community. In fact, in many cultures even today, the grandparents are sought out and highly respected. Especially in Africa and Asia, becoming an elder is an honored position in society. In Hawaii, you are not considered wise until you reach the age of 80 and then there is a great ceremony to honor you.

It's about time we appreciated this resource in America. We can now "adopt a grandparent." What a gift this is to the kids who desperately need guidance and unconditional love. Grandparents are tutoring children in schools, caring for foster-care kids and sharing their skills and years of knowledge. Kids have the opportunity to learn about history from those who have lived it.

Wake up and acknowledge diversity!

It is time to acknowledge this diversity. Why not create Stepparent's Day or "Gotcha Day" (the day you adopted a child) as I describe in my book *The Joy of Family Rituals*? The more we celebrate diversity, the more we will feel connected and part of something larger than ourselves.

When holidays come along, we all think we want the *Leave It to Beaver* nuclear family, complete with grandma baking cookies in the kitchen and the family dog playing with the kids, but the new family rarely fits that description. It's no wonder depression is rampant at these 'special' times of the year. Why aren't we seeing more advertisements with Jamie and his grandparents as well as Susan and her two mothers?

Holidays

Unfortunately, when most of us commemorate holidays, we rarely think about, and in some cases don't even know that many holidays – "holy days" – were originally Pagan, created to mark the changing of seasons and other happenings in nature. Even worse, as our celebrations have become less about meaning and more about material concerns – giving/getting presents or wearing new outfits – holidays can be both stressful and laden with unrealistic expectations.

I would like to suggest that this year let us celebrate from our hearts. The most meaningful rituals are those that strengthen our relationship with The Divine. Such practice helps us to develop the spiritual muscles that ultimately strengthen us in the face of life's greatest tragedies. I pray we all can develop conscious spiritual practices capable of sustaining us during these challenging days ahead and help us to better navigate these uncharted waters.

Sacred Rituals are as basic as all other survival skills.

Key Elements for Creating a Sacred Ritual

- Open your heart
- Pray
- Wherever you are, create sacred space using elements from nature, a picture of your beloved deity or favorite sacred image – anything that connects you more deeply to your heart.

It does not matter if you are in a temple, home, mosque, church, school, office or outdoors with Nature. Spend time wherever you find solace.

Rituals are for the good of all sentient beings. Manipulation must never be used. Rituals are about aspirations and sacred intent. Do not use sacred ritual for revenge or manipulation.

Have a Clear Motivation

The purpose of the ritual is *intention*. Focus your intention. *Consciously creating rituals can keep us centered in the present, allow us to transform the past, and inspires us to set our intention to re-imagine our future.*

Holiday Rituals

- Hug more people.
- Take time to connect and make every encounter meaningful whether it is your bus driver or local shopkeepers.
- Create alters to peace and wholeness.
- Do simple prayers every time you light a candle.
- Find a meaningful way to serve others and your community and world.
- Be mindful.
- Celebrate the summer and winter solstices.
- Be open to the wisdom of and teachings from all religions.
- Attend a temple, church, mosque or Kwanza celebration.
- Share with others what is most important to you – give gifts from the heart.
- Play music, dance and sing.

Some Clients' Rituals

One neat thing my husband does for my mother is send her flowers on my birthday. He has sent various cuts since we started dating 6 years ago. She always looks forward to it. He even sent her flowers the 2 years we were not dating and living in different parts of the country.

When a friend of ours married, his fiancée decided to let her father-in-law-to-be, William, walk her down the aisle. Her father was never involved in her life and her husband doesn't have any sisters. William said it was the highlight of his life. He'd always dreamed of walking his own daughter down the aisle, but didn't think it would happen since he only had sons. Sadly, he died 2 days after the arrival of their firstborn sons (twins).

Thank you all for sharing your wonderful family traditions. As simple as they may be, they are one of the most important things you can do for your children. If you are interested in learning more about how to draw your family closer together through family traditions, check out this website: www.onceuponafamily.com/melissaday. I have an 11-month-old daughter, and I am so excited to try out so many of the ideas I've learned from this website. One of my favorites is taking a picture of my daughter and my husband's hand together each year on Father's Day, the last photo being when she has her wedding ring on her wedding day. I plan to give both she and my husband these photos in a small album. We are also writing a letter to her each year on her birthday, and then 21 days before her 21st birthday, we'll start mailing her the letters.

On Christmas Eve about half an hour after dinner, the doorbell always rings. It's MRS. Santa, and she drops off new PJ's for everyone in the family. (It used to just be for the females in the family until I had my son, then it became everyone!) Then we all change into the PJ's and open presents from the family and then it's bedtime as we wait for Santa to drop off the 'big' presents.

There are a few winter holiday traditions we'll be keeping up as the years go by with our son and any other children we might have.

From my family there are the stockings that arrive at one's door from Santa with a few gifts to keep the kids playing in their rooms until a reasonable time of the morning (since Mom and Dad often stay up late assembling toys). Hand-in-hand with that, no one goes down to where the presents are until everyone is awake and someone has taken a picture of the presents.

Another ritual is to 'steal' the latkes off the paper towels while they are still hot, 'just to check' that they are seasoned properly.

And to start a new tradition, all presents will be exchanged on the Winter Solstice in our house, so that neither Christmas nor Hanukkah is 'our' holiday – Christmas is time for my family to spoil our child and Hanukkah is his family's time to give gifts. And getting Slurpees every time there is a big snowstorm is one that's all winter long.

This is all amazing to me. I am now a 32-year-old mom of a 22-month-old boy. When I was little, my family and I got together on Saturday nights. We always ordered take-out and played cards. Since I have gotten married, my husband and son have also joined in on this. My husband actually looks forward to it. I know that it really works.

In the evening, about 45 minutes before bedtime, we turn off the TV and put on one of my daughters favorite CDs (right now it happens to be the Wiggles). We dance and play to the music until the CD plays all the way through. It's a great way to wear her out before bedtime and have a fun bonding time.

At the dinner table each night, we tell our highs and lows of the day. It gets good conversations started and oftentimes gives us (Dad & Mom) a better insight into the goings-on in our kids' lives. Recently we added to the high and low, a "what I did nice for someone" topic. This reminds us and helps us tune into the idea that we can help others in many different ways.

Our family watches the videos of our daughters' births each year on their birthdays. They love watching themselves on TV and we get a chance to walk down memory lane (and remember how fast time goes).

Each year on the night of their first day back to school, I plan to take my kids out for a very special dinner to celebrate the beginning of a new school year. I want my kids to look forward to school (even though the first day can be a hard one to get through) and know that their education is worth celebrating. When they get older, maybe I'll have a "Beginning of the Year" party (instead of an end-of-the-year party) to include their classmates and teacher.

I keep a Christmas photo album and matching journal (Old Navy) that I pack away with the holiday decorations. I put copies of any holiday photos in the album and write several entries in the journal. If we have relatives in, I encourage them to write in the journal as well. I think it will be a nice keepsake and a good way to reflect on our lives together over the years. When our girls get old enough to draw and then to write, I'll have them make their own entries. I started this after our first baby and now we have two. Even now, it is very exciting after a year has passed to look at the photos and see how the girls have grown. I read the past journal entries to our girls and they get excited about anticipating Santa's visit as well as other special traditions we share.

My family has carried out the greatest family tradition for over 25 years. It started when my father, his adult siblings, spouses, cousins and my grandparents began an annual family reunion on Columbus Day weekend. We meet every year and now I bring my children – the first great-grandchildren.. It is so awesome. So few families get to know the extended members well enough to spend a weekend together.. My kids love it and it is so great to go for a stroll in the Vermont foliage after our big turkey dinner. To reduce the holiday stress of trying to see everyone, we have an early Thanksgiving meal that weekend. too.

My parents ran a "date" system. Because there were four of us kids; it meant we got one Thursday a month and we would alternate parents. One month the girls would go with mum and my brother would go with dad, the next month we would swap. We had a limit of money (at the time it was $10) which was enough to do the basic things like movies and bowling, but we got to choose what we did. I would always go to the driving range with my dad, and it became our special thing.

And best of all, occasionally there were five Thursdays in a month, so mum and dad got the last one for themselves!

We feel that holidays are too commercial, so to personalize Christmas and make it more about the gift of Jesus, we will find one charity or family or organization, etc. that we can give to as a family. Each year, we will make sure to have a new idea.

I am a Seventh-day Adventist, and every Sabbath after church, we go to my mother-in-law's home for lunch. We've done this every weekend since my firstborn (now four) was in the womb. We set a formal table, serve a potluck lunch and invite people from church and college students as well as 'adopted' family. My 11-month-old gets excited about going to Grama's, and my four-year-old is learning how to set the table and has so many positive adult examples around him (all the 'uncles' and 'aunties'). My husband and I can also relax and enjoy some adult conversation as well as flexing our culinary muscles with the dishes we bring each week.

On her own birthday, my mother would give her mom a rose. Now I always give my mom a rose on my birthday. I hope my child will carry on the tradition too. It's such a beautiful way to honor the person who gave birth to you.

My daughter is 9 months, and we've began some traditions, such as reading at bedtime, family walks, etc. But my favorite tradition growing up was Friday night movie/pizza night. My mom got remarried when I was 12 and it was a difficult transition at a difficult age. It was nice to be able to spend Friday nights getting to know my step-dad, even if he did end up falling asleep twenty minutes into the movie.

I live in Michigan. It was family tradition as a child to go to a local tree farm pick and cut down our own tree. Then we took the horse buggy back to the car. And a church next door served hot chocolate and warm pastries. My son is now two and we have done it every year, including my father and sister. More of an extended family tradition.

My husband's mother died several years ago. She was overweight and told everyone that food was her greatest pleasure. Now, every year on her birthday, we go out to eat and order anything we want, regardless of calories, in her honor.

I am about to start a tradition on my son's first birthday. I have chosen one of my husband's shirts and each birthday I will take a photo of my son dressed in it. That way, there will be a lifetime series of his growth and a very sentimental shirt as well.

We've started a monthly ritual since we first adopted our son and that is to go for a moonlight walk at the first full moon. It has been a great time for us just to take a break from the usual hectic pace of our lives to just be one with Nature and a great time for us to teach our son all about lifecycles. We are expecting baby number two and this is a tradition that will definitely continue.

Every year I put a one dollar coin in a special piggy bank for each of my children – one year old - 1 dollar coin, two years old - two dollars coins, etc. I will give them the banks when they are 18 to let them know they were always thought of throughout the years.

In my family, Friday night became the 'no cooking' night. That meant going out to a restaurant (nothing fancy) as a family. It was a great excuse to get everyone together, a relief not to have to cook, and we looked forward to a family night out.

In my childhood family of four girls, each birthday we were 'queen for the day.' When we awoke on our birthday, the house was decorated with balloons and streamers, complete with a homemade sign that said, "Happy Birthday." Our favorite breakfast and dinner were served. And we waited in anticipation all day to open our presents after dinner and birthday cake. Although sometimes times were very tight, my mom and dad always made a big deal out of our birthdays. Hugs and smiles were always abundant. In a larger family as mine was, it's nice to have one day a year when you're the queen!

Every day, when my husband walks through the door from work, I drop whatever me and the baby are doing and run to the door to greet him. He knows that daddy is more important than anything we are doing. Everyone loves it.

Since all of my immediate family lives in the same town, we get together every Sunday night for dinner.

Sunday Night Tradition: I must admit, our Sunday night tradition started out as a way of me getting out of cooking after our Sunday night church service. Every Sunday night, my son and I swing by Wendy's on the way home from church and then rush into our little home to sit on my bed and watch the Disney Sunday night movie. I never thought my son really cared about it (it was more like a habit than a tradition) until one Sunday when my parents were in town and I said we would go see them after church. My son nearly cried and said, "But, Mom, what about our tradition? You know, just me and you and we get nuggets and watch the movie." Since that Sunday, though our yard has gotten flooded up to our front steps, grandparents blow in and out of town, my pocket book almost empty or full to the brim, my son and I spend Sunday night together with nuggets, a movie and love in our hearts.

After bedtime stories and cuddling, my parents would tell my brother and I, "See you in the morning and remember that I love you." It got to the point where they would only have to say the first part and we would finish the sentence. It always made us feel safe and loved, and we have continued this tradition with our respective kids.

With the birth of each of our children, we make our first trip to the library and got their first library card. My second child had his own card at two weeks old. Each of my children has their own library card so when we have our routine weekly visit, they feel ownership in their choices of literature and value reading.

At dinner each night, we try to each take a turn telling our best and worst part of the day. After one person goes, they pick the next person to tell their worst/best. It's a fun way to get things off our minds that bother us and tell about something exciting or nice that happened. Also, we try to once a week (say on Friday) say something nice about each other or compliment each other. I might say to my son, "That was so nice of you to included your sister in your games with your friends." My son might say to my daughter, "Thanks for helping me with my homework." It is a positive time and they like it.

As part of your plan, make a list of rituals you will do on a daily basis, weekly, monthly and yearly. Both you and the kids will quickly become accustomed to doing them and are able to see the bonding that results. Traditions are a time for remembering, sharing and connecting.

Wisdom in the Family Review

Thinking of Having Kids?
Parenting's Life Lessons

Ok Here is your quiz...

This is an opportunity to check out your view and also to readjust your game plan and personal practices.

If you haven't already done so, go back review the 15 lessons and write them here:

Lesson 1

1.

2.

3.

4.

5.

Lesson 2

Before you finally go ahead and have children, find a couple who already are parents and berate them about their...

1.

2.

3.

4.

Suggest ways in which they might improve their child's breastfeeding, sleep habits, toilet training, table manners, and overall behavior. Enjoy it, because it will be the last time in your life you will have all the answers.

Lesson 3

To discover how the nights will feel...

1.

2.

3.

4.

5.

6.

7.

8.

Lesson 4

1.

2.

3.

4.

Lesson 5
1.
2.
Lesson 6
1.
2.
3.
4.
Lesson 7
1.
2.
3.
4.

Lesson 8
1.
2.
3.
4.
5.
6.
7.
8.
9.
10.
11.
12.
13.
14.
Lesson 9
1.
2.
3.
Lesson 10
1.
2.
3.
4.

Lesson 11

1.

2.

3.

4.

5.

6.

Lesson 12

1.

2.

3.

Lesson 13

1.

2.

3.

Lesson 14

1.

2.

3.

4.

5.

Lesson 15

1.

2.

3.

4.

5.

(Writer Anonymous)

Closing Remarks

Wisdom in the Family is about taking a look at yourself, taking a look at your daily practice. The things that you like about who you are and what you do. How you interact with yourself, with your spouse, with your kids and then giving yourself the opportunity to make choices. To modify your daily practice so that it reflects for you a greater balance in the way that you walk through your day.

Please be aware that it will be different for each one of you. That is where the fun lies. It is also where the work lies.

To achieve this greater sense of balance you must work at it. That means you need to be aware of who you are, then use your own innate and learned tools to shift and then to practice, practice and practice.

This is not an easy job.

But Trust me it will be the most rewarding one of your life.

Let it be known you do not have to make this journey alone. There are friends, family and practitioners here to facilitate this process for you

The first step is to want to do it and then everything else will eventually fall into place.

Family Wisdom is about creating a "Family Plan" It is about being the "NOW" parent who is not afraid to go out and educate themselves about how to be a better person.

Once you do this you will see how the nature of your family will change.

CONGRATULATIONS on becoming a more enlightened being !

Wisdom in the Family: A Life Plan

The following components are those that will make up your Individual/ Family practice plan:

1. The Old Paradigm – What did it look like?
2. What does the new picture look like now?
3. What were/are your blockages (Resistance, Attachment, Stuckness and how are they affecting you achieving your goals?
4. What is Thunder and Lightning and how does it relate to your individual development?
5. What are you doing to empower yourself these days?
6. Have you developed any positive affirmations?
7. Have you made any different choices?
8. What is your dominant Parenting Style? What is your child's temperament and learning style? Based on this view what does your action plan look like now?
9. What does your behavioral plan look like?
10. How has the changes you have made in your body language affected your relationship with your spouse, with your child?
11. Have you noticed changes in the way you communicate and how has that affected your life.
12. Incorporate your Work, Life and Balance plan here.
13. We are each others teachers – You can be as creative as you wish right here.
14. "Through the Eyes of your Children"- Incorporate your new practice.
15. This part of your plan is all about, your body, the foods you are choosing to eat, the exercising you are choosing to do and the relaxation practices you will now incorporate into your new life practice.
16. Last but not least is the rituals you choose to incorporate into your plan.

As you complete your plan, notice the changes in your self, in your relationships, in your family.
Yes it is all about choice. You now have the tools to create a new Life/Family practice.
The magic in this is that life is ever changing and this framework as in life is totally fluid allowing you to change with the winds of time.

My Family Plan – What It Looks Like

Bibliography

American Psychiatric Association (1994), *Diagnostic and statistical manual of mental disorders* (4th ed., rev.) (DSM-1V-R)., Washington, D.C: APA

Anderson, Joan and Robin Wilkins. *Getting Unplugged: Take Control of Your Family's Television, Video Game and Computer Habits*. New York: John Wiley & Sons, Inc., 1998.

Axelrod, Lauryn. *TV Proof Your Kids: A Parents Guide To Safe and Healthy Viewing*. New Jersey: Carol Publishing Group, 1997

Baker, William F., and George Dessart. *Down The Tube*. New York: Basic Books, 1998

Barkley, R.D., New ways of looking at ADHD (lecture 1991) Third annual C.H.A.D.D. conference on attention deficit disorders. Washington D.C.

Baumrind, D. (1991). " The influence of parenting style on adolescent competence and substance abuse." *Journal of Early Adolescence.* 11 (1), 56-95

Blank, R., & Remschmidt, H., "Hyperkinetic Syndrome: The Role of Allergy Among Psychological and Neurological Factors." *European Child and Adolescent Psychiatry, (*1994), 3(4), pp. 220-228.

Bradway, K. (1964. "Jung's Psychological Types," *Journal of Analytical Psychology,* vol.9. Tavistock Publishers. Pp.129-135.

Business Week Magazine. (Feb. 1994). *Computers as teacher and tutor.*

Dahl, Ronald. Charlie and The Chocolate Factory. New York: Alfred A. Knopf, 1964.

Dyer, Wayne , *The Power of Intention (2005)*

Erasmus, Udo. *Fats that Heal, Fats that Kill*. Burnaby B.C. Canada: Alive Books, (1993).

Fast, Julius, 1988. *Body Language,* Pocket Books, Reissue

Ginott, H.G. (1993). *Teacher and Child: A Book for Parents and Teachers,* N.Y. pp: 112, 126, 152.

Glasser W. Control Theory: (1985). *A New Explanation of How We Control Our Lives,* New York: Harper & Row

Goleman, Daniel. *Emotional Intelligence: Why It Matters More Than IQ*. New York: Bantam, 1995.

Healy, Jane. *Failure To Connect: How Computers Affect Our Children's Minds—and What We Can Do About It*. New York: Simon & Schuster, 1998.

Jin, P. (1992) " Efficacy of Tai Chi, brisk walking, meditation and reading in reducing mental and emotional stress." *Journal of Psychosomatic Research.* 36: pp. 361-370.

Jung, C. (1923). *Psychological Types.,* New York. Harcourt Brace.

Khalsa, P., & Karta, S. "Keeping Children Healthy," *Yoga Journal.* (Oct. 1996)

Kiersey, D., & Bates, M., (1978). *Please Understand Me. Character and Temperament Types*. Prometheus Nemesis Book Company, Delmor, Ca.

McClendon, Marie. *Alternatives to TV Handbook*. Denver, CO: Whole Human Beans Co., 2001.

Morris, Desmond. , 1995 *Bodytalk; The Meaning of Human Gestures*

Noznick, Robert. *The Examined Life*. New York: Simon & Schuster, 1989

Onkka, Timothy Ph.D. Director, Alpha Center, Northern Indiana School of Psychology

"Parents'Survival Tips," a pamphlet published by the Minnesota Committee for Prevention of Child Abuse, 1934 University Ave. West, St. Paul, MN 55104.

Packard, Vance. *The Hidden Persuaders*. New York: David McKay, 1957.

Palmer, J The Role of Spirituality - Self Empowerment

Pearce, Joseph Chilton. *Magical Child*. New York: Penguin, 1977.

Pease, Allan. 1984 *Signals: How to Use Body Language for Power, Success and love*. Bantam Books

Phipps, Robert., 2002. Body Language and Parenting , *www.bodylanguagetraining.com*

Popkin, Michael H. Active Parenting Now, Parent's Guide

Robleda, Johanna, S., Special Projects Director, *The Parent Center*. San Francisco, Ca. (1997)

Rich, Dorothy. *Megaskills: Building Children's Achievement For The Information Age*. New York: Houghton Mifflin, 1997.

Sharma, Robin, *The Monk Who Sold His Ferrari,* 2005

Singer, Dorothy and Jerome Singer. *The Parents Guide: Use TV To Your Child's Advantage.* Reston, VA: Acropolis Books, 1990.

Spock, Dr. Benjamin. *Rebuilding American Family Values.* Chicago: Contemporary Books, 1996.

Steyer, James P. The *Other Parent: The Inside Story Of The Media's Effect On Our Children.* New York: Atria Books, 2002.

Stordy, J., & Nicholl, J.M. *The LCP Solution: The Remarkable Nutritional Treatment for ADHD, Dyslexia & Dyspraxia (2000) Random House, New York.*

The Nalanda Institute., Mumbai, India. (2000)

Thomson, John. *Natural Childhood.* New York: Fireside Books, Simon & Schuster, 1994.

Todd, Sheri . 2004., *Improving work, life and balance,* Research report.

Wainwright, Gordon, *Teach Yourself Body language,* McGraw-Hill/ Contemporary Books. 2000

Weiss, L.H. & Schwarz, J.C. (1996). "The relationship between parenting types and older adolescents' personality, academic achievement, adjustment and substance abuse. *Child Development.* 67 (5), 2101-2114

Wells, J. Home Fronts*: Controversies in Not-traditional Parenting*

Winn, Marie. *The Plug-In Drug: Television, Computers and Family Life.* New York: Penguin, 2002.

Work, Life and Balance in the Canadian Workplace *Human resources and Social Development of Canada,* 2006

Young Children (November, 1988): *Ideas That Work with Young Children: Avoiding Me Against You Discipline*

National Organizations:

Educational Resources Information Center (ERIC)
1920 Association Dr.
Reston, Va. 22091-1589
(800) 328-0272

National Association of Private Schools for Exceptional Children
1522 K Street, NW Suite1032
Washington, DC 20005
(202) 408-3338

Related Organizations:

National Association for the Education of Young Children
1509 16th Street, NW
Washington, DC 20036-1426
(800) 424-2460

National Association of School Psychologists
4340 East-West Highway   Suite 402
Bethesda, Md. 20814
(301) 657-0270

Advocacy & Legal Issues:

Council of Parent Attorneys and Advocates
P.O. Box 81-7327
Hollywood, Fl. 33081-0327
(954) 966-4489